Meyerhold's Theatre of the Grotesque

BOOKS OF THE THEATRE SERIES

Oscar G. Brockett, General Editor

Number 8

A Books of the Theatre project of the American Educational Theatre Association

Vsevolod Meyerhold about 1930

James M. Symons

Meyerhold's Theatre of the Grotesque

The Post-Revolutionary Productions, 1920-1932

University of Miami Press

Coral Gables, Florida

All photographs courtesy of NOVOSTI from SOVFOTO.
   The quotation from Mayakovsky's *Mystery-Bouffe* is from *The
Complete Plays of Vladimir Mayakovsky*, translated by Guy Daniels.
Copyright © 1968 by the Washington Square Press, Inc., a division
of Simon & Schuster, Inc. Reprinted by permission of the publisher.

To Judy, with love

We, too, will show you life that's real—
very!
But life transformed by the theatre into a spectacle
most extraordinary!

—Vladimir Mayakovsky
(Introduction to *Mystery-Bouffe*)

Contents

Illustrations

Foreword

The American Educational Theatre Association—as part of a continuing joint project with the University of Miami Press—presents the eighth volume in its Books of the Theatre Series. The present manuscript serves as an excellent companion piece to the seventh volume in the Series (Tairov's *Notes of a Director,* translated by William Kuhlke), shedding, as it does, further light on the Russian theatre of the early Twentieth Century, particularly for American readers.

When in June of 1939 Vsevolod Meyerhold disappeared from public sight, he joined the ranks of "non-people," and his name did not appear in print anywhere in the U.S.S.R. until 1956. Since that time both critical studies and personal memoirs have appeared in Russian, devoted in whole or in part to Meyerhold, and at least one important work has appeared in English. Largely on the basis of these materials, plus a volume of Meyerhold's own articles, letters, and speeches, James Symons has developed the present treatment of the distinguished director's busiest and most important decade: from 1920 to just beyond 1930.

Especially if it is taken together with the Kuhlke translation of Tairov, the Symons volume gives American readers their richest insights into what was actually happening on the Russian stage after the Revolution—what was happening, that is to say, outside the walls of the Art Theatre of Danchenko and Stanislavsky.

H. D. Albright
Editor

Preface

It may be argued that Vsevolod Emilevich Meyerhold stands in relation to the modern theatre as do his contemporaries Isadora Duncan, Igor Stravinsky, and Walter Gropius to dance, music, and architecture. Indeed, critic Louis Lozowick writes of him as "the Picasso of the Theatre."[1] And in a recent article for the *Educational Theatre Journal* Norris Houghton wrote that "Meierhold* has had a far more pervasive posthumous influence on us all than we are quite aware. . . . He made the theatre theatrical again."[2]

Compared to such innovators as Picasso, Duncan, Stravinsky, and Gropius, the study of Meyerhold's career, theories, and influence has been until very recently incidental and for the most part superficial. For more than a decade after Meyerhold's disappearance in 1939 the most extensive and reliable sources of information available were Nikolai Volkov's excellent but incomplete biography covering Meyerhold's life and career only to 1917, and a collection of Meyerhold's writings from 1905 to 1912 under

*When quoting from sources in English I shall leave transliterations unchanged when at variance with my spellings (which follow System I in J. T. Shaw's *Transliteration of Modern Russian*).

the title, *O teatr* [On the theatre]. Beyond this, valuable but inconclusive accounts of Meyerhold's work during and after the Revolution are contained in the eyewitness accounts of Western visitors such as Norris Houghton, Huntley Carter, Oliver Saylor, Andre Van Gyseghen, and Joseph McLeod. Together with a strongly biased account of Meyerhold's "descent" into aestheticism by a former disciple, Boris Alpers (*Theatre of the Social Mask*), a brief chronology of the Meyerhold Theatre from 1920 to 1927 by Alexy Gvozdyev, and two post-Revolution monographs by Meyerhold—*Ampluya aktora* [The emploi of the actor], written with V. M. Bebutov and I. A. Aksenov, and *Rekonstruktsia teatra* [Reconstruction of the theatre]—these accounts by enthralled Westerners constituted the bulk of the material available on Meyerhold's activities after the Revolution.

Not until the biographical study by Yuri Jelagin in 1955, *Temny geny* [Dark genius], and the excellent history of the Soviet theatre by Nikolai A. Gorchakov in 1957 (who was a production assistant of Meyerhold's in the 1920s) was there any detailed study of Meyerhold's entire career. But since Meyerhold's posthumous rehabilitation in 1956, studies by Russian theatre scholars have begun to appear, as well as previously suppressed material from the state archives. As a result, we now have available three very important publications: *Vstrechi s Meyerholdom* [Meetings with Meyerhold], a fascinating collection of essays in recollection of their work with Meyerhold by forty-seven different contributors; *V. E. Meyerhold: statyi, pisma, rechi, besedy* [V. E. Meyerhold: articles, letters, speeches, conversations], an invaluable two-volume collection of Meyerhold's public utterances; and *Meyerhold on Theatre*, the first comprehensive English translation of many of Meyerhold's most important articles plus a highly informative critical commentary by Edward Braun. In addition, it is now permissible for personal memoirs to contain references to Meyerhold, and as a result we now have at least three richly informative and intimate descriptions of Meyerhold's manners and methods (albeit always avoiding his political problems in the 1930s): Boris Zakhava's *Sovremniki* [Contemporaries], Igor Ilinsky's *Sam o sebye* [Myself about myself] and Yuri Annenkov's *Dnevnik moikh vstrech* [A journal of my encounters].

On the basis of these materials the pages which follow describe the work of Meyerhold from his opening of the First Theatre of the R.S.F.S.R. with *The Dawns* in 1920 to his last productions in 1931 just prior to the advent of official Socialist Realism. The starting point of such a study is rather easy to select. His last production before the Revolution was Lermontov's *Masquerade*—a lavish, mystical production which premiered at the Alexandrinsky Imperial Theatre on 25 February 1917, just two days before the Revolution. After concluding the Alexandrinsky season, Meyerhold, like everyone else in Russia, was drawn into the melee of revolution and civil war. Not until *The Dawns,* three years later, did he resume regular work as one of Russia's leading directors and begin to make radical changes in the Russian theatre.

To conclude the study with his productions of 1931 is a much more arbitrary decision. The Meyerhold Theatre itself was not actually closed until 1938. But from 1927 on there was serious and overt government interference in Meyerhold's work. It was not, however, until 1932 that Stalin felt powerful enough to officially demand that all artists adhere to one approach: Socialist Realism. Until this time some artists, such as Meyerhold and Mayakovsky, had continued to go much their own way despite growing pressure. But from 1932 Meyerhold became virtually persona non grata in most Russian theatres and theatre circles, including even the theatre which bore his name. And after losing a dramatic showdown with government censors in 1932 over a proposed production of Nikolai Erdman's caustic satire on contemporary Soviet life (*The Suicide*), the nature of Meyerhold's productions changed noticeably. From his 1932 production of Molière's *Don Juan* to his last work—assisting Stanislavsky on a production of *Rigoletto* in 1939—he restricted himself (or was restricted to) "classics," revisions of earlier productions, and some radio productions.

Consequently, the years between 1920 and 1932 comprise the period when Meyerhold was in his artistic prime, in full authority of his own theatre, and free to go as far as his creative impulse would take him in seeking "an organic form for the given content." His work in this period should reveal, if any period can, that theatrical form which he said "bore all the traits of my particular creative individuality."[3]

During this eleven-year period the public witnessed Meyerhold's staging of eighteen different plays at his theatre on Sadovaya Street and two at the Theatre of the Revolution. In addition, five productions were directed under Meyerhold's general supervision—three at the Sadovaya Street theatre and two at the Theatre of the Revolution. These productions form the basis of this fourfold study: a chronicle of Meyerhold's activities in the theatre during his most active Soviet years; an examination of the motives—artistic and political—which underlay his work in this period; support for the proposition that Meyerhold's theatre was essentially a public laboratory in which he, as chief experimenter, sought to evolve a viable alternative to theatrical realism; and a description of that alternative.

1

An Era Ends, A Career Begins

The usual image of Vsevolod Meyerhold is that of an erratic, brooding, and tempestuous innovator—an anti-hero of Byronesque proportions who discovered too late that the Bolshevism which he had embraced was antithetical to the creative freedom which he had to have in order to live. Such an image is not an entirely false one.

The following words, however, purportedly spoken by Meyerhold at a time when political pressure had already grown to ominous intensity, should be borne in mind in any study of his life and work:

> If, after my death, you have to read memoirs in which I am portrayed as a priest, puffed up with my own importance and uttering eternal truths, I charge you to declare that this is libel, and that I was always a very happy person: in the first place, because I greatly love to work, and when you work, you are always happy; but in the second place, because I know for a fact that what is said in jest is often more serious than what is said seriously.[1]

It is reported that a short time later, at the First All-Union

Congress of Directors in June 1939 he put aside jesting and, in what was supposed to have been a recantation, spoke instead, and for the last time publicly, with the forthrightness and passion that had always been characteristic:*

> At this point, I must talk bluntly: if what you have been doing with the Soviet theatre recently is what you call antiformalism . . . then I would prefer to be what you consider a "formalist.". . . The pitiful and wretched thing that pretends to the title of the theatre of socialist realism has nothing in common with art.
> But the theatre is art! And without art, there is no theatre! 2

Such directness, such blatant nonconformity, such "aestheticism," was no longer tolerated in the Soviet Union of 1939. On the following day Meyerhold disappeared and was never heard from again. Not until 1956 was it even permissible to mention his name in print. At that time it was noted that he had died in prison in 1942. More recently, the date of death has been set at 2 February 1940, but the cause remains a matter of speculation.

He had been placed in the ranks of "non-people" and remained there until after the Stalin era. But like a prince of old Imperial Russia, summarily eliminated in the middle of the night, his ghost has haunted the predictably timid and vapid productions of Soviet theatres. Perhaps more than any other creative artist in Soviet Russia's history, Meyerhold's life and fate exemplify just how brutally the ideal of free expression, nurtured by the October Revolution, was subsequently betrayed. And for those in Russia who dare hint at such betrayal or those who have escaped into self-imposed exile to write and speak openly about it, Vsevolod Meyerhold has become a symbol of martyrdom in the struggle for artistic freedom in Soviet Russia. His speech to the Congress of Directors was, in Harrison Salisbury's opinion, "the last open appeal for honesty in art, for creative freedom, that was to be heard in Moscow for nearly twenty years."[3]

---

*Some have questioned the validity of Yuri Jelagin's "stenographic record" of this speech—which is the only record available—and have gone so far as to suggest that in his speech Meyerhold did in fact recant (see Braun's *Meyerhold on Theatre*, p. 252). However, Meyerhold's subsequent fate would certainly seem to give credence to the general tone of Jelagin's account even though the precise wording may be questionable.

For a man who was destined to become such a famous rebel and iconoclast Meyerhold's childhood was pleasantly bourgeois and supremely uneventful. His father, Emile Fedorovich Meyergold, had as a young man severed connections with both his religion and his native land, converting from Judaism to Lutheranism and moving from his native Germany to Russia. Eight years later, having married the daughter of a poor German-Russian family and settled in a provincial town of Pensa, he had built up a distillery business that established the Meyergold family as one of the first families of Pensa. He was a powerful, outgoing person who took great pride in his accomplishments as a businessman and was quite fond of giving parties for his influential friends and prominent visitors to Pensa.

As might be expected, this Russian brewer of German origin left the care and rearing of his eight children very much in the hands of their mother, Alvina Danulovna Meyergold. Romantic, sensitive, and especially fond of music, she countered the Babbittry of Emile Fedorovich with frequent musical evenings in which all the children participated—including the youngest, Karl Emilevich.* As a young boy Karl was started on piano lessons by his mother and continued studying until well into his gymnasium years.

Second only to music in the household of Alvina Meyergold was the influence of the theatre. This came primarily through the flamboyant gossip of touring actors who visited the Meyergold home when playing in Pensa. These visitors were not always second-raters. As in America in the late nineteenth century, many of the country's best actors regularly toured the provinces, and although Pensa was never one of Russia's most important cities, it was at this time culturally alive. It was a busy trade center on the Siberian route and close enough to Moscow and Petersburg to be popular as a center for political and literary dissidents who found life uncomfortable in the capitals. This atmosphere, frequently brought directly into the Meyergold household in the course of parties and social evenings, was bound to play some part in shaping the personality of young Karl.

---

*At age twenty-one Karl changed his name to Vsevolod (after the writer Garshin) Emilevich (patronimic) Meyerhold (changing the Jewish-sounding "g" to "h").

Karl Emilevich was born 28 January 1874 (Old Style).* Ten years later he entered the Pensa Gymnasium where he studied math and literature. He was regarded as a bright, serious student, but often preoccupied with music, theatre, and what sophisticated visitors to the home called "contributing to the times." While still in his early teens he came under the influence of the socialist critics. Like many young men of his time, he was deeply impressed by Chernyshevsky's *What Is To Be Done?* as well as the writings of Pisaryev and Lavrova-Mirtova.

But his interest in political ideas was more than balanced by his growing fascination with the theatre. He spent as much time as he could at the Pensa theatre, especially when guest artists were on hand. Among others he saw Lensky in *Masquerade,* Zorina in *Camille,* Rossi in Shakespeare, and the popular comedians Shukovsky and Andrey-Burlak. Since the Meyergold family did little traveling, the Pensa theatre with its local actors and guest performers was the primary and perhaps exclusive source of Meyerhold's firsthand knowledge of the theatre until he left Pensa to attend law school in Moscow at the age of twenty-one.

He eventually became more than a spectator at the Pensa theatre. In 1892, at the age of eighteen, he served as assistant director for a Pensa theatre production of *Woe from Wit* and made his acting debut in the character role of Repetilov. (His older brother, Fedor, played the lead role of Chatsky.) The comments from the local critic, A. A. Kosminsky, are interestingly prophetic: he wrote that young Karl was not bad at all in the role of Repetilov, "but regrettably, there was a certain weakness in his playing, judging from the example of certain professional comedians who have played Repetilov's drunkenness with less exaggeration."[4] For the rest of his life Meyerhold's acting and directing would be criticized, often in much harsher terms, on the same basis: a lack of "professional" polish due to a marked tendency toward exaggeration.

The death of his father five days after his debut in *Woe from Wit* seems to have had little effect on him. According to his friend

*In the nineteenth century Old Style (Julian) calendar dates are twelve days behind New Style (Gregorian).

and biographer, Nikolai Volkov, Karl had grown very proud of his Russian nationality and consequently felt that there was a fundamental difference between himself and his German father. His character and tastes, however, were strongly influenced by the German atmosphere in his home. He spoke German and was familiar with the works of Goethe, Shiller, Lessing, and especially Mozart, Haydn, Beethoven, and Wagner. In the same year as his stage debut and his father's death (1892), he heard his first Wagnerian symphony and, by Volkov's account, was profoundly and lastingly moved.

If at this point we note three works which his biographers say made deep impressions on Karl during his formative years, we can begin to see the complex mixture of interests and inclinations that was to become characteristic of his career: Chernyshevsky's *What Is To Be Done?*, Griboyedov's *Woe from Wit,* and the music of Wagner—a combination of social criticism, satire, and mysticism.

In the fall of 1895 Meyerhold entered law school at the University of Moscow but the young provincial was so enthralled with the bustling theatrical life of Moscow—ballet, drama, opera, and concerts—that the study of law was soon of little concern to him. After establishing the Pensa People's Theatre with a group of young social activists in his home town during the summer, he returned to Moscow in the fall of 1896 where he discontinued his law studies and enrolled instead in the drama class of the Moscow Philharmonic Society. There, at the age of twenty-two, he entered upon his first formal theatre training under V. I. Nemirovich-Danchenko who later said of him, "Among the students of the Philharmonic school, Meyerhold was exceptional. . . .The best quality of his acting is a wide variety of characterizations. In the school he played more than fifteen major roles—from powerful elderly characters to ordinary vaudeville—and it is difficult to say which was best."[5]

Upon graduating—he and Olga Knipper, Chekhov's future wife, received the highest graduation marks of 5-plus—Meyerhold was invited by Nemirovich-Danchenko to join a new company being formed with Konstantin Stanislavsky and subsequently known as the Moscow Art Theatre. Thus, at the age of twenty-four, with two years of formal training at the Philharmonic and two years of amateur acting experience with the Pensa People's Theatre, Meyerhold began his professional career as a charter member of a company that was to become world famous and the very antithesis of all that Meyerhold himself would eventually represent.

Meyerhold's acting career with the Moscow Art Theatre started promisingly and proceeded steadily downhill. After playing such important roles as Treplev in *The Sea Gull,* Prince Argonsky in *Shylock (The Merchant of Venice)*, Marquis Forlipopoli in *Mistress of the Inn,* and Groznom in *The Death of Ivan the Terrible* in his first two seasons, he was assigned only one important role in his third season (Tusenbach in *The Three Sisters*) and in his fourth season with the Art Theatre was assigned only two small parts—both so insignificant that he went completely unmentioned by the critics.

By this time—the winter of 1901-1902—it was obvious that Meyerhold's personal style was incompatible with the subtle realism being developed by Stanislavsky and Nemirovich-Danchenko; and when in February the Moscow Art Theatre was reorganized on a contractual basis, Meyerhold and two other members were not listed as part of the new company. In a letter to the *Moscow Courier* Meyerhold and the other two actors explained: "While not wishing to give publicity to the causes which compelled us to leave the Art Theatre, we consider it a duty to state that our resignation . . . was not connected in any way with considerations of a material nature."[6]

Although it may have been true that Meyerhold's disagreement with the heads of the Moscow Art Theatre was aesthetic rather than financial, it is also probable that at the time he had no clear alternative in mind. After his first journey abroad—like most Russian travelers, he immediately fell in love with the warm, colorful climate and culture of summertime Italy—he returned to Russia in the fall of 1902 and with one of the other former members of the Art Theatre formed a company composed of unemployed actors and students from Moscow. They leased the civic theatre in the town of Kerson for the 1902-1903 season, and by Meyerhold's own admission proceeded to imitate the methods and aesthetics of the Moscow Art Theatre. "I began as a director with a slavish imitation of Stanislavsky. Theoretically, I no longer accepted many of his directing methods . . . but practically, having undertaken the business, I at first timidly followed in his footsteps."[7]

In his four seasons with the "Comrades of the New Drama" (as they decided to call themselves in their second season), Meyerhold served his directorial internship. Forced to present a constantly changing bill of theatrical fare in order to attract the same limited provincial audience to the theatre night after night, Meyerhold and his associates staged a rapid and seemingly endless succession of plays and scenes from plays. Although they occasionally did Shakespeare, the emphasis—as the company's name would imply—was on modern drama: Ibsen, Chekhov, Tolstoy, Ostrovsky, and in the later seasons especially the symbolist dramas of Hauptmann, Schnitzler, Maeterlinck, Przybyszewski, and again, Ibsen.

Although by 1905 Meyerhold had actually done very little that could be considered revolutionary, what he had done (primarily, a nonrealistic production of Przybyszewski's *Snow*) resulted in his designation by certain Petersburg symbolist poets as the titular head of the symbolist movement in the theatre. More importantly, he was talking a good game: making it clear in articles and lectures that he intended further and more extensive explorations into the realm of stylized theatre.

But the poets of Petersburg were not the only ones interested in Meyerhold's work. Stanislavsky, who at this time was also seeking an alternative to realism, was keeping an eye on his former employee.

> The difference between us lay in the fact that I only strained toward the new, without knowing any of the ways for reaching and realizing it, while Meierhold thought that he had already found new ways and methods which he could not realize partly because of material conditions and partly due to the weak personnel of his troupe. . . . I decided to help Meierhold in his new labors, which, as it seemed to me then, agreed with many of my dreams at the time.[8]

Thus, on 5 March 1905 Stanislavsky introduced Meyerhold as director of the Moscow Art Theatre Studio on Provarskaya Street.

But in the following fall, after a summer of preparation, it was again evident that, their mutual admiration and friendship notwithstanding, Meyerhold and Stanislavsky were not artistically compatible. Stanislavsky was willing to forego realism and explore the possibilities of stylized theatre, but not at the expense of the individual creativeness of the actor. The work of the director, he said, "was interesting to me only in so far as he helped the creativeness of the actor." And Meyerhold's work in the Studio struck Stanislavsky as a usurpation of the actor's creative prerogatives—under the circumstances, necessary perhaps, but nonetheless contrary to the ideals of the Art Theatre: "The talented stage director tried to hide the actors with his work, for in his hands they were only clay for the molding of his interesting groups and *mises en scène,* with the help of which he was realizing his ideas."9

So, with Stanislavsky's explanation that "a good idea, badly shown, dies for a long time," the Studio opening was indefinitely postponed and Meyerhold and Stanislavsky went their separate ways. For thirty-three years they respectfully disagreed with each other from a distance and never joined forces again until 1938 when, again at Stanislavsky's invitation, Meyerhold joined him in preparing a production of *Rigoletto*—the production destined to be the last for both men.*

Even though the work prepared in the Studio was never opened to the public, Meyerhold had become, more than ever, the *enfant terrible* of the Russian theatre. And through the urgings of her friends—many of whom were numbered among the new school of symbolist poets in Petersburg—the famous actress-manager Vera Komissarzhevskaya decided to thrust her theatre into the vanguard of the movement for theatrical modernism by hiring the director who was too eccentric for the Moscow Art Theatre.

The two seasons Meyerhold spent with Komissarzhevskaya were stormy ones. As a talented and strong-willed actress whom Russian critics compared favorable to Duse, Komissarzhevskaya was unlikely to accede to being "clay for the molding of . . . interesting groups." Meyerhold, on the other hand, was at that point in

*According to Yuri Bakhrushin, one of his assistants at the Opera Studio, shortly before his death Stanislavsky said, "Take care of Meyerhold; he is my sole heir in the theatre—here or anywhere else" (*Vstrechi s Meyerholdom,* p. 589).

his career (age thirty-two, eight years of professional experience) when he felt neither the need nor the desire to compromise with anyone. It is not surprising, therefore, that in the midst of their second season Meyerhold demanded absolute authority over his own productions or he would walk out, and Komissarzhevskaya, in turn, reminded him whose theatre it was and pointed the way to the nearest exit.

But their season and a half of combined efforts had not been without its fruits. After opening the first season on 10 November 1906 with an impressionistic* production of *Hedda Gabler* starring Komissarzhevskaya in the title role, Meyerhold proceeded to stage ten more productions at the Komissarzhevskaya Theatre in the 1906-1907 season.

Although in every production Meyerhold was up to something out of the ordinary (it was usually categorized as Symbolist or Impressionist theatre), several of the productions were comparatively uneventful—e.g., Yushkevich's *In the City*, Przybyszewski's *The Eternal Story*, Ibsen's *Nora* (*A Doll's House*), Gerberg's *Love's Tragedy*, Ibsen's *Love's Comedy*, and von Hofmannsthal's *The Wedding of Zobedy*—while others evoked a strong but mixed reaction from critics and the public: Maeterlinck's *Sister Beatrice* and *The Miracle of St. Anthony*, and the opener, *Hedda Gabler.* Only two of his shows during this first season with Komissarzhevskaya were clearly landmarks and the merit of these was hotly disputed at the time. Andreyev's *Life of Man* concluded the season and was, in the opinion of Vera's brother Feodor (who usually had little good to say about Meyerhold's approach and productions), one of the most successful achievements of the Komissarzhevskaya Theatre.[10]

The production used only a few suggestive set pieces arranged before "a deep, gloomy expanse in which everything stands motionless."[11] This opening effect was achieved by eliminating flats and covering the stage walls with dark drapes and then

---

*Meyerhold offered the following defense of his nonrealistic production: "What is the significance of this setting which gives the impression of a vast, cold blue, receding expanse, but which actually looks like nothing whatsoever? . . . Life is not like this, and it is not what Ibsen wrote. . . . The theatre is attempting to give primitive, purified expression to what it senses behind Ibsen's play: a cold, regal, autumnal Hedda" (Meyerhold, *O teatr*, p. 189).

keeping these draped walls in deep shadows. The lighting effects—highly selective spotlighting with symbolic and atmospheric implications—were, according to Feodor Komissarzhevsky and biographer Volkov, a major innovative contribution to scenic modernism on the Russian stage. Meyerhold himself wrote: "This production demonstrated that the New Theatre is not dedicated exclusively to two-dimensional presentation. The majority was wrong to assume that our whole system consisted merely in reducing settings to a decorative panel with the figures of the actors blending with it to form a flat and stylized bas-relief."[12] The second statement refers to his hieratic productions of Maeterlinck in which he was experimenting with Fuchs' relief-stage idea. The other landmark production, which Meyerhold starred in as well as directed, was Alexander Blok's *The Puppet Booth**—the quintessential production of Meyerhold's pre-Bolshevik years. On opening night, 30 December 1906, there was nearly a riot in the theatre as half the audience yelled invectives while the other half called for repeated bows from Meyerhold and Blok.

The point at issue was basically that of realism versus theatricalism; and *The Puppet Booth,* more than any of his previous productions, resounded through the auditorium of the Komissarzhevskaya Theatre like a theatricalist manifesto.

> The entire stage is hung at the sides and rear with blue drapes; this expanse of blue serves as a background as well as reflecting the colour of the setting in the little booth erected on the stage. This booth has its own stage, curtain, prompter's box, and proscenium opening. Instead of being masked by the conventional border, the flies, together with all the ropes and wires, are visible to the audience. . . .
>
> The action begins at a signal on a big drum; music is heard and the audience sees the prompter crawl into his box and light a candle. The curtain of the booth rises to reveal a box set with doors. . . . Parallel to the footlights is a long table, behind which are seated the "Mystics." . . . By the window is a round table with a pot of geraniums and a

---

*In Russian, *Balaganchik*—diminutive form of *balagan* which means "booth," "show," or "farce." An accurate but clumsy translation would be, *The Fairground Puppet Booth.*

slender gilt chair on which Pierrot [played by Meyerhold] is sitting. Harlequin makes his first entry from under the Mystics' table.[13]

In this way Meyerhold described the production six years later in his book *O teatr.*

Blok's play, which he dedicated to Meyerhold, employed the traditional figures of Pierrot, Columbine, and Harlequin along with an assembly of Mystics and the play's Author and proceeded along the lines of a "buffoonade." His purpose, he said in a letter to Meyerhold, was to "smash right through all the dead stuff"—i.e., the personal masks and communal façades which trap behind them life's vitality and meaningful permanence. "I accept the world—the whole world with its stupidity, obliqueness, dead and dry colors—only in order to fool this bony witch and make her young again. In the embraces of the Fool and the Buffoon the old world brightens up, becomes young, and its eyes become translucent, depthless."[14]

There is no question that Blok's play and his ideas about it struck a particularly responsive chord in Meyerhold and permanently influenced his ideas about the theatre.* In subsequent years he often made reference to *The Puppet Booth* in order to illustrate his ideas and frequently did so in terms similar to those used by Blok. In 1912 he proclaimed: "The new *theatre of masks* will . . . build its repertoire according to the laws of the fairground booth, where entertainment always precedes instruction and where movement is prized more highly than words."[15] And in 1920, at the outset of his Bolshevik years: "Here is our theatrical programme: plenty of light, plenty of high spirits, plenty of grandeur, plenty of infectious enthusiasm, unlabored creativity, the participation of the audience in the corporate creative act of the performance."[16] Even as late as 1935: "Now I would be able to put on Blok's *The Puppet Show* as a *sui generis* theatrical Chapliniad. Read *The Puppet Show,* and you will see in it all the

---

*Blok was not the only influence on Meyerhold at this time. In the fall of 1906 he had read Georg Fuchs' *The Theatre of the Future* and, by Volkov's account, "Fuchs opened to Meyerhold a series of new and interesting problems in the sphere of staging productions," as well as reflecting many of Meyerhold's emerging instincts about theatre art (Volkov, *Meyerhold,* 1:241). In addition, during the summer of 1907 Meyerhold traveled to Germany to observe the work of Reinhardt.

elements of Chaplinesque plots; only the wrappings of everyday life are different. Heine is also akin to Chaplin and *The Puppet Show*. In great art, there *is* such a complex kinship."[17]

On 15 September 1907 Meyerhold opened his second season at Komissarzhevskaya's theatre with Wedekind's *Spring's Awakening* —a mildly successful production noteworthy primarily for further innovations in theatrical lighting effects and the strain it put on the relationship between Meyerhold and Komissarzhevskaya due to his refusal to cast her as the play's teen-age heroine. In their next production, one month later, Komissarzhevskaya had her way and the result was a disastrous production of *Pelléas and Mélisande* in which Komissarzhevskaya was embarrassingly miscast as the young Mélisande. The fault, however, was not entirely hers. Even Meyerhold's admirers admitted that either his attempt at directing the performances in something he called "primitive marionette" style was a boring failure, or he simply lost interest in trying to work with Komissarzhevskaya.[18]

Whatever the reasons, the production was such an abysmal failure that Komissarzhevskaya called a meeting of the company and demanded that Meyerhold admit his errors or leave the company. The problem was not just the *Pelléas and Mélisande* production, but his increasing tendency to employ actors as mere marionettes.

Meyerhold, of course, refused to take all the blame. While the tension increased they did have a successful production of Sologub's *The Victory of Death,* but this was too little, too late, and really beside the point—which now came down to much the same question that separated Meyerhold and Stanislavsky: was the theatre ultimately the province of the actor or the director? Although Meyerhold always talked of the primacy of the actor—especially with regard to the actor's relationship to the playwright or scene designer—his actual practice convinced most observers that he gave primacy to the actor only so long as the actor carried out his explicit instructions.

Three days after the opening of *The Victory of Death* Komissarzhevskaya wrote to Meyerhold, "The route on which you persistently travel is a route which leads to a puppet theatre. ... This is your route, but not mine; and in answer to your own phrase, spoken at the last meeting of our art council: 'Maybe I shall leave this theatre,' I will now say, yes, it is necessary for you to leave." [19] The parting was not amiable. There were bitter charges and pointless attempts to shift the blame for production failures. On December 20 Meyerhold took Komissarzhevskaya to court, suing for breach of contract, but the decision was in her favor. He finished the 1907-1908 season by gathering a troupe of actors and touring the provincial cities of western Russia with the productions he had staged at the Komissarzhevskaya Theatre.

Meyerhold and Komissarzhevskaya never worked together again. Three years later she died, still very popular but in deep financial trouble. Her brother Feodor would always hold Meyerhold partially responsible for the increasing difficulties which led to her exhausted collapse and death in the remote eastern provinces where she was touring (in an effort to clear her debts).

At this point, after unpropitious starts with Stanislavsky and Komissarzhevskaya, Meyerhold's faltering career was given a significant boost from a totally unexpected quarter. "When the painter Golovin came into my office and told me that Meyerhold had been fired from the Komissarzhevskaya Theatre because he almost killed everybody there in his innovator's frenzy, I immediately said to Golovin that I wanted to see Meyerhold without even consulting my artistic advisors," writes V. A. Teliakovsky, Director of the Imperial Theatres in 1907.[20] And on the following morning a rather bewildered Meyerhold was ushered into the offices of this most powerful theatre personage in all Russia.

In spite of the successful independent ventures of producers like Stanislavsky, Nemirovich-Danchenko, Alexander Suvorin, Komissarzhevskaya, and Korsh (since the removal in 1882 of the Imperial Theatres' monopoly on commercial theatre enterprises in Moscow and Petersburg), the Imperial Theatres—namely, the Alexandrinsky, Marinsky, and Mikhailovsky in Petersburg and the Bolshoy and Maly in Moscow—still dominated Russian theatre. With their huge companies and schools, their standard repertoire, and a sizable crown subsidy, the Imperial Theatres were naturally bastions of theatrical conservatism. Consequently, it was with no little surprise that Meyerhold found himself being received by

Teliakovsky. Furthermore, as Teliakovsky writes, "He must have been even more surprised when he left with the appointment as one of the director-producers of the Imperial Theatres."[21]

Some people read the event as a renunciation by Meyerhold of his avant-garde posture; for others, it represented an admission by the Imperial Theatres that whatever the dangers, they were going to have to move in a liberal direction if they hoped to remain a vital force in the modern Russian theatre. In fact, as the future proved, it was a marriage of convenience for both parties and involved a certain amount of compromise from both. In order to bring into the Imperial Theatre system someone who would "wake up the audience,"[22] Teliakovsky was willing to go along with some of Meyerhold's eccentricities and do what he could to get the actors to accept Meyerhold's reputedly autocratic methods. For Meyerhold, it meant that he would have to devise less controversial and less stridently iconoclastic productions for the government theatres and pursue his more experimental innovations on the side—at least initially. But, according to Marc Slonim, this did not necessarily entail a denial of artistic conscience by Meyerhold. "His recent experiences shattered his faith in the symbolist 'temple theatre.' He was also through with statuary, hieratic, pictorial, or linear stasis, and he wanted to get away from Craig's marionettes and Maeterlinck's abstractions."[23]

Although it is doubtful that Meyerhold's change of attitude was quite as abrupt as Slonim suggests, it is true that for whatever reasons—artistic conscience, professional exigencies, or, most likely, a combination of the two—Meyerhold's work at the Imperial Theatres was marked by an increased flamboyance, spectacle, overt theatricalism, and a reduction of cerebral symbolism.

"What attracted him most at this point of his career," writes Slonim, "were the circus and the music hall, bright and brilliant forms of spectacular show, with an emphasis on tragic farce and the comic grotesque."[24] In writing this Slonim undoubtedly had in mind not only Meyerhold's productions but also his essay of 1912, *Balagan* [The Fairground Booth]* in which he wrote,

*The similarity between the title of Blok's play, *Balaganchik* [The Puppet Booth], and the title of Meyerhold's subsequent essay, "Balagan" [The Fairground Booth], was undoubtedly intentional on Meyerhold's part.

Surely the art of man on the stage consists in shedding all traces of environment, carefully choosing a mask, donning a decorative costume, and showing off one's brilliant tricks to the public—now as a dancer, now as the intrigant at some masquerade, now as the fool of old Italian comedy, now a juggler. . . .

The theatre of the mask has always been a fairground show, and the idea of acting based on the apotheosis of the mask, gesture and movement is indivisible from the idea of the traveling show. . . .

The fairground booth is eternal. Even though its principles have been banished from within the walls of the theatre, we know that they remain firmly embedded in the lines of all true theatrical writers.[25]

Underlining this apparent change in his idea of theatrical art from a symbolist aesthetic to that of the theatre of masks and the grotesque* is the fact that after having drawn so often on the works of Maeterlinck, Hauptmann, and Ibsen in the years just prior to joining the Imperial Theatres, from 1908 on Meyerhold never again produced a Maeterlinck or Hauptmann play and left Ibsen untouched for ten years.

Instead, he seemed less concerned with staging a particular literary style (e.g., Maeterlinck, Hauptmann, von Hofmannsthal, Wedekind) and much more interested in developing a style of theatre apart from literature. As a result, his choice of plays began to cover a much wider spectrum of dramatic literature. During his years with the Imperial Theatres—from 1908 to 1917—he staged the works of such writers as Molière, Calderón, Gogol, Gluck, Gozzi, Strauss, Wagner, Tolstoy, and Pinero as well as Blok, Schnitzler, Sologub, Lermontov, and Przybyszewski.

In his Imperial Theatre productions—drama at the Alexandrinsky, opera at the Marinsky—as well as private productions under the nom de plume "Doctor Dapperttuto," Meyerhold sought to realize new forms of and approaches to the new, nonrealistic, consciously stylized art of the theatre about which he and others had recently been theorizing. At the Imperial Theatres the main thrust of his innovations was in the direction of the *mises en scène:* the relationship between performers and scenery and, in turn, the relationship between those two elements and the audience.

*A discussion of the grotesque is an important part of "The Fairground Booth" essay and is examined in chapter 3.

But as Stanislavsky had said of Meyerhold's experiments with the Moscow Art Theatre Studio in 1905, "For the new art new actors were necessary, actors of a new sort with an altogether new technique."[26] Certainly Meyerhold was no less aware of this than Stanislavsky— especially, we may assume, after his difficulties with Komissarzhevskaya and her company. Thus, while utilizing the facilities of the Imperial Theatres to carry out experiments in *mises en scène* and set designing (with considerable assistance from the painter and designer, Alexander Golovin), Meyerhold prepared to develop new acting techniques and, he hoped, a new kind of actor (both in private productions and in the Meyerhold Studio).

Thus in the nine-year period of his work leading up to the Revolution in 1917 Meyerhold experimented with scenic innovations at the Imperial Theatres in productions such as *Tristan and Isolde, Don Juan, Boris Godunov, Orphée,* and *Masquerade;* he experimented with new approaches to acting at the House of Interludes and at friends' apartments in commedia-like productions such as *The Scarf of Columbine, Adoration of the Cross, Harlequin, the Marriage Broker, The Puppet Booth,* and *The Unknown Woman*; he began expounding his views in his journal, *Lyubov k tryem apelsinam* [Love of Three Oranges] (which lasted a little over a year), and the publication in 1912 of his book, *O teatr* (a collection of articles he had written for *Lyubov k tryem apelsinam* and other journals from 1906 to 1912); and he devoted a great deal of time and energy to the primary (although not exclusive) task of the Meyerhold Studio: the training and development of that new kind of actor—a twentieth-century *cabotin**— so essential to the realization of a new, retheatricalized theatre.

It was with these matters that Meyerhold was concerned when, on 27 February 1917—two days after the highly successful premier of his latest production at the Alexandrinsky, Lermontov's *Masquerade*—the Russian Revolution began. From that point on, nothing would ever be the same in Russia—including matters artistic.

---

*Cabotin: troubadour or minstrel; "a strolling player; . . . a kinsman to the mime, the histrion, and the juggler" (from "Balagan" in *O teatr*, p. 147).

2

October Comes to Sadovaya Street

Theatre in the New Soviet State

It is necessary for a Western observer—particularly an American—to understand that the theatre in Russia, like poetry and the novel, has always carried the potential for considerable social impact. It is perhaps inevitable that theatre, public readings, and church rites would play a prominent part in shaping attitudes and opinions in a country where the populace is largely illiterate (about eighty percent of the population on the eve of the Revolution) and those wishing to influence and govern them constitute a sophisticated and well-educated minority. For many Russians, especially in the provinces, the theatre was exceeded only by the church as a source of both diversion and enlightenment.

Immediately following the Revolution, the stage in Russia took on yet another function: it became a platform for essentially extemporaneous "productions"—indigenous or imported—which exuberantly proclaimed the victory of the proletariat, the "freeing of the toiling masses," and the duty of all to join in the building of a new society. According to Huntley Carter's figures, the number of theatres in Russia increased from 240 to over 6,000 between

1914 and 1920.[1] Marc Slonim states that in 1920 the armed forces alone had 1,200 theatres and 911 dramatic groups.[2]

Allowing for the probability that the figures given Carter and Slonim were bloated, the fact remains that by 1920 the theatre in Russia was, more than ever, a very important means of communicating to and instilling in the people the particulars of a cultural ideology. But in the Politburo definite conclusions had not yet been reached regarding just what the shape and content of this ideology should be.* Consequently, for a time the theatre artists were at liberty to thrash it out among themselves. The result was that splendidly fervent decade of Russian theatre history, the 1920s.

It would be misleading to suggest that in the chaos of the early 1920s there were certain clearly defined groups in contention for ultimate influence in the theatre. But allowing for considerable flux and overlap, the contending ideological forces can be categorized under three general headings. (I would disavow Huntley Carter's three-way division of "Left-Center-Right"[3] not only because of the possible confusion resulting from the political connotation of the terms, but also because it appeared to be more of a two-way split—the old versus the new with the latter being subdivided into two contending groups—rather than an equally balanced three-way split.)

First, there were those such as Stanislavsky, Nemirovich-Danchenko, Blok, and, significantly, Lunacharsky, who supported the established Russian theatre institutions. They contended that however valid the political change might be, the theatre must remain a thing apart and in the hands of trained artists whose business was art and not politics. At first this included an argument for the right to ignore modern propaganda drama for the sake of preserving the classics. Stanislavsky, for instance, directed only one Soviet propaganda play in his entire career: *Armored Train 14-69* in 1927—the Moscow Art Theatre's first production of a play with strictly Soviet subject matter.

*Even though Lenin himself had troubled to nationalize the property of all the theatres in Russia by the decree of 26 August 1919 in order to subordinate the theatres to the Bolshevik ideology ("On the Unification of Theatre Work"), he was still much too occupied with matters of international politics, civil war, and a devastated economy to work out any particulars regarding cultural affairs.

The other two categories were composed of those who sought to remake the theatre in a new Soviet image. But there were two different schools of thought on just how to go about it. On the one hand were those who reflected the old anti-Western attitudes of the Slavophiles and Scythians.* They wished to take the theatre out of the hands of the aristocrats, professionals, and imitators of Western traditions and return it to "the masses" where it would become simple, direct, participatory, and improvisational. Only in this way, they argued, could it once again really belong to and be a true expression of the Russian people.

On the other hand, there were those who sought to remake the theatre not by eliminating the professionals entirely but by broadening the scope of theatrical professionalism in such a way that eager, industrious young men and women could "take a job" in the theatre in much the same way that they would be employed in a factory. The proponents of this approach were interested in neither preserving the classics nor returning the theatre to the form of a rural roundelay. For them the new theatre of Soviet Russia would be the theatre of the machine age, the theatre of the proletariat, the theatre exploring the future rather than returning to the past.

It is in this last category that we find Meyerhold in 1920—along with Mayakovsky, the Futurists, and the Proletarian Culture Movement (*Proletkult*). For a brief time they carried the day. For a while they seemed to represent for most Western observers all that was so bright and hopeful in the "Great Russian Experiment." But the seeds of their destruction lay within: they were too closely linked with similar developments in the West, and the esoteric nature of much of their work made it unsuitable as a propaganda tool. This left them open to charges of aping "decadent capitalism" and of being guilty of obscurantism and formalism. In the early 1920s such phrases were only attempts to

---

*Slavophiles: members of a Russian intellectual movement which flourished in the 1840s, 1850s, and 1860s. They held that Russia's strength lay in her non-Western antirationalist, pre-Petrin roots.

Scythians: a group of writers and intellectuals who continued the Slavophile tradition in the early 1900s. They supported the Bolsheviks in 1917—not because they agreed with the aims of Marxism but because they believed the Revolution would sweep away the harmful traditions of European influence.

insult and discredit. But by 1932 they would carry the lethal weight of an official denunciation, and the Russian theatre was well on its way along the sterile route of Socialist Realism.

Meyerhold Joins the Bolsheviks

From an aesthetic point of view, the Meyerhold of 1920 seems almost irreconcilable with the Meyerhold of 1917 and before. At first glance, at least, it is hard to see anything but the obvious contradiction between his advocacy of *Proletkult* and Futurism's machine aesthetic in 1920 and his earlier dedication to the theatre of Appia, Fuchs, Wagner, and Maeterlinck. It is easy to see why Meyerhold might be accused of having made a complete about-face.

But from the political point of view there is no real basis for a similar charge of self-contradiction. It is true that as a director at the Imperial Theatres from 1908 to 1917 he served audiences of the aristocratic, intellectual, and bourgeois elite, but it would be wrong to infer from this that he endorsed their politics. On the contrary, from the time the young Meyerhold was first introduced to the liberal ideas of the Social Democrats by guests in his parents' home in Pensa he was on the side of "the people." One of his earliest ventures into the theatre was when, at the age of nineteen, he joined with some other concerned young people in his hometown to establish a theatre for the working classes—the Pensa People's Theatre.

His interest in social causes, however, was soon outstripped by his interest in the theatre. On the occasion of both the aborted revolution in 1905 and the successful one in 1917, he was so totally involved with the Studio project of the Moscow Art Theatre at the time of the former and his production of *Masquerade* for the Alexandrinsky at the time of the latter, that he was completely disengaged from the events taking place in the streets. But his neglect of political matters was due simply to his preoccupation with theatre rather than any personal opposition to the cause of the revolutionaries, and when the Revolution materialized there was no question where his sympathies lay.

In December of 1917—one month after the take-over by the

Bolsheviks*—the head of the newly created Commissariat of Education, Anatoly Lunacharsky, invited the most prominent Russian writers, painters, and actors to a conference on the arts in order to form a Department of Art within the Commissariat of Education. Of the one hundred and twenty invited, only five accepted. One of them was Meyerhold. One month later he was appointed head of the Petrograd (formerly Petersburg and subsequently Leningrad) branch of Theatre Section of the People's Commissariat of Education—known as TEO *Narkompros.*

Eight months later, in August of 1918, Meyerhold joined the Communist party. Through all the tribulations in the years which followed there is no evidence that he ever regretted it—his running battle with party bureaucrats, critics, and censors notwithstanding.

Three months after joining the party he presented the first Soviet drama. On the evening of 7 November 1918, at the Petrograd Theatre of Musical Drama, Meyerhold and Vladimir Mayakovsky initiated the history of the Soviet theatre with a production of Mayakovsky's *Mystery-Bouffe* in honor of the first anniversary of the Bolshevik revolution. The brawling, sprawling, cartoon-like political parody of a biblical mystery play based on the Flood was, according to Nikolai A. Gorchakov, "a noisy demonstration of the brilliant director's transition to Bolshevism."[4]

But due to the spread of disease to epidemic proportions and the shortages of fuel, food, and water, the city of Petrograd was becoming virtually uninhabitable and in 1919 Meyerhold left with his family for the southern part of Russia. Once there, however, in territory openly contested by the anti-Bolshevik White Army, Meyerhold began urging others—some of whom had left Petrograd for political reasons—to take sides with the Bolsheviks. As a result, he was arrested and nearly executed.**

---

*As soon as they were in power the Bolsheviks put Russia on the New Style (Gregorian) calendar used by the rest of Europe which in the twentieth century is thirteen days ahead of Imperial Russia's Old Style (Julian) calendar. Thus, the "October Revolution" (O.S.) took place in November (N.S.).

**Two men arrested with him were indeed executed. Unlike Meyerhold, they had no influential friends who would intervene at the last moment in their behalf.

Eventually the area was liberated by the Red Army. Meyerhold immediately felt the call of duty, proudly donned the Red Army uniform, and set about making plans for theatrical contributions within the ranks. But late in the summer of 1920 Lunacharsky called him to Moscow (which had replaced Petrograd as the capital of Russia) and appointed him to replace Olga Kameneva, Trotsky's sister, as head of TEO *Narkompros*. The appointment was officially announced on 16 September 1920.

His first concern was to find himself a theatre. While others debated which theatres should be nationalized and subsidized, and how much and to what end, Meyerhold commandeered the old Zon Opera house, introduced himself to the company which had recently been gathered there,* announced plans for the premier production in less than two months, and christened the enterprise the First Theatre of the R.S.F.S.R. (Russian Socialist Federative Soviet Republic).

R.S.F.S.R. I Opens: *The Dawns*

The old theatre stood in the midst of the Moscow theatre district at Number Twenty Sadovaya Street [Garden Street]. Inside the unheated derelict—with its flaking paint, broken and moldy seats, and water-soaked walls—the aristocratic nature of its past was suggested only by the traditional horseshoe-shaped loge at one end and a gaping hole of opera stage proportions at the other. The proscenium opening, framed by a proscenium arch which literally arched across the top in a slight curve, was approximately fifty feet wide and forty feet high. The Zon had never been one of Moscow's really elegant houses and now, in its stripped and dilapidated condition, its atmosphere was more that of an ordinary meeting hall with a monstrous stage than an opera theatre.

All in all, it was perfectly suited for Meyerhold's purpose: the establishment of the First Theatre of the R.S.F.S.R.—a theatre in

---

*A theatre collective composed of three groups formerly known as the Free Theatre, the New Theatre of KPSRO, and the State Showcase Theatre had been assigned to the Zon. It had yet to produce anything.

the spartan, ascetic spirit of the October Revolution and the very antithesis of the old insulated pockets of luxury amid deprivation that characterized the theatres of Imperial Russia. The First Theatre of the R.S.F.S.R. was to be, in every respect, nonillusionistic. If living quarters in Moscow were cold, damp, and in need of repair, so was the theatre. If noisy crowds of ragged soldiers and workers constantly puffing on foul-smelling, cheap cigarettes filled the political meeting halls of Moscow and Petrograd, they were welcome to fill the auditorium of the First Theatre of the R.S.F.S.R.

Even if there had been funds available for immediate refurbishing—and there probably weren't—Meyerhold, in a state of revolutionary idealism, might well have refused them. He wanted a harsh, open, rugged theatre that was clearly established to serve a much different clientele than the quietly comfortable interiors of the Maly, the Bolshoy, the Kamerny, and the Moscow Art Theatre. Whatever else might be said about the theatre at Twenty Sadovaya Street, it was unquestionably something quite different from the established "temples of art." Boris Alpers, a frequent and enthusiastic visitor, described it thus:

> It was an ordinary meeting hall, with damp spots on the walls, and a damp and bluish atmosphere. There were no ticket collectors at the doors of the theatre. . . . They were wide open and, in winter, snowstorms would sometimes invade the lobby and the corridors of the theatre and make the audiences turn up their overcoat collars. . . . The railings were stripped off the loges. The seats and benches for the audience had been greatly knocked about, and they were no longer arranged in rows. One could crack nuts or smoke cheap tobacco in the lobby. Red Army units and groups of young workers constituted the new audiences. They received their tickets by allotments, and they filled the theatre with noise and excitement.[5]

Of course, such conditions did not last for very long. The young Communists were proud of their suffering and sacrifices in the name of the Revolution, but like anyone else they preferred heated buildings, good tobacco, and comfortable clothing. And by the time its name was changed to the Meyerhold Theatre (in

1923), the theatre, although still comparatively unadorned, was heated, refurbished, and under at least a few administrative regulations. But during its brief history as the First Theatre of the R.S.F.S.R., the theatre at Number Twenty Sadovaya Street was clearly a participant in as well a product of the revolutionary times.

The inaugural production was Meyerhold's Sovietized version of *The Dawns* by the Belgian playwright Emile Verhaeren. Without revision *The Dawns* would have been an appropriate play for the Kerensky era of constitutional socialism. Written in 1898, the original play had not foreseen Bolshevism and the Soviet regime. Instead, it was directed against militarism, imperialism, and parliamentarianism; the proletarian mass was depicted as passive—deserving of sympathy—rather than overpowering. The protagonist, Erenian, emerges as the hero due to his success at reconciling the angry but inarticulate working masses with the wealthy but frightened capitalists.

In the adaptation by Meyerhold and his assistant, Georgy Chulkov, Erenian became a model Bolshevik, leading the masses to overthrow class enemies and establish the dictatorship of the proletariat. In expanding the role of the proletariat, Meyerhold and Chulkov added several completely new scenes. They modernized and Sovietized the play to such an extent that it became nothing less than a slightly abstracted account of the Russian Revolution (although conveniently ignoring the Kerensky interval between the overthrow of the Tsar and the Bolshevik assumption of power).

One of the most memorable aspects of the production was the appearance at every performance of a messenger who would read the latest dispatches from the fronts of both the civil war and the war against Poland. This would be followed by comments and discussions between the cast and the audience.*

Considering the content of the production, the absolutely nonillusionistic atmosphere created by the messenger's reports and the general condition of the theatre, it is somewhat surprising that the design of the production was not the nonillusionistic actualism

*Although this is sometimes regarded as a Meyerhold hallmark, he actually used it only in this particular production.

of later productions. Instead, it was what might be called Futuristic Cubism. On a stage of metallic gray cubes, flats, and ramps, actors dressed in metallic gray uniforms roamed about in a manner resembling a cross between ballet and military drill. The abstract decor of Vladimir Dmitriev filled the space above the stage floor with contra-reliefs, metallic triangles, shimmering strips of tin, and a pair of red and gold disks.

The scenic conception of *The Dawns* belonged more to Dmitriev than to Meyerhold. When he was writing about the stage form of *The Dawns* six years later (in 1926), Meyerhold stated that the idea for the setting originated with Dmitriev when he was a Meyerhold student in 1918. This was a course of instruction in the arts of designing and directing which was established by Meyerhold in the summer of 1918 under the auspices of TEO *Narkompros* (Theatre Section of the People's Commissariat of Education). Two years later Meyerhold brought Dmitriev into the founding of the First Theatre of the R.S.F.S.R. and they set to work on *The Dawns.* According to Meyerhold,

> In 1920 the First Theatre of the R.S.F.R. realized this work of Dmitriev. In this the attempt was made to conclusively break with the decorative canons of the Italian Renaissance theatre. But in making revisions to the traditional stage form Dmitriev stopped halfway. He put on the stage in place of decorative flats (painted and unpainted), various geometric forms, crisscrossing ropes, and so forth.[6]

And he went on to say that since the abstract design failed to really connect with the stage action, certain critics were not far from wrong when they spoke of the design as being a conglomerate of theatrical trinkets.

It must be remembered that Meyerhold made these comments from six years' hindsight. During these intervening years his purely constructivist productions were realized. But at the time of *The Dawns* the challenge was to break loose from the painted flats and backdrops of both the Art Nouveau and Naturalism (which Meyerhold regarded as nothing more nor less than a continuation of the decorative canons of the Italian Renaissance theatre). The production of *The Dawns* did in fact use a painted backdrop and even a curtain between acts (the last time Meyerhold was to use one). But the solid geometric forms, the arrangement of hanging ropes and pieces of metal, the large stairway between house and stage, and the abstract costumes all attracted the attention of and provoked comments by the audience and critics.

Notwithstanding the production's ardent pro-Soviet, agitprop nature,* the Communist critics did not care for *The Dawns*. It was to be expected that the defenders of realism would not find such a production to their tastes, but even Meyerhold's fellow Futurist, the prominent writer Victor Shklovsky, objected:

> Verhaeren has written a bad play. The revolutionary theatre is being created in haste, and hence the play has been hastily accepted as revolutionary. . . . The action has been made contemporary, although I cannot say why the Imperialist War takes place with spears and shields. In the middle of the second act, it seems, a messenger comes on and reads a dispatch about the losses of the Red Army at Perekop. . . . But because the action has been made contemporary, the dispatch is torn out of its context and the artistic effect which it was supposed to produce is not achieved.[7]

And as if an attack by Shklovsky were not a bitter enough pill to swallow, a few days later in the pages of *Pravda* there appeared a disparaging article by Natalia Krupskaya, the wife of Lenin.

Since Krupskaya rarely took time to address herself to artistic matters, that she wrote the article at all is some indication of the notoriety of Meyerhold's first offering at the First Theatre of the R.S.F.S.R. Unlike Shklovsky, Krupskaya admired Verhaeren's play; it was what Meyerhold did to it that distressed her:

> A wonderful tale is turned into a trivial farce, while all the charm of *Les Aubes* disappears. . . . In a Russian environment, in the environment of the class struggle, Erenian is a traitor, a traitor who has taken the bait of flattery. A hero outside of time and space can be overlooked, but to have the Russian proletariat act like Shakespeare's crowds—whom any conceited fool can lead wherever he feels like it—is an insult.[8]

But Meyerhold, who in his time had crossed swords with more than a few prominent personages, would not be put off even by

---

*agitprop—"Short for agitation-propaganda; pertaining to mobile dramatic troups which aim primarily at propagandizing their audiences" (Mordecai Gorelik, *New Theatres for Old*, p. 475).

Lenin's wife. He told his company that all the commotion caused by their production of *The Dawns,* far from being a discouragement, should actually reinforce their determination. He said that the critics may as well get used to the idea that this was to be a theatre which sought to arouse and agitate the audience rather than soothe it. And without mentioning her name he replied to Krupskaya: "It has been said that we destroyed Verhaeren's beautiful creation. I say, *nyet*; with Comrade Bebutov we did not go too far in this reworking process, in which it is necessary to go ever further, and if we failed to complete our work on Verhaeren, then that is only due to lack of time."[9]

These remarks were part of Meyerhold's contribution to a public discussion of the production on 22 November 1920, two weeks after the opening. The discussion turned into a debate between Meyerhold and Mayakovsky defending the production and Lunacharsky, critic S. A. Margolin, and others attacking it. It is worth noting that in the stenographic record of Meyerhold's remarks he makes no real attempt to defend the performance of the actors, which most critics described as the work of rank amateurs. In fact they were amateurs—rank or otherwise—and at this point Meyerhold was apparently more interested in using them as obedient warm bodies in an effort to realize his production concept than in training them as performing artists. His belief that "theatre is acting"[10] had been temporarily put aside in the name of agitprop theatre.

But with regard to the production of *The Dawns* in particular and the approach of the First Theatre of the R.S.F.S.R. in general, he was steadfast in their defense. To the suggestion by one of the disputants that *The Dawns*, having come under critical attack, should be moved to a less auspicious theatre, Meyerhold retorted, "We would be glad to offer Verhaeren's *The Dawns* to the [Moscow] Art Theatre and let them review their own repertoire. If they decide it is necessary for them to change their repertoire we will give them this play, choose another work and strive to introduce even more cubism, suprematism,* and tear out even more footlights."[11]

---

*Suprematism: one of the first systems of purely abstract pictorial composition, based on geometric figures. Its founder was the Russian artist Malevich who designed the set for the 1918 production of *Mystery-Bouffe*.

He concluded his defense with one of the oldest and best arguments that an innovative director sometimes has at his command for use against his conservative critics: the public was packing the theatre for every performance. And to underscore this he read a letter from a Red Army unit thanking him for offering them the kind of theatre and the kind of production which they felt was really theirs. The quiet decorum of the Moscow Art Theatre was all well and good for some people, said Meyerhold, but *Uncle Vanya* had nothing to say to the men of the Red Army, whereas *The Dawns* did.

A Theatrical October

All the hoopla raised by the inaugural production of the First Theatre of the R.S.F.S.R. was really part of a much broader ideological debate going on at the time over the appropriate relationship between the Revolution and the arts. With regard to his particular field, Meyerhold believed that it was time for an "October in the theatre." One month after the opening of *The Dawns* he published an article in the December 14 issue of the *Theatrical Herald* calling for all Russian theatres to become politically and conclusively revolutionary. He said it was the duty of the theatre to become "one of the tools in the revolutionary struggle and the development of socialism. The Theatrical October is a phenomenon of enormous proportions: revolutionizing the theatre professionals, creating [new] dramatists, regisseurs, and skilled actors, experimenting in the areas of an independent Red Army theatre . . . all this as well as revolutionizing and modernizing the theatres of the provinces."[12]

Throughout his career Meyerhold performed as an inveterate maximalist: once having decided on the appropriateness of an action, idea, or method—be it in the arts or politics—he was inclined to pursue it relentlessly to its limits. Believing as he did in the October Revolution of 1917—in which the Bolsheviks "maximalized" the political revolution of the preceding February by overthrowing the provisional government of Kerensky in the name of the proletariat—Meyerhold's call for a "Theatrical October" was his effort as head of TEO to carry into the realm of the Russian theatre what the Bolsheviks' October had accomplished in the spheres of Russian politics and economics.

He took his cue from one of the resolutions adopted by the Eighth Congress of the Communist party in 1919. It was entitled, "On Proletarian Culture," and said in part, "In the Soviet Workers' and Peasants' Republic, every educational endeavor, both in politics and in education generally—and in art particularly—must be permeated with the spirit of the proletariat's class struggle for successfully accomplishing the aims of its dictatorship."[13] But if Meyerhold read into the goals of such a resolution a tacit encouragement to proceed with the same means that had carried the day in 1917, then he failed to grasp the tenor of the changing times. The wide-eyed Bolshevik maximalism which in 1917 had swept aside everything in its path was by 1920 being tempered by the practical concerns of trying to defeat a counterrevolutionary force and stabilizing a nation torn by wars internal and external.

No sooner had Meyerhold unfurled his banner for a "Theatrical October" than he was made to realize that things were not as they had been in 1917. His immediate superior, Anatoly Lunacharsky, responded to Meyerhold's call for an October in the theatre with the statement, "I can entrust Comrade Meyerhold with the destruction of what is old and bad and with the creation of what is new and good, but I cannot entrust him with the preservation of what is old and good."[14] That such a highly placed spokesman for the party could speak of something being both old—i.e., a product of Tsarist Russia—and good must have come as a shock or at least a disappointment to Meyerhold.

But it shouldn't have. Like any revolutionary force once it obtains power, the Communist party's dictatorship was conservative and mortally afraid of unbridled flights of free thought. Furthermore, it was well-known that Lenin's personal artistic tastes were quite conservative. It was therefore no surprise that Meyerhold's call for a "Theatrical October," coming after the Communists had been in power for three years, received something quite less than enthusiastic support from the party. As Lunacharsky arrogantly remarked, "Now that the tiny theatrical October is arriving, it would, of course, be ridiculous to give it the valuables* which were preserved not without great labor at the time of the gigantic tempests in the real October [of 1917]."[15]

At the same time that Meyerhold was struggling to get his "Theatrical October" project underway there appeared in the party's official publication, *Pravda (Truth)*, an energetic denunciation by the Central Committee of the Communist party of new art, including the *Proletkult* movement, Futurism, and the production of *The Dawns* in particular: "In the region of art, workers are innoculated with an absurd distortion of taste."[16] And with an eyewitness account of *The Dawns* as a case in point, the article accused the intelligentsia of fostering half-bourgeois ideas and philosophies. Although such statements by the Central Committee in December 1921 did not have the ominous ring that they would a few years later, it was nonetheless perfectly clear that further efforts in this direction would not be well received.

Meyerhold rode out the polemical storm through the rest of the winter of 1920-1921. But with the coming of the spring thaw, a season which has aroused the freedom instinct in winter-bound Russians since time immemorial, Meyerhold decided it would be best to put at least a little distance between himself and the political machinery of the Communist state. On 8 April 1921, less than a year after having been appointed, he resigned as head of TEO.

This was not the occasion of a bitter split with the party. As a dedicated Communist he continued to champion the Soviet cause and continued to have several good friends in the official hierarchy. Although his resignation from TEO was followed by the indefinite postponement of his plans for an open-air mass spectacle, *Battles and Victories* (in which he planned to surpass Evreinov's 1919 production of *The Taking of the Winter Palace*), he was destined to do several Soviet agitprop productions in the years ahead.

Nevertheless, biographer Yuri Jelagin is probably right when he says that the production of *The Dawns* represents the high point of Meyerhold's enthusiasm for Communism and agitprop theatre.

---

*Lunarcharsky was referring to such theatres as the Moscow Art Theatre, the Bolshoy, and the Maly, which Meyerhold and the *Proletkult* sought to liquidate or take over.

The critical attacks which followed both *The Dawns* and his proposal for a "Theatrical October" did not embitter him, but for a man of his temperament the job of trying to comply with the party line in the theatre was too restrictive. Consequently, while remaining loyal to the party and its general goals he sought to establish a certain amount of independence for himself with regard to matters of art and the theatre.

For a while such an independent attitude was viable for a few people like Meyerhold and Mayakovsky whose revolutionary credentials and party contacts were strong enough (even though Mayakovsky, unlike Meyerhold, never joined the party). But such viability was destined to crumble away. With the reaction to *The Dawns* the handwriting first appeared on the wall, and according to Gorchakov, this was the beginning of Meyerhold's personal tragedy: "The extremely brilliant director had joined the Party and given all his creative strength to the Party theatre. He now turned out to be alien, too wise and incomprehensible for the proletarian 'supermen,' and so he worked alone."[17]

Mystery-Bouffe, Second Edition

By the very nature of the idea which motivated its coming into being, the First Theatre of the R.S.F.S.R. either functioned as an obedient representative of party tastes or it ceased to have a raison d'être. The production of *The Dawns* indicated a clear difference of opinion in this regard and the theatre's future was to be very brief. The ambitious repertoire* which Meyerhold had planned for the theatre's first season was never to be realized. But before concluding its brief existence the First Theatre of the R.S.F.S.R. offered a second production of historical significance: a new edition of the Meyerhold-Mayakovsky production of 1918, *Mystery-Bouffe.*

Meyerhold's resignation from TEO in April did not include resignation from the directorship of the First Theatre of the R.S.F.S.R., and less than a month later, on 1 May 1921, his new

---

*The Dawns, Mystery-Bouffe, Hamlet, Great Catherine (Shaw), *Golden Head* (Claudel), and *Women in Parliament* (Aristophanes).

staging of Mayakovsky's revised script premiered. In the sequence of productions at the First Theatre of the R.S.F.S.R. *Mystery-Bouffe* followed *The Dawns*; but as Huntley Carter has rightly observed, "*Mystery-Bouffe* . . . really preceded *The Dawns* in the logical order of illustrations of the course of current events. It [*Mystery-Bouffe*] reflected the Revolution as The Deluge sweeping away one social order and introducing another. After The Deluge, 'The Dawn.' " [18]

In the sequence of Meyerhold's post-Revolution productions, *Mystery-Bouffe* actually did precede *The Dawns* when in 1918 Meyerhold and Mayakovsky staged their first version of it in Petrograd. But in spite of the fact that the 1918 production is regarded as the first production of a Soviet play, it is the 1921 version at the First Theatre of the R.S.F.S.R. that has become canonical.

The production of 1918 was offered as part of the activities celebrating the first anniversary of the October Revolution. The poster of the Petrograd Theatre of Musical Drama announced, "We poets, artists, regisseurs, and actors celebrate the anniversary of the October Revolution with a revolutionary spectacle." It went on to describe the five scenes of the forthcoming spectacle:

Scene I. Whites and blacks run from the red flood.
Scene II. An Ark. The clean palm off an unclean Tsar and republic.
   See for yourself what results from this.
Scene III. Hell. The workers send Beelzebub to the devil.
Scene IV. Heaven. A great discussion between a farm hand and Methusaelah.
Scene V. A sunny communal holiday of things and workers.

Finally, at the bottom of the poster, came the title:

"! *Mystery-Bouffe*! "
Heroic, Episodic, and Satirical
Portrayal of Our Epoch, made by
V. Mayakovsky [19]

In the middle of the poster was a drawing of the globe with the label "Old World" printed across it. Through this was drawn a large, black X.

In the 1921 revision the revolutionary euphoria was qualified somewhat as the satire embraced not only the Western capitalists but Soviet speculators and bureaucrats as well. Also an account of the Soviet regime's struggle against the counterrevolutionary White Army, which had taken place during the 1918 to 1921 interval between productions, was included. But the general idea was still the same: a mystery play spoof depicting the Great Flood of the new millenium, followed by something like a Moses of the body-proletariat leading the downtrodden away from the sinking golden calf of the capitalist exploiters and into the promised land of Bolshevik milk and honey.

Before the production got under way one of the proletarian characters stepped forward and delivered a delightful and rather unusual prologue. Since it so accurately and succinctly reflects the mood of *Mystery-Bouffe* as well as the general theatrical attitude of both Mayakovsky and Meyerhold (in 1921 and the years beyond as well), and since it contains a summary of the play which would be hard to improve upon, I shall quote it in full.

In just a minute
we'll present to your view
our *Mystery-Bouffe.*
But first I must say a few words.
This play
is something new.
Without help, nobody has yet succeeded
in jumping higher than his head.
Likewise a new play must be preceded
by a prologue, or else it's dead.
First let me ask you:
Why is this playhouse in such a mess?
To right-thinking people
it's a scandal, no less!
But then what makes you go to see a show?
You do it for pleasure—
isn't that so?

But is the pleasure really so great, after all,
if you're looking just at the stage?
The stage, you know,
is only one-third of the hall.
Therefore,
at an interesting show,
if things are set up properly,
your pleasure is multiplied by three.
But if the play isn't interesting,
then you're wasting your time
looking at even one-third of what's happening.

For other theatrical companies
the spectacle doesn't matter:
for them
the stage
is a keyhole without a key.
"Just sit there quietly," they say to you,
"either straight or sidewise,
and look at a slice of other folks' lives."
You look—and what do you see?
Uncle Vanya
and Auntie Manya
parked on a sofa as they chatter.
But we don't care
about uncles or aunts:
you can find them at home—or anywhere!
We, too, will show you life that's real—
very!
But life transformed by the theatre into a spectacle
most extraordinary!

The gist of Act One is as follows:
the world is leaking.
Then comes a stampede:
everyone flees Revolution's flood.
There are seven pairs of The Unclean,
and seven pairs of The Clean
(that is, fourteen poor proletarians
and fourteen important bourgeois),
and in between,
with a pair of tear-stained cheeks,

a miserable little Menshevik.
The North Pole is flooded,
the last refuge is gone.
So they all begin building,
not just an Ark,
but a great big super-duper one.

In Act Two the public
takes a trip on the ark:
here you'll find both autocracy
and a democratic republic.
Finally,
while the Menshevik howls,
The Clean are thrown overboard head over heels.

In the Third Act we show and tell
how the workers
have nothing to be afraid of—
not even the devils in Hell.

In Act Four—
laugh till it brings tears to your eyes! —
we show the bowers of Paradise.

In Act Five, Devastation or Chaos,
opening wide her huge yap,
destroys things and gobbles them up.
But we, though we worked in semi-starvation,
succeeded
in conquering Devastation.

In the Sixth Act
comes the Commune.
Everyone
must sing out at the top of his voice!

Look as hard as you can!
Is everything ready—
both up in Heaven
and Down Below?
(*voice from offstage*: Rea-dy!)
On with the show! 20

The belly-laugh satire, the overt theatricalism, the disregard for plot suspense, the contemporaneous comments—characteristics which would remain applicable to all of Mayakovsky's future work and much of Meyerhold's—are contained in this sprightly prologue. And in two lines Mayakovsky summed up a theatrical aesthetic which would be appropriate for nearly every production his friend Meyerhold would stage in the decade ahead: "We, too, will show you life that's real—/ very! / But life transformed by the theatre into a spectacle / most extraordinary."

For the set and costumes of the 1921 production Meyerhold and Mayakovsky called upon Vladimir Kiselyev, A. Lavinsky, and V. Khrakovsky. Filling nearly the entire downstage area was a huge half-cylinder representing the North Pole. Upstage of this were several ramps, platforms, ropes (looking like something left over from *The Dawns*), and poles. All this was backed by a backdrop representing the deck of a steamship. No curtain was used, and the large half-cylinder, with some adjacent platforms, was thrust out through the proscenium opening onto the apron and nearly into the laps of the audience.

The costuming gave a two-dimensional, posterlike effect which was deemed appropriate for the kind of performances given by Meyerhold's "troops." Mayakovsky's script did not call for individualized characters but rather "a Menshivik," "a Bolshevik," "an American," "a German," and so forth.[21] And certainly Meyerhold's eager amateurs played with the broadness and lack of subtlety which was suitable for caricature rather than characterization.

On opening night an aspiring young actor, Alexander Fevralsky, was seated in the audience. Forty-five years later he looked back on the event and described it this way:

> Although the construction of the stage was cumbersome and excessively conditional,* although the musical accompaniment seemed to be in discord with the play, although not all of the performers gave

---

*Fevralsky uses the word *uslovnoy* which can be translated as "conditional" or "conventional." Meyerhold used the same word in the title of an article (c. 1907) in which he sought to explain his efforts at the Moscow Art Theatre Studio in 1905: "Perviya popytki sozdaniya uslovnago teatra" [First attempts at creating a conditional (conventional?) theatre] (*O teatr*, p. 35). In *Meyerhold on Theatre*, Edward Braun translates the term as "stylized" (p. 49).

consistent characterizations or were able to capture the rhythm of Mayakovsky's verses, and although the movement was seldom unified—all the same, the show produced a great impression. The abstract and static nature of *The Dawns* was overcome. The shortcomings of the production receded into the background and artists, inspired by the passionate words of the play and seized by the excitement of a First of May holiday, played with great enthusiasm.22

Although historian Marc Slonim and Meyerhold's biographer, Yuri Jelagin, both label *Mystery-Bouffe* as unsuccessful (Slonim describes it as "this unhappy enterprise"),[23] this account certainly suggests something other than a grim failure.*

Fevralsky recalls that on opening night at the end of the first act the audience broke out in such a roar of applause that the success of the production was hardly in doubt. And at the conclusion of the last act the playing and singing of the *Internationale* (with new lyrics by Mayakovsky) was followed by a virtual frenzy of stomping and cheering. Mayakovsky and Meyerhold, arms linked, bowed continuously in response to the cheering as the actors and even the technicians were called out onto the stage to join them. Fevralsky, who went on to become one of the leading actors of the Soviet stage, concludes, "After forty-five years it is difficult to recall another performance which was greeted with such enthusiasm from the audience."[24]

This was not just the opening night enthusiasm of a crowd of friends. The show ran for over one hundred performances—including one performance in German in a circus arena for the Third Congress of the Communist Internationale for which the excessive cost of the *mise en scène* earned Meyerhold a reprimand from party authorities—and later toured extensively in the provinces. Fevralsky writes that he attended several of these subsequent performances and that the audience response was no less enthusiastic. Such evidence would seem to belie the opinion that *Mystery-Bouffe* was anything but a success.

But there are two kinds of success in the theatre: the success of

---

*And his account is of considerable value. According to the editors of the recently published collection of Soviet theatre historical documents, the press was almost completely silent concerning the *Mystery-Bouffe* production and the only detailed account available is Fevralsky's (*Sovietsky teatr—dokumenty i materialy, 1917-1967*, 1:142). Since it was not printed until 1966, neither Slonim nor Jelagin had access to it.

a "hit" that for a time is all the rage, and the success that is marked by permanence in a repertoire. Some productions have both, while others achieve one or the other. And it is probably safe to assume that historians tend to give priority to the latter whereas performers themselves—and certainly first night eyewitness observers—tend to favor the former. If this is true, it may account for the difference of opinion regarding the success of *Mystery-Bouffe*. While there can be no doubt that it was quite an event when it appeared—otherwise it would hardly have been presented for the Third Congress—it is also true that, unlike productions of other lesser Soviet plays, it never became an item in the permanent repertoire of any theatre.

If the First Theatre of the R.S.F.S.R. had continued, perhaps *Mystery-Bouffe* would have continued with it. But it was a unique kind of show—even Mayakovsky and Meyerhold never did anything quite like it again—and not the kind of play or production that another theatre would pick up and put into the repertoire. Like many of the writers and artists of that time, its destiny was to blaze very brightly but very briefly.

R.S.F.S.R. I Closes

As head of the Theatre Section of the Commissariat of Education Meyerhold had been in a position to defend the theatre he founded. After resigning his political authority, however, his theatre was at the mercy of a host of squabbling bureaucrats.

But even before his resignation the theatre had been lowered in rank by means of a transfer in March 1921, to the hostile supervision of the Moscow Division of National Education (MONO). Following Meyerhold's resignation in April and the opening of *Mystery-Bouffe* in May a specially designated commission of political education spokesmen decreed that all theatre performances were to be immediately prohibited and the theatre closed. This decision was motivated, according to recently published documents of Soviet theatre history, by "the immense expenditures and by the lack of shows representing the interests of the working people."[25]

Lunacharsky, although frequently at odds with him over

particular productions, had a high regard for Meyerhold and did not care to see the First Theatre closed out. So on June 10 Lunarcharsky pulled rank on MONO and returned the enterprise to Meyerhold's personal authority under the Political Education Department's "Workshop of Communist Drama."

But a considerable campaign in the press was started in late June against the "bourgeois aestheticism" of Meyerhold's theatre and Lunacharsky could only go so far in protecting the venture. Furthermore, Meyerhold was not very fond of the solution since it placed him and his theatre directly under the Chief of Political Education, V. F. Pletnyev. As usual, Meyerhold was not receptive to the idea of someone else directly supervising his theatre, and after ignoring several "suggestions," received two angry letters from Pletnyev in the month of September. In them, he informed Meyerhold that all decisions relating to artistic matters and repertoire were henceforth to follow rules laid down by the Chief of Political Education—Pletnyev.

With that Meyerhold packed his bags and walked away from what was left of the First Theatre of the R.S.F.S.R. The only thing that was left was the final performance of his production of Ibsen's *League of Youth.* He had put it together during that summer of bureaucratic boondoggling and it opened on 7 August 1921 only to close after twenty-two performances when Meyerhold left. In the material presently available on Meyerhold productions there exists no description of it and in most instances it is not even mentioned.

With the departure of Meyerhold—and with him most of his students and associates—the First Theatre of the R.S.F.S.R. concluded its brief existence. Few critics were to feel anything other than relief. But whether they sensed it or not, Vsevolod Meyerhold's career as a gadfly on the rump of Soviet theatre was just getting started.

In December of 1921, following Meyerhold's departure, the theatre building at Number Twenty Sadovaya Street was renamed the State Theatre of Communist Drama. However, nothing was produced, and in the middle of the theatre season the building was standing idle. Since there was apparently no need as yet for a national theatre dedicated to Communist drama, it was decided to put the old building at the service of young students and the experimental productions growing out of their workshop activities—specifically, the students of Meyerhold's Free Workshop and the students of Neslobin's Actors' Theatre. Thus in January of 1922 the theatre at Number Twenty Sadovaya Street became known as the Actors' Theatre.

3

Cabotin Emerges

O A Change of Context

ne of the difficulties facing the student of any aspect of Soviet
history is the profusion of titles that come and go and shift about
with such frequency that it is almost necessary to create one's own
cross-reference guide when going from one document or study to
another. This is true in everything from the history of the secret
police to agricultural policies to the names of theatres.

We have just been looking at the First Theatre of the
R.S.F.S.R., which then became the First Theatre of MONO, but
was then retitled First Theatre of the R.S.F.S.R., and was finally
named the Theatre of Communist Drama before being labeled the
Actors' Theatre—all in the space of sixteen months. Understand-
ably, some commentators choose to ignore all this and talk of the
"Meyerhold Theatre" starting with his production of *The Dawns*.
On the other hand, an historian like Nikolai A. Gorchakov
acknowledges the First Theatre of the R.S.F.S.R. and doesn't talk
of an actual Meyerhold Theatre until the production of Crommelynck's *The Magnificent Cuckold* in 1922.

But the fact is that there was no theatre formally named after
Meyerhold until 1923. Crommelynck's play, like a production of
Ibsen's *A Doll's House* a week earlier, was done at the Actors'

Theatre. This was followed by *The Death of Tarelkin* at the GITIS (State Institute of Theatre Art) Theatre, and finally, on 4 March 1923 by *The Earth Rebellious* at the officially designated Meyerhold Theatre.

Since these changing names actually refer to the same theatre building it is convenient to merely note them in passing and regard Meyerhold's work during this period as an essentially uninterrupted sequence of productions at Number Twenty Sadovaya Street. However, this would be misleading in at least one important instance: the change of name in January 1922 from First Theatre of the R.S.F.S.R. to the Actors' Theatre. For this represented a change in the basic nature and purpose of Meyerhold's productions at Twenty Sadovaya Street. And in proceeding from his productions at the First Theatre of the R.S.F.S.R. in the foregoing chapter to his productions at the Actors' Theatre in this one it is important to recognize that the political context of his work, so significant in the former instance, is of only peripheral relevance to his productions at the Actors' Theatre. Instead, the new source of motivation was aesthetic rather than political. *The Dawns* and *Mystery-Bouffe* were productions which grew out of Meyerhold's enthusiasm for the Revolution. He had approached the stage as one dedicated to bringing it into the service of the state.

But the subsequent productions of *The Magnificent Cuckold* and *The Death of Tarelkin* grew out of Meyerhold's enthusiasm for a frankly theatrical aesthetic* of the theatre. In these productions he approached the stage as an experimenter dedicated to the regeneration of the theatre through a rediscovery of theatrical essences in terms of the twentieth century. And for Meyerhold the essence of theatricality lay in the antics of the cabotin—the strolling player of medieval Europe who linked the classic theatre of Greece and Rome to that of the Renaissance: "It was with his help that the Western theatre came to full flower in the theatres of Spain and Italy in the seventeenth century."[1] For Meyerhold, the tradition of "cabotinage" was not merely a

---

*Due to its connotation of bourgeois decadency, the term "aesthetic" was an anathema to Bolshevik artists—including Meyerhold. I intend no such connotation; I use it here merely to suggest an apolitical attitude vis-à-vis agitprop theatre.

stylistic option; he regarded it as the theatre's one and only viable tradition. "If there is no cabotin, there is no theatre either; and, contrariwise, as soon as the theatre rejects the basic rules of theatricality it straightway imagines that it can dispense with the cabotin."[2]

Of course, these different motives were not as exclusive and separate as this may suggest: there were artistic motives in his work on *The Dawns* and *Mystery-Bouffe* just as there were political rationalizations for *The Magnificent Cuckold* and *The Death of Tarelkin*. But whereas the former productions were an immediate reflection of his involvement in politics, the latter were a direct result of his workshop experiments in theatrical art. Consequently, just as an explanation of the prevailing political situation was a necessary context for a discussion of *The Dawns* and *Mystery-Bouffe*, so a look at Meyerhold's workshop approach and methods (for which we must return to the pre-Revolution period of his work where he begins such activities) is a prerequisite to examining the productions which resulted.

The Meyerhold Studio, 1913-1917

In his account for *Harper's Magazine* of a recent visit to the Soviet Union, Arthur Miller speaks of "the earthiness, the bodiliness, so to speak" of the acting he discovered in the Soviet theatres. He was struck by "the physicalness of Russian acting, its mortal quality."[3] Describing a production of *Ten Days That Shook The World*, he writes, "Much of this production is sheer choreography and neither better nor worse than its counterparts elsewhere, but there is always some explosive conception which instantly speaks of this particular Russian genius for physicalizing."[4]

But this "particular Russian genius for physicalizing" is not an indigenous tradition of the Russian theatre. On the contrary, before Meyerhold the Russian stage had always been quite "wordy." When Meyerhold's instincts* took him to a much more robust and physical theatre he had to find his precedents outside

---

*The larger-than-life, theatrical theatre came naturally to Meyerhold. A discussion of his earliest activities in the theatre is not within the scope of this study, but these years clearly indicate his inclination toward overt theatricalism. (See "Introduction," p. 22.)

the history of the Russian theatre. But starting with the productions of Meyerhold, bodiliness—as Miller calls it—became one of the dominant features of productions in the Soviet theatre.

It is sometimes stated that, unlike Stanislavsky or Vakhtangov, Meyerhold failed to leave any "school" of disciples behind him. This is not really true. The official insistence on Socialist Realism and particularly the official discrediting of Meyerhold from 1939 to 1956 prevented, until recently, any public recognition of his influence.

But since 1956 memoirs and testimonies have begun to appear which bear witness to the considerable influence he had and continues to have on the Russian theatre and its artists. This influence is derived not so much from his writings as from the lessons and ideas first absorbed from Meyerhold by young playwrights, performers, designers, and directors through their contact with him in his productions and workshops, especially in the 1920s. Such innovators and artists as Nikolai Okhlopkov, Boris Zakhava, Ruben Simonov, Nikolai Petrov, Vsevolod Vishnevsky, Igor Ilinsky, and many others—including, of course, Sergei Eisenstein and Eugene Vakhtangov—worked under Meyerhold in their formative years.*

Just as it is difficult to find any time when a director is not also a teacher, so it is difficult to point to a time when Meyerhold did not use the stage more or less as a theatrical workshop. From his first work as a young director in the provinces with the "Comrades of the New Drama" from 1902 to 1906, including his attempts to establish the Moscow Art Theatre Studio in 1905, to his unorthodox presentations at Vera Komissarzhevskaya's theatre from 1906 to 1908, Meyerhold took a workshop approach to his productions. In his productions he was invariably experimenting, on a trial and error basis, with new ideas and approaches (or old ones, rediscovered) instead of functioning as general coordinator for a "normal" turn of the century production.

*The book which contains many personal testimonies to this influence, *Vstrechi s Meyerholdom* [Meetings with Meyerhold] was published in 1967 and has been an invaluable source for this study. Harrison Salisbury, on a recent visit to the apartment of film director Gregory Kozinstev (*Don Quixote* and *Hamlet*), recalls, "In a prominent place—as on the table of many writers in Moscow and Leningrad—is a big new volume called *Meetings with Meyerhold.*... 'Yes,' said Kozinstev, 'Meyerhold is a great influence today' " (*The Soviet Union: The Fifty Years,* ed. Harrison Salisbury, p. 194).

But it wasn't until 1913, while directing public productions at the Imperial Theatres, and private ones—as "Doctor Daperttuto"—at friends' apartments, that he established a separate workshop for theatre training. The Meyerhold Studio, a school of acting, opened in the fall of 1913 in a large apartment at Number Thirteen Troitska Street, Petersburg. It was destined to exist until 1917, although in its last year or so activities fell off considerably.

The primary emphasis of this pre-Revolution studio was the training and indoctrination of young performers in the concepts and methods of the commedia dell'arte. Meyerhold's earlier attempts at finding an alternative to theatrical realism had taken the form of theatrical impressionism and symbolism. But by 1913 he had become convinced that a regeneration of the theatre would have to take an even more overtly theatrical form and came close to renouncing the very symbolism that he had previously introduced into the Russian theatre:* "Andrei Bely is right. Reviewing the symbolist theatre of today [1912] he comes to the conclusion: 'Let the theatre remain the theatre, and the mystery—the mystery.' "[5]

In Meyerhold's opinion, a renaissance of true theatre lay with the restoration of the cabotin.

> The cabotin is a strolling player; the cabotin is a kinsman to the mime, the histrion, and the juggler; the cabotin can work miracles with his technical mastery; the cabotin keeps alive the tradition of the true art of acting. . . .
>
> In order to rescue the Russian theatre from its own desire to become the servant of literature, we must spare nothing to restore to the stage the cult of cabotinage in its broadest sense.[6]

Through his experimental productions as "Doctor Daperttuto" (an Italian mask character from E. T. A. Hoffmann's *Adventure on New Year's Eve* meaning "Doctor Everywhere"), through his short-lived but influential journal, *Love of Three Oranges* (again the commedia motif, taken from Gozzi's fable of the same

---

*By Yuri Jelagin's account, Meyerhold's symbolist production of Przybyszewski's *Snow* in 1904 was the first experiment in conventionalized, anti-naturalistic theatre in Russia (*Temny geny*, p. 90).

name—the passages just quoted first appeared in it), and especially through the training of young performers at the Meyerhold Studio,* he set about restoring this "cult of cabotinage" in the Russian theatre.

In the Studio he surrounded himself with capable teachers in the various fields of knowledge he considered essential for the modern cabotin. On the technical side there was Yuri Bondi—a close friend of Meyerhold's at the time and the designer for some of his Daperttuto productions as well as a partner in the journal, *Love of Three Oranges.*** In the Studio Bondi taught "the material elements of theatrical production: building, furnishing, lighting the stage floor, costuming the actor, make-up, and properties."[7]

The chief scholar, historian, and theorist was Vladimir Solovyev, "a knowledgeable historian of world drama and theatre from ancient Attic comedy to contemporary."[8] Although Meyerhold himself was deeply interested in commedia dell'arte, it was Solovyev who undertook the teaching of it at the Studio in a course titled "Methods of Staging Commedia dell'Arte Performances."[9] In the class "Technique of Speaking Poetry and Prose," Karl Vogakha taught poetic analysis in terms of meter and rhythm, how to harmonize the poetic elements in oral presentation, and how to discover the rhythms peculiar to prose.[10] Meyerhold himself taught "Stage Movement."[11]

As might be expected, the study of commedia dell'arte was not for the purpose of faithful reproductions. Rather, "commedia dell'arte was an aide of considerable richness in terms of ideas of theatrical tradition, means of studying the purpose of theatre, and in the practical area of staging techniques."[12] It was therefore something like a theoretical foundation for what Meyerhold pursued in his own class: "For Meyerhold, Solovyev's class was like a step towards his [Meyerhold's] goal."[13]

According to Alexy Gripich, Meyerhold's class, "Stage Movement," was more precisely a class in acting and directing skills:

*The Meyerhold Studio was the name of his pre-Revolution organization; his similar organization after the Revolution was called the Meyerhold (Free) Workshop. The distinction is intended when upper case is applied to "studio" and "workshop."

**Bondi probably provided a fair amount of the financial backing for the Studio and journal. He was virtually codirector with Meyerhold in the Studio. His brother and sister were also involved in the Studio, but none of the Bondis were professional.

Meyerhold began with the techniques of stage movement and gesture with controlled examples on stage. Exercises were transformed into etudes, and from etudes arose the pantomimes. Thus, from the exercise "shooting a bow" arose the etude "The Hunt," and subsequently a pantomime in which all "generations" of the Studio were involved. Several of the exercises and etudes became "classics" and later entered into the teaching of biomechanics.[14]

In general, the curriculum of the Studio was designed for the fulfillment of five goals: (1) study of the technique of stage movement, (2) study of the basic principles of staging techniques of improvizational Italian comedy, (3) employing in the modern theatre the traditional methods of the seventeenth and eighteenth centuries, (4) musical reading in drama, (5) practical study of the material elements of production: building, furnishings, lighting, properties, and makeup.[15]

Theatre as Grotesquerie

If there was something like a general aesthetic of the theatre which gave conceptual continuity to these goals and which served to link the study of commedia with the challenges of the twentieth-century stage and thereby prevent such study from being only an exercise in historicism, it was Meyerhold's idea of the grotesque. One of the students, Alexandra Smirnova, recently recalled that "Meyerhold was very fond of the grotesque, and we in the studio were fascinated with this form of performance. The grotesque is the means of transforming any of the most ordinary and realistic state of affairs, making it unusually sharp, and strongly influential and memorable."[16] Incomplete as this may be as a definition of the grotesque, it does suggest how one of the students in the Studio understood Meyerhold's intention and practice with regard to the grotesque.

In "The Fairground Booth"—that seminal essay of Meyerhold's, written in 1912, to which reference has been made (pp. 32-33)—Meyerhold himself spoke of the artist who approaches his art with the attitude of the grotesque:

> This attitude opens to the artist some marvelous horizons.
> He concerns himself first with himself, with his own personal attitude towards the world. He selects the material of his art, not according to verisimilitude, but according to his artistic fancy.

In the first stage he treats reality stylistically, always taking into consideration, to a certain extent, probability. "Schematisation" implies a certain impoverishment of the concrete which it reduces to the typical.

The grotesque, advancing beyond stylization, is a method of synthesizing rather than analyzing. In turning away details, the grotesque recreates the fullness of life (in a perspective of "improbable suitability," according to Pushkin's expression).

In reducing the richness of the empirical world to a typical unity, stylization impoverishes life whereas the grotesque refuses to recognize only one aspect—*only* the vulgar or *only* the elevated. It mixes the opposites and by design accents the contradictions.* *The only effect which counts is the improvised, the original* [emphasis Meyerhold's].[17]

This section of the Meyerhold article contains the essential idea which underlies his experimental work during his pre-Revolution period—the improvizations, the etudes, the interludes, the pantomimes, the plays of Alexander Blok, and the entire program of study at the Meyerhold Studio.

Furthermore, as we shall see, there is nothing in his future work which fundamentally contradicts this attitude of the grotesque. On the contrary, it is this idea of the grotesque which constitutes the conceptual consistency in nearly all of the work of Vsevolod Meyerhold. From the passage quoted above such phrases as "not according to verisimilitude, but according to his artistic fancy," "a method of synthesizing rather than analyzing," "improbable suitability," "mixes the opposites," "accents the contradictions," and "the improvised, the original"—are expressions as appropriate to *The Forest* (1924), *The Inspector General* (1926), *Woe to Wit* (1928), and *The Bathhouse* (1930) as they are to *Don Juan* (1910), *The Scarf of Columbine* (1910), and *The Puppet Booth* and *The Unknown Woman* (1914).

Proceeding from such an attitude, it is not suprising that nearly all of Meyerhold's productions would be categorized as satire or

*Cf. Victor Hugo's discussion of the grotesque in his "Preface to Cromwell." For Hugo the grotesque was the opposite of the sublime with which it could be joined to form a dynamic literary dualism: "In truth, in the new poetry, while the sublime represents the soul as it is, purified by Christian morality, the grotesque plays the part of the human beast" (*European Theories of the Drama*, ed. Barrett H. Clark, p. 360). For Meyerhold, on the other hand, the grotesque was not synonymous with the beastly half of "Beauty and the Beast" but rather the effect of their coming together.

farce. By its very nature the attitude of the grotesque preempts the sentimental, the romantic, and by most definitions, the tragic. When Meyerhold states, "The art of the grotesque is founded on the opposition of substance and form,"[18] he is virtually echoing Henri Bergson's idea of the comic.* But we would seriously misconstrue Meyerhold's idea if we took this to mean that he was exclusively or even primarily interested in comically entertaining theatre as an end in itself. As he said late in his career, "I know for a fact that what is said in jest is often more serious than what is said seriously."[19]

For Meyerhold the grotesque was the most dynamic means at the disposal of theatre artists for giving expression to the joie de vivre which is all too often missing from man's daily life. And it must be understood that for Meyerhold the joy of living was to be found not so much in the simple pleasures and quiet contentedness as in the fireworks of life's contrasts, conflicts, and dissonances. Furthermore, the grotesque was not to be construed simply as a manifestation of skepticism or ironic detachment; rather, it was for him the artist's involvement in a search for meanings: "Beyond that which we see, existence is composed of an immense domain of mystery. The grotesque seeks the supernatural, synthesizes the quintessence of contraries, and creates the image of the phenomenal. Thus it urges the spectator to attempt to penetrate the enigma of the inconceivable."[20] And finally: "In handling the grotesque, the artist attempts to cause the spectator to suddenly pass from a plane with which he is familiar, to another plane which is unexpected."[21]

For Meyerhold, then, the theatre was not to be a mirror which reflects upon us our own daily lives, nor was it a place to depict life as viewed through glasses romantic, sentimental, comic, or tragic. It was, instead, *a place for confronting an audience, through conventionalized means peculiar to the theatre, with a synthesized distillation of life's extremities in conflict with one another*—and let the laughs, gasps, and squirming arise as unexpectedly as the events on the stage.

*I have found no evidence that Meyerhold was acquainted with Bergson's essay, Laughter (published in 1900), nor is there any mention of Bergson in Meyerhold's writings.

In 1917 the Meyerhold Studio—along with nearly every other form of organized social activity—was terminated by the Revolution. In 1918 and 1920 he was briefly involved with TEO-sponsored workshops, but it wasn't until the fall of 1921 that his workshop activities resumed in earnest. It was at this time that the State Workshop for Advanced Directing (GVIRM) was established and placed under his supervision.

At first glance it might appear that Meyerhold's post-Revolution Workshop at GVIRM, out of which came the principles of biomechanics and scenic constructivism, evinces an entirely different approach from his commedia-based work in the pre-Revolution Meyerhold Studio. For those who would see Meyerhold's work as being divided into two distinctly different phases—pre-Revolution and post-Revolution—each with its own concepts and methods, the two different workshops serve ostensibly as a case in point. But the fact is that the basic concept of theatre underlying the Meyerhold Workshop at GVIRM was essentially the same aesthetic concept which had informed his experiments in the Meyerhold Studio: the theatrical grotesque.

In 1922 GVIRM published a pamphlet—*Ampluya aktora* [The *emploi* of the actor]—written by Meyerhold and his chief assistants at GVIRM, Valery Bebutov and Ivan Aksenov. The opening pages of this pronouncement of GVIRM's ideas and intentions contained the following statements.

> [The grotesque is] a deliberate exaggeration and reconstruction (distortion) of nature and the unification of objects that are not united by either nature or the customs of our daily life. The theatre, being a combination of natural, temporal, spatial, and numerical phenomena, is itself outside of nature. It finds that these phenomena invariably contradict our everyday experience and that *the theatre itself is essentially an example of the grotesque* [emphasis mine]. Arising from the grotesque of a ritual masquerade, the theatre inevitably is destroyed by any given attempt to remove the grotesque—the basis of its existence—from it.[22]

Thus Meyerhold conceived of the theatre as "essentially an example of the grotesque" in 1922 (and, I submit, throughout the rest of his career) as well as in the years prior to the Revolution.

And the idea of the grotesque in the theatre was not for Meyerhold a choice of mode or convention; for him, the theatre was inherently a grotesquerie: i.e., "a deliberate exaggeration and reconstruction . . . of nature and the unification of objects that are not united by either nature or the customs of our daily life." Consequently, to say that Meyerhold practiced a theatre of the grotesque would be, by his definition of theatre, a redundancy. Once this is understood the seeming discrepancies between the commedia practices of the Meyerhold Studio and the Futuristic biomechanics and scenic constructivism of the Meyerhold Workshop at GVIRM can be easily reconciled.

The Meyerhold Workshop: GVIRM

Yuri Jelagin may have been right when he said that Meyerhold lacked, in the final analysis, the qualities essential to a great teacher.[23] On the other hand, Alexander Fevralsky (who, unlike Jelagin, was actually a student of Meyerhold's), recalls, "From the very outset of the 1920s Meyerhold was surrounded by young people who believed in him, studied with him, and helped him in his quests."[24]

It was just such a group of young people who, along with some eager newcomers from the provinces, followed Meyerhold out of the dissolving First Theatre of the R.S.F.S.R. and into the formation of GVIRM. This was in the fall of 1921. Less than a year later, in April of 1922, they would present one of Meyerhold's most successful and precedent-shattering productions: *The Magnificent Cuckold.*

GVIRM was located in a large hall at Number Thirty-two Novinsky Boulevard. It was headed by Meyerhold, Valery Bebutov (Meyerhold's right-hand man and codirector), and Ivan Aksenov (poet, playwright, and primarily known as a Shakespearean scholar and translator).* According to Alexander Fevralsky it was

*The staff also included a Mongolian by the name of Inkinzhinomov who was a special consultant on Asian theatre. Just as Solovyev had served as Italian theatre specialist in the Meyerhold Studio, so Inkinzhinomov introduced the methods and aesthetics of Oriental theatre conventions to GVIRM. According to Gorchakov (*The Theatre in Soviet Russia,* p. 204), he was influential in developing the theory of biomechanics.

something like a model communist school: "Teachers and students formed a united family; all work was developed through genuinely intimate collaboration. Meyerhold's fame did not in the least prevent the establishment of a sincere friendship between 'The Master' and his students."[25] This doesn't sound like the Meyerhold of old. But perhaps after the discouraging rebuff he had just received at the hands of party authorities and critics, he was less inclined to be so dogmatic.

On the other hand, the recollections of another student, Sergei Yutkevich, suggests that Meyerhold had not lost his grip entirely. At least in the process of selecting applicants the congenial atmosphere was not yet the order of the day. Behind a long table sat Meyerhold, Bebutov, and Aksenov. One at a time students would enter the room and take a seat before them. "Applicants had to present either their own special project and design sketches . . . or submit themselves to an oral colloquial in order to establish their level of culture. If the candidate appeared suitable, then the exam route took him to a second level which consisted of exercises before the directing and acting masters [presumably, Meyerhold and Bebutov]."[26]

But Fevralsky states that the atmosphere of the Workshop itself (providing one got accepted) was quite open, free, and creative.

> The students were not asked for prepared conclusions, but were required to blaze trails, together with Meyerhold and his staff, towards the creation of new concepts of the theatre. . . .
> Many of the students entered the Workshop seeking a new theatre. Meyerhold consolidated their aspirations, opened a wide perspective, and set concrete tasks. The students of Meyerhold considered themselves as pioneers of new directions in art, and with great earnestness defended and propagandized the principles of a new theatre.[27]

These "principles of a new theatre" did not begin and end with the well-known scenic constructivism and biomechanics, but these two items are (perhaps unfortunately) the most immediately recognizable aspects of Meyerhold's efforts to revamp the twentieth-century Russian theatre.

Actually they are nothing more nor less than means to a desired end. Starting with *The Magnificent Cuckold* and continuing for about two years, they existed as raw manifestations of an idea of theatre that Meyerhold had been attempting to realize for several years. The prestige of scenic constructivism and biomechanics belies the fact that they were employed by Meyerhold in their "pure" state (I would prefer to call it "raw" state) in only three or four productions over a period of less than two years. After this experimental period he began to integrate the concepts of scenic constructivism and biomechanics with other experiments in more conventional stage traditions and attitudes.

Biomechanics and Scenic Constructivism

The writings on the subject of biomechanics, by Meyerhold as well as others, are frankly much less interesting and provocative than Meyerhold's earlier writings about acting when he was more directly under the influence of the commedia dell'arte. One is reminded of the comparison between some of Brecht's tiresomely tendentious writings on playwriting and the plays themselves. If Meyerhold's actors had been as coldly pseudoscientific and regulated as his writings suggest, it is hard to imagine that they would have aroused the kind of enthusiastic response they did.

But unlike the case of Brecht, wherein we have the actual plays to compare with his writings about playwriting, we can only surmise from photographs, eyewitness accounts, and most importantly the undeniable success of the productions, that there must have been a great deal more life and excitement in biomechanical performances than the dry tracts describing its methods would suggest. And it must be remembered that at this time Meyerhold was still anxiously trying to free the theatre from what he considered the grip of decadent, stultifying, psychological realism. Before the Revolution he had been pretty much on his own and forced to rely on the authority of historical precedent (commedia, Oriental theatre, etc.). Now he sought to align himself and his ideas with the Soviet ideologies of materialist science, mechanized efficiency, and the virtues newly assigned to the proletarian man.

I do not mean to suggest by this that Meyerhold was consciously trying to sell his aesthetic ideas under the guise of a proletarian manifestation, but rather that, like Brecht, Meyerhold at this time continued to function as a creative artist in spite of himself. As a director, he practiced something quite different from what he was preaching—or at least practiced a great deal more than he wrote about.

Most of Meyerhold's writings on the subject of biomechanics are found in three sources: his caustic review of Alexander Tairov's book, *Notes of a Director,* published in the March 1922 edition of the journal, *Pechat i revolutsia* [Press and revolution]; an article entitled "Aktor budushchego" ["The actor of the future"], written for the June 1922 issue of *Ermitazh* [Hermitage] magazine; and the GVIRM pamphlet (see p. 68 above), also published in 1922, by Meyerhold, Bebutov, and Aksenov, entitled *Ampluya aktora* [The *emploi* of the actor].*

The following, taken from *Ampluya aktora,* indicates how Meyerhold in 1922 sought to explain the elements of acting as conceived under the principle of biomechanics. It comes close to being an outright refutation of Stanislavsky's approach, and Meyerhold undoubtedly meant it to be just that.

A necessary and special trait in actors is their ability to respond to stimuli applied to their reflexes. . . . The stimulus is the ability to fulfill an assignment received from the outside through feelings, motion, and language. To co-ordinate the reactions to stimuli is what constitutes *acting.* The separate parts of this are *the elements of acting,* each of which has three stages: 1) Intention; 2) Accomplishment; 3) Reaction.

Intention is the intellectual perception of the assignment received from the outside (from the author, the dramatist, the director, or on the initiative of the performer himself).

Accomplishment is the series of volitional, mimetic, and vocal reflexes.

Reaction is the lowering of the volitional reflex in accordance with the realization of the mimetic and vocal reflexes. The volitional reflex is prepared to receive a new intention and proceeds to a new element of *acting.* 28

*The term *"ampluya"* gives some difficulty in English. It can be translated as "role" or "part," but can also suggest an actor's "line of business." Since the cognate *"rol"* is normally used in Russian to designate the character which an actor plays in a particular drama, we may assume that in using the term *ampluya* instead of *rol* the authors' intention was to stress what might be called "the business of performing in the theatre" rather than strictly character development. Hence, the use of the French term, *"emploi."*

Then, as if to make unmistakeably clear the proletarian nature of this approach, the following statement is made. "A person who possesses the necessary ability for reflex stimuli can be or can become an actor; he can fulfill one of the roles in the theatre in accordance with his natural and physical talents. He can be given a position that is determined as appropriate by the stage functions."[29]

Thus did Meyerhold, Bebutov, and Aksenov seek to bring the "art" of acting right into line with the Communist Golden Rule: from each according to his abilities, to each according to his needs. The idea that all a person needs to be an actor is "ability for reflex stimuli" is, despite its mechanized terminology, something that even Stanislavsky might agree with. The difference, of course, is whether one is interested in describing what it takes to be an actor or what it takes to be a *good* actor. But to distinguish between poor, fair, good, and excellent actors would be an act of discrimination. And certainly in 1922 no loyal party member, his eyes firmly fixed on that glorious future of a classless society, would be caught advocating such a bourgeois and reactionary thing as discrimination.

In a society, however, where everyone is equal (including actors in competition for roles), some will usually be a little more equal than others. Knowing this, and yet wishing to avoid hypocrisy, one must say something to the effect that each "equal" person "can be given a position that is determined as appropriate." Appropriate to what? His talent, of course. And who makes this determination? The man in the theatre who is more equal than anyone else—the director. Thus, we are right back to old-fashioned discrimination again. And it was this "reactionary hypocrisy" that prevented Meyerhold's theatre from degenerating to the level of tasteless mediocrity achieved by the real *Proletkult* theatres that actually practiced nondiscrimination.

But Meyerhold's "stage algebra"* approach to acting and the theatre did have one distinguishing effect.[30] It tended to reduce reliance on the individual creative effort of the actors for the

---

*Meyerhold said that the actor embodied in himself both the organizer and that which is organized: "$N = A_1 + A_2$ (where $N =$ the actor; A_1 the artist who conceives the idea . . . ; A_2 the executant who executes the conception of A_1)" (*V. E. Meyerhold,* 2:487).

success of a production. The "assignment"—i.e., creative concept—was usually given in complete detail by the director to the actor whose job it then was to execute it as precisely and effectively as his talents enabled him. This is why many have accused Meyerhold of trying to turn actors into automatons or marionettes. ("Note his admiration of Gordon Craig!" they were apt to say.) It is necessary, however, to remind oneself that what he was proposing was not much different from what is done in the ballet—and ballerinas are not regarded as automatons. But in the theatre, one will say, we are dealing not just with movement but with the conflict of vocalized ideas between highly individualized characters.

This, in fact, points to an important—perhaps basic—distinguishing characteristic of Meyerhold's theatre at this time in particular and throughout his entire career in varying degrees. Meyerhold, having been influenced early in his career by such antiliterary theatre reformers as Fuchs, Appia, and Craig, was less concerned about the words—i.e., the "literary" aspect—of a production than directors in the tradition of Stanislavsky and Nemirovich-Danchenko. Secondly, having been influenced by the commedia dell'arte and Oriental theatre, he was more interested in broad character types than in sharply individualized characters.

It follows, then, that two aspects of the realistic theatre which normally distinguish it from ballet—vocalized ideas and carefully individualized characters—were not so very important for Meyerhold. And if biomechanics hindered the realization of these two aspects, the result in Meyerhold's eyes was not a marionette or automaton but an actor on whom physical demands were far greater than on more traditional actors; consequently, the biomechanical actor partook more of the discipline of the dance. It was, in fact, a "dancing" quality which linked the good biomechanical actor with the efficient laborer: both attempting to remove superfluous and unproductive motions and rhythms, and to correctly locate the center of gravity in the body. In the article for *Ermitazh* ("Aktor budushchego") Meyerhold wrote,

> The motions constructed on these bases are distinguished by a *dansant*
> quality. The labor process by experienced workers always resembles the

dance. Here, work verges on art. The sight of a person who is working correctly produces a certain satisfaction.

This applies completely to the work of the actor in the theatre of the future. We are always dealing in art with the organization of material. Art must be based on scientific principles; all the work done by the artist must be conscious.[31]

Thus did Meyerhold seek to blend both his pre-Revolution aesthetic convictions concerning the theatre of the physically dynamic actor with the ideology of the "new Soviet Man" in all his robust efficiency, dexterity, and organizational cooperativeness.

The result was, according to Nikolai A. Gorchakov, "the lively, mischievous, and unbridled gaiety of the comedians who enacted *Le Cocu Magnifique* with a controlled virtuosity over their bodies."[32]

It was as if the band of comedians had just raced out of a sunny square into the gloomy theatre, had joined in tossing all the trashy rags out into the street, had taken the stage in battle, and, in unrestrained happiness at having the space of an open stage under their control, had given themselves up to the most "crazy jokes of the theatre." It furnished clear and convincing proof that the actor himself contained the magic power of transforming the wasteland of the stage and the abstract constructions into something living.[33]

This was, without a doubt, the theatre which Meyerhold was seeking. A theatre where all the hokum of illusionism and internal psychologizing was abruptly dismissed by the irreverent and demystifying mimicry of an irrepressible company of buffoons. The fact that such staging techniques could be justified in terms of Soviet Stakhanovite* ideology was to prove less important than his success in proving his approach to be a viable and exciting alternative to the theatre of realism.

Along with biomechanics, the other famous product of GVIRM

---

*Nicholas Stakhanov was a coal miner virtually canonized by Stalin as a "Hero of Socialist Labor" for cutting out 102 tons of coal (fourteen times his quota) in one shift. Subsequently, a Stakhanovite was a person of total and unreserved commitment to the "New Age."

was scenic constructivism. Oddly enough, scenic constructivism seems to have found a much more prominent place in the theatre lexicon than biomechanics. The oddity lies in the fact that Meyerhold himself made much less of it than biomechanics. He rarely bothered to discourse on scenic constructivism either orally or in print—either as a separate innovation or in connection with biomechanics. And in the recollections of former GVIRM students the biomechanic theory of acting plays a prominent part while the concept of scenic constructivism is usually relegated to an afterthought, when it is mentioned at all.*

The reason for this undoubtedly lies in the fact that scenic constructivism in its clearest and most familiar forms—the productions of *The Magnificent Cuckold* and *The Death of Tarelkin*—was much less the product of Meyerhold's thinking than that of the two constructivist artists he invited to design the productions: Lyubov Popova, *The Magnificent Cuckold,* and Varvara Stepanova, *The Death of Tarelkin.* This is not to say that scenic constructivism was merely a gimmick employed by Meyerhold in an effort to capitalize on a popular item currently the subject of considerable discussion among Soviet artists and intellectuals. It is quite clear that for several years his concept of set designing had been developing in the direction of just such an idea as scenic constructivism. As early as 1910, several years before the constructivist sculptors and architects pronounced their theories,** Meyerhold had written, "The director has a flat surface (the stage) and wood from which, like an architect, he constructs the essential practical stage fittings—plus the human body (the actor); his task is to combine these elements to form a harmonious, integrated work of art, a stage-picture."[34]

*Former student Fevralsky: "Two methods new for theatre schools, which Meyerhold called scene-conducting and biomechanics, formed the basis of Meyerhold's future theatre work; in the workshop [GVIRM] was also developed the principle of scenic constructivism" (*Vstrechi s Meyerholdom,* p. 185).

**The first instance of constructivist art was Vladimir Tatlin's "Relief Construction" in 1914; however, the beginning of constructivism is usually dated as 1917 when Tatlin decorated the Cafe Pittoresque in Moscow with constructivism. In 1920 a schism developed between the "functionalist" and "abstractionalist" constructivists and from about 1920 to 1923 both camps were busy publishing manifestos and articles. Tatlin, Popova, and Stepanova belonged to the "functionalist" group.

Nevertheless, the evidence of his previous productions, the nature of the curriculum in his workshops, and the fact that he invited Popova to essentially reproduce, in stage terms, what he had seen of her work at a constructivist exhibition in 1921, makes it clear that the scenic constructivism of *The Magnificent Cuckold* and *The Death of Tarelkin* was not so much Meyerhold's conception as Popova's and Stepanova's. Thus scenic constructivism should not be regarded as immediately attributable to Meyerhold; rather, the infusion of his theatrical concepts into the activities at GVIRM and the Actors' Theatre made the Workshop and its theatre uniquely receptive to the proposals of the constructivists.

There was yet another explanation for the scenic constructivism of *The Magnificent Cuckold* and *The Death of Tarelkin*: it was a very inexpensive method of setting the stage. By Meyerhold's own admission (in a recollection written by him four years later), the nature of *The Magnificent Cuckold*'s production was as much a matter of making a virtue of necessity as a manifestation of artistic credo:

> After the closure of the First Theatre of the R.S.F.S.R. we were left without a theatre and began to work on production problems without a stage.
>
> This manner of working was strongly reflected in the character of the production which we were then preparing. We never did have much money, and at that time we had none at all. The entire production of *The Magnificent Cuckold* cost 200 roubles.[35] *

Of course biomechanics need not be attributed to these conditions, but it is quite possible that the starkness of the original scenic constructivism was, as much as anything, a financial solution.

Further evidence of this is indicated by the rather humorous circumstances surrounding a one-night production by Meyerhold's GVIRM students at the Actors' Theatre just a few days before the

*At today's rate of exchange, about $200. Perhaps more indicative is the fact that while at the Imperial Theatres before the Revolution, Meyerhold was paid 500 roubles for each opera he directed—in addition to his regular salary.

opening of *The Magnificent Cuckold*. On the evening of 20 April 1922 they presented, under Meyerhold's direction, Ibsen's *Nora (A Doll's House)*: "a tragedy about Nora Helmer, or about those wives from bourgeois families who preferred freedom and work."[36]

This production is rarely noted by commentators on Meyerhold—and rightly so. Although it is part of his official record of productions,[37] it should be regarded as an exercise-demonstration to which the public was unfortunately invited—probably in an effort to raise a few roubles. It does, however, offer a candid glimpse of Meyerhold improvising *in extremis*. Student Sergei Yutkevich recalls the situation: "Productions were resumed in the theatre on Sadovo-Triumphali [Number Twenty Sadovaya Street]; but Meyerhold, enthusiastically involved with his teaching, rarely put in an appearance there. He presented, for one evening only, Ibsen's *Nora* . . . demonstrating for us how it is possible to bring a production into being in three days."[38]   Only three days' preparation. And what passed as the "set" was also conceived and "mounted" in these three days (or about thirty minutes of one of them).

It was a better example of ingenuity than innovation—although some of the audience may have thought they were seeing the latter. Again, Yutkevich's recollections:

> He especially surprised us with the form of the decoration. There was not time for the preparation of the decoration, and of course funds were not plentiful, so he reversed some old canvas flats, leaned them against the bare brick walls of the theatre, erected from all this nothing very comfortable, but according to his assertions, it represented the disintegration of bourgeois life, those petty bourgeois modes against which Nora mutinies. [39]

One hopes that there was a certain tongue in cheek in Meyerhold's transparent justification of the improvised set.

The hastily prepared, slapdash production of *Nora* gave but little hint of what was coming just five days later: one of the most daringly innovative and successful experiments in the history of the Russian theatre—Meyerhold's constructivist-biomechanical production of Crommelynck's *The Magnificent Cuckold*. Few historians of the theatre would argue with Gorchakov's declaration that "Meyerhold's forms and devices in this production exercised a profound and prolonged influence on both the Soviet and non-Soviet European theatres."[40]

4
Stylistic Extremes

The Magnificent Cuckold

In the GVIRM rehearsal halls on Novinsky Boulevard Meyerhold and his Workshop students* had been developing their experimental ideas for seven months prior to the opening of *The Magnificent Cuckold*. The dissolution of the First Theatre of the R.S.F.S.R. in the fall of 1921 had left Meyerhold without a theatre and he was forced to restrict his activities to the rehearsal halls. Although the old theatre at Number Twenty Sadovaya Street was shortly available to him again—the result of its being rechristened the Actors' Theatre and placed at the disposal of GVIRM and Neslobin's Actors' Theatre in January of 1922—it wasn't until the evening of 22 April 1922 that Meyerhold's students from GVIRM made their first public appearance (discounting the one-night production of *Nora*).

In Fernand Crommelynck's *The Magnificent Cuckold* Meyerhold had found an almost perfect vehicle for the theatre form

---

*On paper, the Meyerhold Workshop was but one division of GVIRM; in practice, however, nearly everything at GVIRM revolved about the Workshop and in many recollections the Meyerhold Workshop and GVIRM are practically synonymous.

which he was developing. Four years later, in 1926, Meyerhold recalled, "With this production we hoped to lay the basis for a new form of theatrical presentation with no need for illusionistic settings or complicated props, making do with the simplest objects which came to hand and transforming a spectacle performed by specialists into an improvised performance which could be put on by workers in their leisure time."[1] The utilitarian motive of developing a form of theatre "which could be put on by workers" and the practical matter of a severely limited budget—these extenuating considerations notwithstanding, *The Magnificent Cuckold*'s production was an immediate outgrowth of Meyerhold's continuing efforts to rediscover the elemental joie de vivre of theatrical art.

In Crommelynck's play, first produced in Paris in 1920, the ritual of a jealous husband testing the faithfulness of a beautiful wife is extended to the point of grotesque absurdity. Bruno, a miller, is obsessed with both the unmatched beauty of his wife and the conviction that any woman so beautiful is bound to yield to the temptations of infidelity. And the more his wife, Stella, protests her innocence, the more convinced he is that she has a lover. Finally, he declares that the only way that she can prove that she is not being faithful to a lover is to put herself at the disposal of any and all males in the village. But despite her distraught willingness to accommodate all the eager offers that come pouring in, he refuses to believe that she is actually going through with it. The result is scandal, the mayor intervenes, and the women assault Stella. And in the end, despairing of her husband, she leaves him for a young shepherd. But does this finally convince Bruno? No. He remains unconvinced and feels that this is but another of Stella's "tricks" in her effort to conceal the identity of the lover to whom she is still faithful.

Crommelynck himself said that the play could be produced as either farce or tragedy.[2] In the Meyerhold production (of Aksenov's translation) there was little question which way it was being interpreted: "Babanova, Ilinsky, and Zaichikov enacted Crommelynck's tragic farce without a drop of the 'tragic.' They used the gay mockery of mischievous comedians and circuslike devices."[3] The cast members were dressed alike in blue coveralls.

On the bare stage sat the first "machine for theatre"* in the Russian theatre. How much of the idea was Meyerhold's and how much was that of the credited designer, Popova, is impossible to tell. Meyerhold often predetermined much of the designer's work with his own concepts and floor plans; on the other hand, he is not listed here as codesigner, as he is for some of his later productions. It would probably be reasonable to assume that lack of funds ruled out a new, extensive setting; Meyerhold thus chose to do it "bare" and three-dimensional rather than paint up some of the old flats in the theatre; and Popova determined the dimensions and details of the actual set.

The result was a completely denuded stage—no curtains, no backdrops, no masking pieces whatsoever. On this stage sat an uncovered construction of platforms and inclined surfaces joined together by ramps and stairs, and surrounded by wheels, rolling discs, windmill sails (an item of representation!), a trapeze, and a viaduct. Slightly upstage of all this was a giant red and blue disk with large Latin letters, CR MM L NCK, printed in white on it. Each time Bruno would begin to fume in a jealous rage, the wheel would start turning furiously with a loud clumpity, clumpity sound.

What did all this amount to? Nothing. Nothing, that is, until put to use and consequently brought to life by the actors. This was the theatre of the actor. The set was a machine for his use. And like the stage of the commedia dell'arte, it was nothing in itself, but was created into something by the talents of the actor working in conjunction with the imagination of the audience. In the Workshop the actors had been studying their craft from a highly physical and presentational perspective: acrobatics, juggling, tumbling, fencing, boxing, dancing, and, of course, mime. These actors were to be the twentieth-century, machine-age versions of that cabotin of whom Meyerhold had spoken so fondly in 1912.

---

*"Machine for Theatre": in scene design, the principle that a stage setting is a machine which functions during the period of a performance, serving the actors and the requirements of the script." Later, in speaking of the Soviet designer's penchant for the "machine for theatre" Gorelik says, "He [the Soviet designer] thinks of the setting not as a picture of an abstract mood, but as something intimately related to the physical movement of the actor" (Mordecai Gorelik, *New Theatres for Old*, pp. 353, 485).

The effect must have been not unlike the early films of Charlie Chaplin—of whom Meyerhold was to become a great admirer—and Mack Sennett's Keystone Cops.

> As though by way of jesting, Meyerhold threw out upon the streets . . . whole stores of dusty linen settings and cardboard properties . . . turned the stage into a desert and put upon it a man, one without any makeup, without any colorful theatrical costume, a half athlete, a half mime of the newest formation, one full of laughter. . . . The strong, agile, physically robust mime actor filled the stage with his self-possessed impetuous movements. It was as though he impersonated the new man freed from the power of things, from the power of an inert immobile environment. . . .
>
> The actor was rebuilding his house—recreating his art out of plain, expeditious and frolicsome movements of the human body.[4]

But this vivid, fun-filled picture which Boris Alpers draws of the production seems almost incompatible with a statement made, at a much later date, by Meyerhold. In 1933 Meyerhold talked of the production to a British correspondent from the *London Observer* who quoted him as saying, "My central idea was to show the brutal repression of wives as human beings. The heroine—Stella—is shown as a sacrifice to such brutal instincts that the audience concludes the need for socialist order."[5]

Such a tendentious reading of *The Magnificent Cuckold* is possible and, given Meyerhold's sincere enthusiasm for socialist revolution, it is also possible that in 1922 he actually saw it as a kind of *Lehrstück*. But it is much more likely that the increasingly hostile atmosphere of suspicion which prevailed when he gave the interview in 1933 compelled Meyerhold to stress, for public consumption, a socialistically "correct" interpretation of his earlier work. For if his "central idea" had really been so pedantic it is hard to believe that the production would have been so "full of laughter," so "frolicsome," and "greeted with delight" by the general audience while at the same time frightening "a section of critical opinion."[6]

The fact of the matter is that Meyerhold's concept of the theatre was inherently contradictory to the cultivation of ideological propaganda. And the reason for the suspicion of some party critics that there was something amiss in the ostensibly agitprop productions of *The Dawns* and *Mystery-Bouffe* becomes explicable—at least from hindsight—in light of *The Magnificent Cuckold.*

Demystification of Ritual

For Meyerhold to attempt to integrate his own idea of theatre with the concept of theatre as a propaganda tool was not to practice deception—except in the sense that he may have been deceiving himself by thinking that the two could be compatible. To recall a statement made by Meyerhold in his 1939 speech, "All my efforts were directed at finding an organic form for the given content."[7] But, as we have seen, there was something about the form of his productions of *The Dawns* and *Mystery-Bouffe* that deeply disturbed the very people whose ideas he thought he was promoting.

The problem was actually in the relationship of form and content. Even Meyerhold himself probably did not realize at the time of *The Dawns* and *Mystery-Bouffe* the implications of the particular form of theatre that he was developing. But with *The Magnificent Cuckold* and subsequent productions he seems to have grasped, intellectually or intuitively, the attitude inherently implied by his idea of form and to have gone about the business of applying it to appropriate plays.

What this attitude was—and is—has been described in an essay by the Polish critic Jan Kott. In "Theatre and Literature," Kott states that the classical definition of theatre which declares it to be an imitation of an action is true, he believes, but only in the sense that it is "the imitation of an action by another action, the imitation of a body by another body." Having underscored this difference between the imitator and the thing being imitated, Kott goes on to make this assertion: "The Mass is a ritual, a repetition of sacred words and gestures. What would happen if a Mass were played on the stage? An actor on the stage does not play a priest saying a Mass, he *mimes* the gestures of the priest. As such the performance is not a ritual, but a profanation of the ritual."[9]

Kott's contention that a mass played by an actor on the stage would necessarily be a profanation might certainly be challenged by proponents of the realistic stage. It is quite conceivable that the actors at the Moscow Art Theatre could have staged a mass that would not have communicated a sense of profanation except to the most rigidly orthodox Catholic. But in the "theatrical" theatre (which for Kott is the only one worth talking about), the material of life is used for the purposes of the theatre: i.e., subordinate to the theatre qua theatre. In this case, the potential for profanation becomes very real, if not inevitable. Consequently, "the *theatrical* mime of a sacred mime played on the stage by an actor is shocking—it is a demystification of ritual."[10] And finally, "To mime a Mass is a profanation, but to mime love is also a profanation. . . . To play love is to imitate love, but to mime love is to demystify love, to mime power is to demystify power, to mime ritual is to demystify ritual."[11]

Although Kott makes no use of it, he might very well have referred to the history of Soviet theatre as an excellent case in point. The commissars felt profoundly ill at ease in the presence of Meyerhold's theatrical theatre of mime and mask, even though the subject matter might be all in the favor of the Communist state. On the other hand, the same subject matter treated in the realistic manner of, say, the Moscow Art Theatre, seemed suitable and properly respectable. The eventual result was the official insistence on Socialist Realism.

The authorities sensed there was something wrong about *The Dawns* and *Mystery-Bouffe*. Meyerhold was—quite unintentionally—demystifying the "ritual" of Soviet ideology and the Revolution by miming rather than playing it. But when Meyerhold switched subject matter from Soviet to bourgeois society, then the demystifying nature of the theatrical mime had, in the eyes of the authorities, a legitimate target. This is why *The Magnificent Cuckold* was accepted and even lauded by many of the same critics who had reacted negatively to *The Dawns* and *Mystery-Bouffe*.

Profanation, demystification, and satire are inherent in the form of theatre art which Meyerhold was developing—the theatre of masks, mime, and the grotesque. Meyerhold said that he was not a formalist because he accepted the content as given and then sought an organic form appropriate to it. This may have been true in the case of any particular production which he staged, but it is also true that he believed in a general definition of theatre which was at odds with a completely organic approach. In other words, he had no qualms about switching subject matter from the pro-Soviet *The Dawns* to the antibourgeois *Magnificent Cuckold,* but he could not switch the definition of his theatre from the satirical and demystifying theatre of the grotesque to a more positive and myth-promoting form of theatre—e.g., Realism or Symbolism.

From GVIRM to GITIS

The success of *The Magnificent Cuckold* was followed seven months later by a similarly staged production of Alexander Sukhovo-Kobylin's *The Death of Tarelkin.* The obvious similarity between the two productions emphasizes the fact that the biomechanics and scenic constructivism of *The Magnificent Cuckold* were not just one-shot experiments—or, if they had been so intended, they certainly proved successful enough to repeat. About *The Magnificent Cuckold* Meyerhold said, "The fact that the stylistic extremes displayed by this production—although they frightened a section of critical opinion—were greeted *with delight* by the widest possible audience, proved that an urgent desire for such a theatrical style was felt by this new audience."[12] Although there were no discernable changes in Meyerhold's methods or concepts in the interval between the two productions, there were some administrative developments that should be noted before examining *The Death of Tarelkin.*

The Magnificent Cuckold opened in the spring of 1922. In the following summer GVIRM (actually, GVITM—the term "Directing" having been replaced by "Theatrical") was dissolved and in its place was established the State Institute of Theatrical Art (GITIS). To make a very general analogy, GITIS was to GVIRM (or GVITM) what a university is to a college: the former embraces several of the latter. GVIRM was a workshop composed of various divisions, whereas GITIS was an institution composed of the State Institute of Musical Drama, what was formerly GVIRM, and eight smaller workshops. In GITIS Meyerhold conducted some classes for beginning students and, more importantly, supervised his personal branch of the institute, the Meyerhold Workshop.

The theatre at Number Twenty Sadovaya Street, which as the Actors' Theatre had been available to GVIRM and Neslobin students, was now attached to the institute and on 1 October 1922 was appropriately renamed the Theatre of GITIS. It was also during the interval between *The Magnificent Cuckold* and *The Death of Tarelkin* that Meyerhold became associated with the Theatre of the Revolution. This theatre had originated among the political workers in 1919 as a loosely organized group bent on staging agitprop plays. At the time Meyerhold became the theatre's artistic director in the summer of 1922 the name was changed from Theatre of Revolutionary Satire to the more general Theatre of the Revolution.

In the fall of 1922 work on Toller's *Machine Wreckers* began at the Theatre of the Revolution under the direction of P. P. Repin. Apparently, all was not going well and Meyerhold stepped in to take charge of the production. This, his first work with German Expressionist drama, was uneventful except for the fact that it marked the beginning of his work at the Theatre of the Revolution. For the next year and a half Meyerhold used this theatre to realize his overtly political productions of agitprop and Expressionist drama while developing a more "aesthetic"—or at least apolitical—theatre on Sadovaya Street.

At the Sadovaya Street theatre, now known as the Theatre of GITIS, the actors of the Meyerhold Workshop shared the stage with another GITIS division, the Experimental-Heroical Theatre of Ferdinandov and Shersheniyevich. Not surprisingly, the prominence of Meyerhold's name, the nature of his personality, and the success of *The Magnificent Cuckold* caused the Workshop to overshadow the Experimental-Heroical Theatre and it wasn't long before the latter chose to go elsewhere. Before they did, however, the other tenants—the Meyerhold Workshop—scored another success with their biomechanic and constructivist radicalism: Sukhovo-Kobylin's *The Death of Tarelkin.*

The Death of Tarelkin

The matter of Meyerhold's irreverent treatment of Russian classics is usually first raised with regard to his production in 1924 of Ostrovsky's *The Forest*. Actually, it is with the opening of *The Death of Tarelkin* on 24 November 1922 at the Theatre of GITIS that he took the initial plunge into the business of audaciously reviving traditional Russian plays. It is interesting to note that in his "revivals" he worked his way back through the Russian repertoire in exactly reverse chronology. He started with *Tarelkin* (written in 1869 but not produced until 1900), then did two plays by Ostrovsky, *A Lucrative Post* and *The Forest* (both first produced in the second half of the nineteenth century), and finally Gogol's *Inspector General* and Griboyedov's *Woe from Wit* (both products of the first half of the nineteenth century). There is probably more coincidence than logic to this inverted sequence, but it might be noted in passing that as Meyerhold worked his way back through the Russian repertoire from *The Death of Tarelkin* in 1922 to *Woe from Wit* in 1928 his revivification procedures reflected a lessening of interest in "proletarianizing" the classics and greater interest in "conventionalizing" them; in other words, a decrease in political and an increase in aesthetic considerations.

The Death of Tarelkin is the third play in a trilogy by Alexander Sukhovo-Kobylin known simply as *The Trilogy*—the first two being *Krechinsky's Wedding* and *The Case*. This trilogy and its author form a fascinating chapter in the history of Russian drama—a chapter usually noted for its Kafkaesque quality. In the second quarter of the nineteenth century Sukhovo-Kobylin (1817-1903) was a handsome Moscow aristocrat with a fashionable interest in belles lettres, philosophy, and beautiful women. But in 1850 an event occurred which transformed his life into a grotesque nightmare.

The mutilated body of his French mistress of ten years was found in a pile of snow on the outskirts of Moscow. The trials and retrials which followed for the next seven years made the case one of the most infamous in the history of pre-Revolution jurisprudence. During this period Sukhovo-Kobylin was twice incarcerated as guilt was alternately shifted from his shoulders to those of his servants. Finally, with the personal intervention of Empress Alexandra herself, the case was resolved in October of 1857 with a verdict of not guilty for both Sukhovo-Kobylin and his servants.

The Trilogy is a direct outgrowth of his seven years of

anguished struggling to find his way out of the bureaucratic maze which constituted the Russian legal system of the 1850s. It starts with a relatively innocent comedy of manners in the style of Eugène Scribe and the *pièce bien fait, Krechinsky's Wedding.* In this play a scheming but impoverished nobleman, Krechinsky, seeks to solve his financial problems by marrying the daughter of a wealthy provincial landowner.

The second play, *The Case,* begins a downward spiral through the maze of bureaucratic corruption as the landowner and his daughter, innocently implicated in the dealings of Krechinsky, try to extricate themselves. But the more they struggle and the more they try to go along with the system of bribes and perjury, the more desperate becomes their plight until the half-crazed landowner finally drops dead of exhaustion.

The final play, *The Death of Tarelkin,* continues the downward spiral. But now it is no longer a struggle between good and evil but between the agents of evil themselves, Tarelkin and Varravin, as they fight over possession of the late landowner's bribe money. Tarelkin has stolen some papers incriminating to Varravin, his superior. With these he hopes to blackmail Varravin out of the competition for the landowner's money. But Varravin is on to him, so Tarelkin tries to throw him off the trail by counterfeiting his own death (complete with dummy corpse stuffed with reeking dead fish for the sake of olfactory verisimilitude as well as discouraging close inspection), and assuming the identity of a recently deceased neighbor.

Varravin discovers the plot but pretends ignorance. Instead, he arrests Tarelkin (now identified as Kopylov) on suspicion of being a vampire which according to rumors is terrorizing Moscow and Petersburg. Under intensive and ingenious grilling Tarelkin-Kopylov finally reveals himself, relinquishes the incriminating papers, and is set free by Varravin. But he is set free as Kopylov, Tarelkin being officially dead, and is left standing onstage facing the audience, out of work, out of money, out of schemes: "Gentlemen, perhaps you need someone to manage your estate?"[13]

In his last years at the Imperial Theatres Meyerhold had staged all three plays of the trilogy—*Krechinsky's Wedding* in 1917, just one month before *Masquerade* and the Revolution, and *The Case* and *The Death of Tarelkin* seven and nine months later, respectively. *The Death of Tarelkin* had first been presented on the Russian stage in 1900 after Sukhovo-Kobylin made many amendments to his originally censored script of 1869. In Meyerhold's 1917 production, which was realized in the immediate aftermath of the overthrow of the Tsar, the vicious satire of the original script was restored and the drama was produced in an onstage atmosphere of grotesque farce and nightmarish absurdity.

In 1922, however, the old Tsarist bureaucracy was clearly a thing of the past and Bolsheviks like Meyerhold, no longer anxious about its possible return, regarded it with the derisive laughter of confident conquerors. And compared to his 1917 version, Meyerhold's 1922 staging of *The Death of Tarelkin* reflected this change of attitude. Instead of frighteningly vicious schemers, Varravin, Tarelkin, and their associates were satirized as thoroughly corrupt bunglers whose stupidity was exceeded only by their greed. The entire production was in the tone of a loud and merry repudiation of the whole pre-Revolutionary lot of them.

On a brightly illuminated and completely stripped stage sat an assortment of "acting instruments" painted white. According to Alexy Gvozdyev: "In this production Meyerhold continued to develop his struggle against the traditional theatres. The single machine of *Cuckold* was separated into a series of individual installations, theatrical devices capable of becoming the supporting points for the unusual playing of the actors."[14]

As in *The Magnificent Cuckold,* the "devices" which constituted the setting for *The Death of Tarelkin* were not wholly nonrepresentational.* Instead, these devices were—like the acting done in, on, and around them—unadorned caricatures of the real thing interspersed with a few strictly utilitarian items: "For example, the police torture-chamber was represented by means of an undecorated apparatus which consisted of a latticed cage with a rotating wheel which transferred the prisoner from one part to

*Meyerhold's constructivist sets never were completely nonrepresentational. In fact, few such sets exist in the entire history of the modern theatre. Projects of this nature were offered by such people as Tatlin and Ekster but rarely were they realized in actual production. One such realization was the setting by Gabo and Pevsner for Diagliev's *La Chatte* in 1927.

another. Wooden crates with lids made possible the development of the stage in the manner of "Petrushka" [Jack-in-the-box], which intensified the frightening appearance of the "vampire."[15]

The actors, outfitted in Varvara Stepanova's baggy, striped costumes, romped about the stage in a biomechanical version of circus clowns and strolling players—that is, choreographed miming, tumbling, chasing, and fighting. Tarelkin, a pathetic victim in the 1917 production (and in Sukhovo-Kobylin's script), became something like the Head Clown and had a grand time making fools of his captors: "Tarelkin, bound hand and foot in prison and frantic with thirst, tried in vain to reach a cup of water held by a warder—then suddenly he winked broadly at the audience and took a long draught from a bottle of wine he had concealed in his pocket."[16] Sukhovo-Kobylin's script calls for no such respite for the suffering Tarelkin. It is a good example of just how far Meyerhold was going at this time with the idea of mockery.

Nothing was above ridicule: not the script, the author's intentions, or even the character which the actor was portraying. In one moment the actor would appear to be sincerely portraying the character's feelings and attitude, and then in a flash he would suddenly do something totally out of character and situation, as if to say to the audience, "Weren't these people an absurd lot! " It was the idea of actor-commenting-on-his-character carried out in the most obvious fashion.

In spite of a few refinements and some new gimmicks—collapsible furniture, spring-loaded chairs, stools that set off blank cartridges—it was all pretty much what the audiences had seen earlier in *The Magnificent Cuckold.* As a result *Tarelkin,* although not a failure, did not enjoy the success of *The Magnificent Cuckold.*

There were those who were willing to come to the theatre and enjoy the actor's antics in much the same way that they would enjoy those of a clown: the repetition, with some variations, of a certain bag of tricks. But for others the novelties in Meyerhold's production of *The Magnificent Cuckold* were not something that could be imposed on a succession of plays without a diminution of effect. In the commedia dell'arte the actors relied heavily on a set bag of tricks—the *lazzi*; but unlike Meyerhold's biomechanical actors in *The Magnificent Cuckold* and *The Death of Tarelkin*, the

commedia actor specialized in a particular character—e.g., Panta-
lone, Harlequin, Brigellia—who continued to appear in scenario
after scenario. The stories changed, but the characters remained
the same. But from *The Magnificent Cuckold* to *The Death of
Tarelkin* both the story *and* the characters changed while the
presentational performances remained essentially the same. As a
result, attention was focused on the performer qua performer at
the expense of story and character. And once this was done the
theatre ceased to be theatre and became a circus. For those who
came to *The Death of Tarelkin* looking for the experience of the
theatre, the results left something to be desired.

Apparently Meyerhold also recognized the results for what they
really were; in subsequent productions he began to modify what
he himself called "the stylistic extremes"[17] of *Cuckold* and
Tarelkin. Having taken the actor as far as possible from Stanislavsky's lifelike characterizations, he now began to reverse his steps as
he sought what would be for him the proper balance between the
actor's performance and the playwright's character.

NEP and Agitprop: *The Earth Rebellious*

The opening of *The Death of Tarelkin* in November 1922 took
place exactly two years after the opening of *The Dawns.* A great
deal transpired in that twenty-four month period: Meyerhold's
leadership of an subsequent resignation from TEO; the establishment and subsequent dissolution of the First Theatre of the
R.S.F.S.R.; his appointment as artistic director of the Theatre of
the Revolution; the establishment of GVIRM and then GITIS;
and, of course, his productions at the theatre on Sadovaya Street.
In the midst of all this he left his wife Olga for a young actress
who had joined his workshop in 1920, Znaida Raikh. Znaida, in
turn, had left her husband, the poet Sergei Yesenin, who in his
turn became the lover of Isadora Duncan.*

In matters more prosaic, it was also during this period (in 1921)

---

*In the years of civil war immediately following the Revolution the Soviet citizenry
found nearly everything difficult to obtain except propaganda leaflets and divorces. To
nullify a marriage a husband or wife needed only to notify the district commissar (a post
card would do) that he or she didn't wish to be married any longer. What the other
partner thought about it was beside the point. Thus, Meyerhold's first wife—with him
since 1896—fades from the picture and we never hear of her again.

that the NEP—New Economic Policy—was instituted by Lenin. This policy amounted to a temporary relaxation of the Communist strictures against the profit motive of capitalist economics. The combined effects of World War I, the Revolution, the civil war, the blockade of the new Soviet State by Western countries, and the general administrative ineptitude in the ranks of the new government had resulted in an almost total breakdown of the production and distribution of goods and services. In an effort to get the country back on its feet the NEP allowed a limited version of capitalism, sought the cooperation of the bourgeois administrators, managers, educators, and intellectuals, and set out to improve relations with the Western countries.

This relaxation of strict Communist ideology was to continue until 1928. For some, this period was recalled as "The Golden Age of the NEP"; for others (the more orthodox Marxists) it was a brief and unfortunate time characterized by the greed and exploitation of "Nepmen"—those who set about the business of making a fat profit off the misfortunes of a country and people racked by the combined devastation of a world war and a civil war.

Although there was undoubtedly much truth in the charges leveled against the Nepmen—even those who disagreed with some of the hard party line preceding the NEP, such as Meyerhold, reserved some of their bitterest satire and vilification for the profiteering Nepmen—it is equally certain that much of the creative experimentation in the arts during the 1920s would never have taken place but for the ideological relaxation accompanying the NEP. Certainly Meyerhold, who in 1921 was already at odds with the party line to some extent, would never have been able to achieve distinction and prominence as a highly honored Soviet director with the kind of productions he did in the 1920s had it not been for the tolerant conditions of the NEP.

The implementation of the NEP may explain the slight but significant reversal of Meyerhold's fortunes two years after the demise of the First Theatre of the R.S.F.S.R. and his resignation from TEO. It is important to emphasize that Meyerhold did not break with the party nor did he cease to advocate theatre for the proletariat. Nevertheless, his determination to proceed with freewheeling experimentation did not bode well for his future in a tightly controlled society. It was therefore something of a respite that the NEP relaxations granted Meyerhold from 1922 to 1928; and it was during this time that his production concepts and methods reached their full maturity.

After putting *The Death of Tarelkin* into repertoire with *The Magnificent Cuckold* at the Theatre of GITIS, Meyerhold again turned his attention to the activities at the Theatre of the Revolution. He began working on an agitprop play with a trio of proletarian playwrights: Nikolai Asyev, Sergei Gorodyetsky, and Sergei Tretyakov. It was to be called *Verturnaf* (an acronym for "Versailles Tourists on a Landmine"). But for reasons which apparently have gone unrecorded the production was never given a public performance. Instead, he took over the direction of a Toller play already in rehearsal—as he had done a few months earlier. This production, *Man and the Masses,* opened 26 January 1923. Unfortunately, the sources now available fail to indicate the nature of this production or Meyerhold's contribution to it.

By the spring of 1923 he was ready to present his next production at the Theatre of GITIS; however, it no longer went under that name. In the interval between the opening of *The Death of Tarelkin* in November 1922 and his next production the following March, the cotenants (The Experimental-Heroical Theatre of Ferdinandov and Shersheneyevich) had dissolved and the company from the Meyerhold Workshop became the sole occupants. Consequently, the name of the theatre was changed once more—from the Theatre of GITIS to the Meyerhold Theatre. For the first time in his career, which now stretched back over twenty-five years, Meyerhold was at work in a theatre which officially bore his name. It would continue to do so for fifteen years.

For his first production in the theatre bearing his name Meyerhold offered a helter-skelter conglomeration of nearly all the ideas he had been working on since 1920: agitprop, Expressionism, biomechanics, and scenic constructivism. The play was Marcel Martinet's verse drama, *The Night,* as translated and revised by Sergei Gorodyetsky and Sergei Tretyakov—two of the writers Meyerhold had been working with earlier on the aborted production of *Verturnaf* at the Theatre of the Revolution. It was called

Zemla dibom—variously translated as "the earth rebellious," "the world upside down," "the earth in turmoil," and (most literally) "the earth on its hind legs."

The revision of *The Night* was no less drastic than that of *The Dawns*. However, this time Meyerhold took the precaution of changing the name, perhaps in order to ward off the kind of critical comparison with the original that was leveled by Krupskaya against his version of *The Dawns*. Instead of sticking with Martinet's story of an aborted mutiny during an imaginary imperialist war, Meyerhold and his adapters filled the play with topical allusions in line with recent Soviet history. The allegorical dialogue was sharpened and laconicized into the agitprop declamatory style. Parading Red Army units, motorcycle units zooming down the aisles and onto the stage, Red Cross workers carrying wounded Red soldiers, slide projections on screens hung from the proscenium arch, trucks, bicycles, small cannons, and a gigantic piece of construction by Popova (designer of *The Magnificent Cuckold*) which resembled a gantry crane—all took their turn on the same bare stage under the glare of the same unfiltered light which served *The Magnificent Cuckold* and *The Death of Tarelkin*.

Unlike *Cuckold* and *Tarelkin*, however, *The Earth Rebellious* was not an exercise in the satirical grotesque. Like *The Dawns* it was conceived as a pageant of celebration and was dedicated to the Red Army and its founder, Lev Trotsky. With regard to this there is an interesting account by Yuri Annenkov, a painter and friend of Meyerhold's, of an incident which occurred on the night he attended the show.

In his memoirs Annenkov recalls that excitement was particularly high that evening (he doesn't remember the exact date) because Trotsky himself was in the audience.

> During one of the acts, happening to glance towards the seat of Trotsky, I saw that he was no longer there. I assumed that the production was perhaps not to his tastes and that he had decided to leave the theatre. But after two or three minutes Trotsky suddenly appeared *on the stage* and, in the same setting which contained the actors, delivered a short speech regarding the fifth anniversary of the founding of the Red Army which fit right in with the action of the

play. After thunderous applause the action on stage continued as if without interruption and Trotsky again returned to his seat.[18]

Accounts of the production are quite sketchy and Annenkov's anecdote suggests, as well as any other description, the show's style and atmosphere. Especially unclear is just how much slapstick and parody of the Imperialists was included. Gorchakov[19] and Slonim[20] mention the presence of buffoonery but also agree with other accounts that the prevailing tone was one of heroic pageantry. As such it was probably a production much more in the manner of *The Dawns* than of *Mystery-Bouffe.*

The explanation for such essentially heroic productions as *The Dawns* and *The Earth Rebellious* lies in the fact that they were both anniversary shows: *The Dawns* for the third anniversary of the Revolution, *The Earth Rebellious* for the fifth anniversary of the founding of the Red Army. Unless this is understood they would appear as unexplained anomalies in the midst of Meyerhold's transition from his pre-Revolution ironic grotesque to his post-Revolution satiric grotesque.

It must also be recognized, however, that the basically heroic nature of *The Earth Rebellious,* different as it was from the satirical nature of *The Magnificent Cuckold* and *The Death of Tarelkin,* did not cause Meyerhold to set aside many of the production concepts and methods realized in these two shows: biomechanics, scenic constructivism, bare stage, and general illumination formed the production basis for *The Earth Rebellious* just as they had for *The Magnificent Cuckold* and *The Death of Tarelkin.* But in addition, Meyerhold employed real objects—guns, motorcycles, lorries, field telephones, stretchers, a harvester, a mobile kitchen—and costumes appropriate to the real apparel of the characters: Red Army and Red Cross uniforms, workers' overalls, and the assorted garb of early twentieth-century bureaucrats.

The realism of props and costumes marks a departure from Meyerhold's four previous productions beginning with *The Dawns.* It marks the first modification of his previously unabated drive towards increasingly abstract and nonrepresentational staging. After *The Earth Rebellious* introduced the realism of costumes and props into his post-Revolution work, he never again returned to the nearly total abstraction of them as in *The Magnificent Cuckold* and *The Death of Tareklin.*

After having been previewed for units of the Red Army in February and presented for the public in March, the production was removed from the stage of the Meyerhold Theatre. It had never been planned as an item for the permanent repertoire, but subsequent to its production at the Meyerhold Theatre it was frequently performed as an open-air spectacle similar (on a reduced scale) to the unrealized plans he had made for a mass spectacle in 1920, *Battles and Victories.*

The Earth Rebellious was to be Meyerhold's last agitprop play in the heroic manner until late in 1929. *Roar China,* a 1926 production, might be placed in this category, but it was actually staged and directed by a Meyerhold student. Such productions of the 1920s as *Lake Lyul, Give Us Europe!* , *Teacher Bubus,* and *The Warrant* are, in a sense, agitprop plays, but they make their point by satirizing the bourgeoisie rather than championing the Soviet man, his revolution, and his values. Thus their agitprop quality is negative and implied rather than explicitly stated as in *The Dawns* or *The Earth Rebellious.* But Meyerhold continuously sought to justify his satirical productions as forms of educational agitprop theatre: if Tsarist bureaucrats were enemies of the state, and if *The Inspector General* ridiculed these bureaucrats, then *The Inspector General* was an agitational production in the cause of Communism.

This line of argument worked for a while, at least through the NEP period. But by the late 1920s the Soviet authorities were no longer concerned about any threat from "former people" (Tsarist followers) and were more interested in promoting Soviet ideology. And as discussed earlier, the very nature of Meyerhold's theatre aesthetic (the demystifying nature of the mime and the grotesque) made it unsuitable for the promotion of any ideological myth.

Furthermore, in the late 1920s it became clear that Meyerhold had no intention of restricting himself to the ridicule of stupid, self-serving Tsarist bureaucrats but considered those in the Communist bureaucracy as equally fair game—as in *The Bedbug* and *The Bathhouse.* This, as much as anything, was his undoing.

Like many other old-line revolutionaries of 1917, he failed to understand (or refused to accept) the fact that what was evil and in need of exposure under the Tsar became sacrosanct and defensible simply by virtue of the fact that it was now a part of the Soviet system. As late as 1938 Ilya Ehrenburg says[21] that Meyerhold, like others such as Boris Pasternak, still believed that the purges and the general oppression were the work of conniving functionaries and that if only Stalin could be made aware of what they were doing he would put a stop to it and root out such betrayers of the Revolution.

Would Meyerhold's fate have been different had he stuck to the heroic agitprop line of *The Dawns* and *The Earth Rebellious*? Quite possibly. It is not unreasonable to assume that his career might have gone more in the direction of his student, Sergei Eisenstein, who practically made an artistic virtue out of heroic agitprop (e.g., *The Battleship Potempkin*).

But Meyerhold's artistic intuition did not move in this direction. And unlike some, such as Bertolt Brecht, he was unable to justify the compromising of his artistic integrity and his creative intuition with the dictates of a political ideology. He no doubt believed in the cause of Communism as strongly as Brecht; but unlike Brecht, Meyerhold's first love and most fundamental commitment was to the art of the theatre rather than a particular social or political cause. And in Stalin's Russia of the 1930s a man who put anything—even truth—ahead of party-dictated ideology was in serious and probably fatal trouble.

5

"Back to Ostrovsky"

Ostrovsky Meets Meyerhold, I : *A Lucrative Post*

In the spring of 1923 no one would have guessed the tragic outcome of Meyerhold's career. On the contrary, after a slight fall from grace due to the conflicts over the First Theatre of the R.S.F.S.R., Meyerhold's star was again in ascendance. On the night of 2 April 1923, one month after the production of *The Earth Rebellious,* Meyerhold became the recipient of one of the highest honors the Soviet government could bestow upon its artists. At an evening in his honor at the Bolshoy Theatre in Moscow he was granted the title of People's Artist of the R.S.F.S.R. and thus became the first stage director and only the sixth Soviet artist of any kind to be so honored.

The evening celebrated his twenty-fifth anniversary on the Russian stage with a program presented by his students and company. It consisted of the second act from his production of *Man and the Masses,* the third act of his *Magnificent Cuckold,* and the second act of his *Death of Tarelkin.* In addition, the promotion poster listed something called "The Workshop Forgery" featuring a jazz band and a "dancing machine."[1] This sounds like a parody of the Meyerhold Workshop; if it was, it suggests the pleasing image of a man who, even on such an auspicious evening as this, was not one to become puffed up with seriousness about himself.*

Following the production of *The Earth Rebellious* and the celebration of his twenty-fifth anniversary, Meyerhold devoted a great deal of time to activities at the Theatre of the Revolution. While work proceeded rather sporadically on two productions at the Meyerhold Theatre (a dramatization of Prosper Mérimée's short story *Jacquerie* and the Bizet opera which was based on another Mérimée short story, *Carmen*), Meyerhold, surrounded by some of his best students, set to work on two productions at the Theatre of the Revolution: Alexander Ostrovsky's *A Lucrative Post,* codirected by A. B. Vielishev, and Alexy Faiko's *Lake Lyul,* codirected by A. M. Rume. Both productions were designed by Meyerhold's friend and frequent design assistant, V. A. Shestakov. This was to be one of the last times that a Meyerhold production would give full design credit to someone else. In nearly all of his subsequent productions Meyerhold himself was listed as designer of the set plan. (However, this may have been nothing more than open acknowledgment of what had always been the case anyway.)

More important, these two productions were also to be Meyerhold's last work at the Theatre of the Revolution. But his influence by this time was firmly established in this theatre and after liquidation of the Meyerhold Theatre in 1938 it became the closest thing to a bearer of the Meyerhold tradition.**

By Lunacharsky's proclamation, the focus of Russian theatre in the year 1923 would be on the centennial celebration of Alexander Ostrovsky's birth. The slogan was to be "Back to Ostrovsky! " But Lunacharsky had in mind something of broader implications than just a centennial observation: "By the slogan 'Back to Ostrovsky,' I wanted to talk about the need for returning

---

*See his remarks about this on p. 19.

**In 1957 the name was changed from the Theatre of the Revolution to the Theatre of Mayakovsky. More recently, according to Norris Houghton (*ETJ,* May 1971, pp. 117-126), the Taganka Theatre, under the direction of Yuri Liubimov, has emerged as the most likely successor to the Meyerhold tradition.

to the realistic theatre which was socially psychological and . . . socially interesting. This was a suitable technique of expression."[2]

Most of the major theatres contributed to the centennial with a production of one of Ostrovsky's numerous plays (he was by far the most prolific of major Russian playwrights). But just what treatment or approach should be taken in order to please Lunacharsky and other Soviet authorities was very much in question. Either the mode of production desired by the authorities was unclear or the various theatres simply accepted the letter of the proclamation and disregarded the spirit.

At the Moscow Proletkult Theatre, Meyerhold's former student, Sergei Eisenstein, staged Sergei Tretyakov's very free adaptation of Ostrovsky's *Enough Simplicity for Every Wise Man* as a "montage of attractions"[3] complete with a tightrope act by one of the characters. At the Maly Theatre, director N. O. Volkonsky "rejuvenated" Ostrovsky in "Party-style" by changing the characters in *A Lucrative Post* from minor civil servants to important members of Tsarist society. But due to his reluctance to tamper with the dialogue, the result was confusion and, according to Gorchakov, the production was nearly charged with being counter-revolutionary.[4] Tairov's Kamerny Theatre was on tour in Europe during the first part of the 1923-1924 theatre season, but upon its return to Russia in 1924 offered its contribution with a surrealistically designed production of *The Storm*. Ostrovsky was a permanent part of the realistic repertoire of the Moscow Art Theatre and it was their approach that Lunacharsky probably had in mind. Ironically, the Moscow Art Theatre was on tour in America from January 1923 to May 1924 and consequently missed the entire centennial.

Not to be outdone by all this, Meyerhold planned not one but two Ostrovsky productions during the 1923-1924 season: at the Theatre of the Revolution, *A Lucrative Post,* and at the Meyerhold Theatre, *The Forest.* For Lunacharsky and his purpose of "returning to the realistic theatre which was socially psychological," this bit of news was probably something less than reassuring. And sure enough, Meyerhold proceeded to make it quite clear that even with Ostrovsky he had no intention of returning to realism or the "socially psychological"—whatever that was supposed to be.

On 15 May 1923—one month after the celebration in his honor at the Bolshoy—the newly designated People's Artist presented Alexander Ostrovsky's *A Lucrative Post* at the Theatre of the Revolution. This play, like so many Russian comedies of the nineteenth century, follows in the *Inspector General*'s tradition of satirizing the greed, gullibility, and pretentiousness of provincial civil servants. Thus, after having put together the heroic and sentimental *Earth Rebellious,* Meyerhold was back in his natural idiom of parody and satire.

Unfortunately, *A Lucrative Post* is another Meyerhold production of which the accounts are very sparse. In the accounts of Meyerhold's work during this period by Gorchakov, Braun, Jelagin, Alpers, Slonim, Houghton, Gvozdyev, Zakhava, and even in the collection of material in *Vstrechi s Meyerholdom* and *V. E. Meyerhold: statyi, pisma, rechi, besedy* there are only occasional references to this Ostrovsky production. Instead, the chronicler usually proceeds directly from *The Earth Rebellious* to the much more famous Ostrovsky production of eight months later at the Meyerhold Theatre, *The Forest.*

The general disregard of *A Lucrative Post* (and of *Lake Lyul* which followed it at the Theatre of the Revolution) may be due to the fact that Meyerhold was working with a codirector—something he rarely did except when working with Mayakovsky on one of his plays—and it is therefore impossible to tell how much of the production can be accurately attributed to Meyerhold. But the account by Bolislav Rostotsky in his recent study, *O rezhissor-skom tvorchestve V. E. Meyerholda* [About the creative director, V. E. Meyerhold], suggests that the position of codirector notwithstanding, the production was in the hands of Meyerhold. According to Rostotsky, the production of *A Lucrative Post* was "an excellent example of the manifestation of all that was best in connection with Meyerhold's efforts to be innovative in his approach to the classics."[5]

As mentioned earlier, Meyerhold's first post-Revolution production in the direction of revised classics was his biomechanical-constructivist production of *The Death of Tarelkin.* Now, less than a year later and with only *The Earth Rebellious* produced in the meantime, Meyerhold reduces significantly the initial blatancy of biomechanics and constructivism. "If in the production of *The Death of Tarelkin* the attempt to stress the social aspect resulted in distortion through futuristic eccentricities, it was a different matter in the production of Ostrovsky's *A Lucrative Post*. . . . This production was a splendid directorial success."[6]

In the rare photographs of this production* and in Shestakov's design sketches there appear to be no constructivist units employed at all. Instead, the stage comes much closer to resembling the bas-relief concept of Georg Fuchs. A solid-looking wall extends from one side of the stage to the other and rises from the stage floor into the flies until it is out of sight. It appears to be parallel to the edge of the stage apron and set back to a depth of about fifteen feet. According to Shestakov's sketch, the top half of this wall is painted in a light tone and the bottom half is composed of a series of wooden panels. It is broken only by a single doorway about two-thirds of the way up in the center. Extending out and down from the doorway is a long stairway which reaches to the stage floor.

The sketch and photographs show this wide but shallow playing area occupied by only a few items of realistic furniture: a couple of tables and some straight-back chairs. And perhaps most striking of all in comparison with *The Death of Tarelkin* is the costuming: it is quite clearly accurate period attire for the time of Ostrovsky's story (mid-nineteenth century). This is the first time since his call for a "Theatrical October" in 1920 that Meyerhold employs realistic period costumes.

Although Rostotsky's account and the photographs offer admittedly flimsy substaniation, it does appear that along with constructivism and stylized costuming, the biomechanical approach to acting may also have undergone substantial modification. In the photographs, even without allowing for the usual exaggeration in posing, the attitudes of the actors appear much more realistic and less choreographed than in photographs of *Tarelkin* and *Cuckold*. Rostotsky states: ' Of course there were

---

*Some new ones have just appeared at the time of this writing in Konstantine Rudnitsky's *Rezhissor Meyerhold* [Meyerhold the director] (Moscow, 1969), pp. 288-300.

also eccentric performances in the production of *A Lucrative Post,* but they were different according to each character. The eccentricity of characters was subordinate to artistic truth and they were not transformed into something automated."[7]

Meyerhold's return to a degree of character delineation, as suggested in this passage from Rostotsky's study, is a very important development. In his productions since 1920—*The Dawns, Mystery-Bouffe, The Magnificent Cuckold, The Death of Tarelkin,* and *The Earth Rebellious*—Meyerhold had rigorously subordinated the individual personalities of the dramatic characters to the uniformity of biomechanics or to superficial categories such as Soviet Man, Former People, and Bourgeois Capitalists. At the most, delineations were made, as in *Mystery-Bouffe,* on the basis of "A Menshivik," 'A Bolshevik," or "An American." But now, with this seldom-noted production of *A Lucrative Post* in 1923, he returned to the mode of theatrical characterization that he had been developing in the years immediately prior to the Revolution.

This was not, of course, the capitulation of a theatricalist innovator to the forces of psychological or socialist realism. Rather, it was the resurgence of his original inclination in the direction of a theatre aesthetic based on the principles of the commedia dell'arte. Says Rostotsky, "While completely preserving the passion for innovation . . . Meyerhold proceeded in the present case not by way of external forms of innovation, but by way of delving deeply into the material of the dramatist and boldly revealing the content in all its richness."[8] But the way in which the actors, through their characterizations, revealed this content continued to offer a clear alternative to realism. "Instead of showing psychological characters, Meyerhold at this time sought to reveal typical psychological traits as a sharp and effective method of social exposure."[9]

Rostotsky goes on to describe, through references to leading actor Dimitry Orlov's account in *The Moscow Theatre of the Revolution,* how Meyerhold directed his performers in this production. In one example Orlov, as the character Yusov, was to enter the study of his superior in a servile manner. In order to convey this attitude with broad, commedialike strokes, Meyerhold directed Orlov to shuffle into the room in a squatting position. Later in the play as the same character gleefully burned some incriminating papers, Meyerhold isolated him in a single pool of light as he broke into a stylized jig. (This suggestion of selective lighting was also something that Meyerhold had not been employing in his most recent productions.)

All in all—in set design, costumes, props, lighting, and acting—the production of *A Lucrative Post* at the Theatre of the Revolution on 15 May 1923 represents a major turning point in Meyerhold's post-Revolution career. In all of his much more famous productions to come he continues to stage plays in a manner quite consistent with the approach taken in *A Lucrative Post* and never again returns to the impersonal nature of *The Dawns* and *The Earth Rebellious* or to the degree of abstractness in the nearly pure biomechanics and scenic constructivism of *The Magnificent Cuckold* and *The Death of Tarelkin.*

Highrise Agitprop: *Lake Lyul*

Following the opening of *A Lucrative Post* in May, Meyerhold and Znaida Raikh partook of the growing Soviet interest in the Western countries with a summer vacation in western Europe. This was not a new interest for Meyerhold; he had made several trips outside of Russia prior to the Revolution. However, this was his first journey abroad since the events of 1917. For the first few years immediately following the Revolution, Soviet Russia had been virtually quarantined from the rest of the world. This isolation was partly self-imposed and partly the result of the reluctance by capitalist countries to accept the Communist government as legitimate.

It was not until about 1922 that it became unmistakably clear that the counterrevolutionary forces had been defeated and that Lenin and his Communist Party were in complete control. At the same time, it became clear to Lenin that for at least a while it would be necessary to relax the strict Communist ideology not only through the NEP within Russia but also in terms of Russia's relations with America and Western Europe. This compromise with ideological enemies was rationalized along these lines:

although the wealthy capitalist exploiter is and always will be the enemy, there is nothing wrong with admiring and learning from the scientific and industrial accomplishments of Western workers —who are, after all, potential comrades-in-arms with the Russian proletariat.

One of the results was a relaxation of travel bans between Russia and the countries of the West. And along with the imported goods and returning Russian travelers came an influx of morals, manners, and cultural tastes from the rapidly modernizing Europe and America of the 1920s. The fox-trot, the Charleston, tap-dancing, and especially American jazz came to symbolize for the Russian the morals and manners of the Western bourgeoisie. The figure of Western decadence was shifted from one of paunchy self-righteousness to that of finger-snapping, daringly-dressed "slickers" who spent most of their time dancing from one nightclub to another.

It was no trouble for Meyerhold, an ebullient man of action, to communicate in his productions an attitude of satirical condemnation for the former figure of Western decadence; but as for Western "slickers," his critics charged that his satirical portraits of them contained as much admiration as condemnation—or at least the audiences evinced an undue fascination with them and their evil ways.

Meyerhold first peopled his stage with caricatures of these modern decadents in his last production at the Theatre of the Revolution on 7 November 1923. This was Alexy Faiko's *Lake Lyul,* which Faiko himself described in this manner:

> In the spring of 1923 I wrote my first major play, *Lake Lyul,* a romantic melodrama in five acts. Location: somewhere in the Far West or perhaps in the Far East. Many characters. Crowd scenes. White, yellow, and black races. Hotels, villas, shops. Advertisement hoardings and lifts. A revolutionary struggle on an island. An underground movement. Conspiracies. The basis of the plot—the rise and fall of the renegade, Anton Prim. [10]

Except for his association with Mayakovsky this was one of the first times that Meyerhold worked on a play in the presence of its author. And Faiko's recollection of that experience offers an amusing and perhaps indicative glimpse of Meyerhold at work.

Faiko writes that as fall arrived in 1923 and plans got underway for production of *Lake Lyul,* Meyerhold had still not returned from Europe. "In the press appeared detailed notices about the forthcoming new production. The stage had been completely freed for *Lake.* . . . But Meyerhold had still not returned. Around the theatre the rumor circulated that Vsevolod Emilevich would not participate in the production but intended only to polish the prepared show."[11] Faiko says that despite his own apprehension everyone else was calm and going about the business of preparing the stage according to some basic ideas of codirector Abe Rume. But then: "All of a sudden he appeared. Unexpectedly and casually. As if coming to a regular rehearsal."[12]

Meyerhold was fifty years old at this time but Faiko recalls that he didn't look his age at all.* Rather, he was quite sporty "in his grey suit, short golf trousers, leggings or puttees. In all he was a cool, boney, and slightly ungainly figure . . . but in his gestures he was somehow both unconstrained and very refined."[13]

Faiko goes on to say that in his first meeting with Meyerhold the famous director was not inclined to ceremony, "but conducted himself as if he had known me for a long time, although he didn't make anything important out of it."[14]

> "You have been to the rehearsals? " he asked me.
> "Yes. Almost every one."
> "But 'almost' is not enough. If it happens that the author is living then everything possible must be drawn from him . . . and then some."
> "But what if he is dead? "
> Meyerhold thought for a second.
> "The same is true . . . only from someone else."
> And with that he quickly started upstairs. But I wanted to find out more about this master and I overtook him.
> "Vsevolod Emilevich, how do you . . . how do we . . . aside from this . . . relate to each other with regard to my play?"
> Meyerhold suddenly stopped and asked, as if amazed:
> "But you know I have already accepted it. You know it's in

*Photographs certainly bear Faiko out on this point, e.g., *V. E. Meyerhold,* illus. following 2:80.

rehearsal, yes? Haven't you been informed of this? "

Meyerhold leaped two steps and, half turning, shouted:

"In my opinion, it is interesting. Yes? Or no? What's your opinion? Is it not interesting? Huh? " And not waiting for an answer, he briskly continued up the stairs, disappearing into the darkness.[15]

And thus began Meyerhold's rehearsals on *Lake Lyul* at the Theatre of the Revolution. "The atmosphere," recalls Faiko, "at once became electric." [16]

Lake Lyul was decidedly different from *A Lucrative Post* in only two aspects: it was a new play in a contemporary setting which satirized modern Western degeneracy, and it employed a bare stage with a constructivist setting. In the lighting, costumes, props, and acting, the same subtlety of exaggeration (subtle in comparison to his previous productions) prevailed as in *A Lucrative Post.* Faiko describes the visual aspect of the production in this way:

> The back wall of the theatre was bared. Girders stuck out and wires and cables dangled uncompromisingly. The center of the stage was occupied by a three-storied construction with receding corridors, cages, ladders, platforms, and lifts which moved horizontally and vertically. There were illuminated titles and advertisements, and silvered screens lit from behind. Affording something of a contrast to this background were the brilliant colors of the not altogether lifelike costumes: the elegant toilettes of the ladies, the gleaming white of starched shirt-fronts, aiguillettes, epaulettes, liveries trimmed with gold.[17]

This was Meyerhold's most extensive use to date of large platforms at varying heights. There were seven large playing areas, not counting the stage floor, with the uppermost at a height of about twenty feet from the floor. These platforms, which were completely unmasked, were connected one to the other by ladders at frighteningly steep angles (and without handrails). Any actor who lacked the physical agility of an athlete would certainly have broken his neck in due time.

But the physical training of biomechanics made the use of such a dynamically constructed stage feasible. It was for this purpose rather than acrobatics for their own sake, as in *Magnificent Cuckold* and *The Death of Tarelkin,* that Meyerhold now utilized the extensive physical training of his actors. The capacity of his actors to work with confidence on such a stage resulted in the physical gusto and dynamism peculiar to the Meyerhold productions of this period.

Ostrovsky Meets Meyerhold, II: *The Forest*

If the academicians had been upset over Meyerhold's unconventional attitudes towards Ostrovsky in *A Lucrative Post,* his production of *The Forest* eight months later at the Meyerhold Theatre must have left them aghast.

On the other hand, by January of 1924 they must have known what to expect from Meyerhold—and he didn't fall short of their fearful expectations. With his semiconstructivist production in the tradition of the theatre of masks, Meyerhold made it clear that he was quite willing to do the plays of Ostrovsky and other Russian classics, but that he had no intention of going "back" to anything.

The eminent historian of Russian literature, D. S. Mirsky, states that *The Forest* is equalled only by *The Storm* as Ostrovsky's masterpiece: "It is the one in which the essential nobility of man is most triumphantly asserted. But it also contains the most unsweetened types of cynical and complacent meanness and selfishness in the whole of Russian literature."[18] It was this latter quality of the play which interested Meyerhold.

According to his English translator and editor Euguene Bristow, Ostrovsky's first draft of the play (in 1870) was conceived as essentially a domestic comedy. But as he continued working on it he changed the plot and "added elements to increase the social *byt* ("mode") and eliminated details to decrease the family *byt.* In short, Ostrovsky changed the play from a domestic to a social comedy."[19]

So one might argue, as Meyerhold's supporters did, that Meyerhold's reworking of the play in the direction of even stronger social satire was only an extension of what Ostrovsky himself had done. The basis of Meyerhold's corruption, as his critics preferred to regard it, was to break the five act comedy into thirty-three episodes and rearrange them in such a way that one scene would be juxtaposed with another in order to most effectively satirize the former. The result was a montagelike progression in which two or even three episodes might be going on at the same time.

Meyerhold's raw material was a play about two strolling players —Schastlivtsev ("Fortunate") the comedian, and Neschastlivtsev ("Unfortunate") the tragedian—barnstorming the backwoods of provincial Russia. They come upon an estate in which they find the landed gentry embroiled in the agonies of thwarted romances and devious lovers' plots. Recognizing these romantic role-players for what they are, the two actors involve themselves in the machinations, unravel the gordian knot of amorous entanglements, and then go merrily on their way in the confidence that there is a greater sense of reality in their life of illusion than in the illusion of life experienced by such landed nobility.

Considering Meyerhold's idea of theatre and the grotesque, it is not difficult to see even from this brief summary why he would be attracted to *The Forest*. Not only did it offer a satire on the old gentry and their sentimentality, but it also suggested a fundamental aspect of his idea of life and the theatre: role-playing is the true reality and to ignore this or be in ignorance of it is to be immersed in unreality. We are only what we pretend to be and can experience reality only in terms of the role we play. This is the ultimate grotesquerie: life is a masquerade. Meyerhold said as much in his productions time and time again, often quite explicitly in the productions of *The Puppet Booth, The Scarf of Columbine, The Life of Man, Masquerade, The Death of Tarelkin, The Forest,* and later, *The Inspector General* and *Woe to Wit.* * Of course most thoughtful people realize this; the difference is whether one takes this role-playing seriously or not. Stanislavsky did, Meyerhold didn't, and therein lies the philosophical and aesthetic difference between the two.

Whether role-playing is taken seriously or not depends on whether one considers role-playing a by-product of an unnatural,

*One is naturally led to wonder if Meyerhold was aware of Pirandello's work—by 1923 Pirandello's *Six Characters in Search of an Author, Henry IV,* and *Right You Are!* had been published and translated. But there is no evidence that Meyerhold was ever interested in Pirandello or even knew of him.

contrived society or as an unalterable aspect of the human condition. For the Russian Marxist of the 1920s it was the former. And insofar as Meyerhold was a sincere Communist he regarded the bourgeoisie as the role-players and the New Man of the Soviet state as the irresistable truth of the future. The problem was that his productions—especially when considered in light of his pre-Revolution work—seemed to reveal, perhaps unwittingly, a conviction that the masquerade was inherent in the human condition and by implication that the Communist was no less a role-player and no closer to "truth" than his bourgeois counterpart. In Mayakovsky's *The Bedbug* and *The Bathhouse* in 1929 and 1930 he finally makes such a statement about Soviet bureacrats in a very explicit manner.

As for what attitude Meyerhold took toward this human proclivity for role-playing, a significant clue is offered in his direction to the actors playing Schastlivtsev and Neschastlivtsev in *The Forest.* He told Igor Ilinsky (Schastlivtsev) and Mikhail Mukhin (Neschastlivtsev) to think of themselves as history's two greatest role-players: Sancho Panza and Don Quixote.[20] But this did not mean that in Meyerhold's production they were to become the focus of ridicule. Quite the contrary. As in Ostrovsky's script, it was through and by these two conscious performers (Schastlivtsev and Neschastlivtsev) that the unconscious "performers" (the love-struck gentry on the estate) were revealed and satirized.

Consequently, for Meyerhold it was not a matter of being or not being a role-player, but how well and to what end one played a role. Only with this attitude can Don Quixote be regarded as a splendid figure; otherwise, he is but a deluded and funny old man. And from Meyerhold's conception of Neschastlivtsev as a Don Quixote figure it is clear that he did not see the Knight of the Woeful Countenance as a deluded old man.

Unfortunately, this discussion of the philosophical implications of Meyerhold's theatre aesthetic must remain essentially speculative. He was not inclined, at least publicly, to pursue the philosophical ramifications of his aesthetic. But insofar as the theatre of Meyerhold was such a pronounced reflection of the man himself, consideration of his philosophical attitude—albeit by conjecture—seems warranted.

Meyerhold's production of *The Forest* continued in the line of modified biomechanics and scenic constructivism which first appeared eight months earlier in *A Lucrative Post.* Historians and commentators on Meyerhold's work don't always agree on the nature or degree of this modification and few offer any explanation for it. According to Nikolai Gorchakov, "In *The Forest* he rejected the constructivist asceticism of his earlier productions."[21] But Marc Slonim states that "The setting was basically constructivist"[22] while Norris Houghton and Boris Alpers are not hesitant to lump *The Forest* together with *The Magnificent Cuckold* and *The Death of Tarelkin* when describing the nature of Meyerhold's scenic constructivism.[23]

But this disagreement is more apparent, or semantic, than real. In the context of a general study of the modern Russian theatre in which Meyerhold's work is being compared to that of other directors—as in Houghton's *Moscow Rehearsals*—the setting for *The Forest* is but another example of scenic constructivism (or in Slonim's phrase, "basically constructivist"[24]). On the other hand, when considered in the limited context of Meyerhold's own work the setting for *The Forest* is clearly a departure from his earlier scenic constructivism. As Edward Braun states in his excellent commentary, "The permanent setting [for *The Forest*] with its dynamic function was a refinement of Meyerhold's earlier, more overtly constructivist manner."[25]

As it had been for *A Lucrative Post,* the stage for *The Forest* was quite bare except for one long, descending stairway. Unlike those for *The Magnificent Cuckold, The Death of Tarelkin,* and *Lake Lyul,* the setting for *The Forest* did not consist of a multileveled "machine for acting" or a series of such constructions. Instead, the flat stage floor and the broad, curving stairway—which occupied most of stage-right by starting at its highest point up-center (about fifteen feet from the floor) and making a gentle descending curve across the stage-right area before terminating in the center of the orchestra pit—this floor and stairway comprised the playing area for *The Forest.*

When compared with the elaborate constructions of Popova, Stepanova, and Shestakov for *The Magnificent Cuckold, The Death of Tarelkin, The Earth Rebellious,* and *Lake Lyul,* this stage plan—which was Meyerhold's own design—implies a distinctly different approach to the stage setting and the production staging in general. With neutral curtains enclosing a bare, flat playing area, Meyerhold's stage for *The Forest* once again suggests the stage of the commedia dell'arte rather than futuristic mechanization.

Bits and pieces of realistic props and furniture appeared from time to time on the stage—again, as they did in *A Lucrative Post*—but were not always used in the usual way: a table might be used as a bridge, a chair as a knoll, and so on in the manner of Chinese opera stage conventions. Furthermore, these occasional props and pieces were used to transform temporarily a certain area of the neutral stage into a specific locale:

> This transformation of the neutral constructional equipment and its separate parts takes place continuously during the whole show. The actor changes, by his enactment, the very meaning and significance of these constructions and apparatuses. . . . The park bench placed behind a trellis in the rendezvous episode, or a table and a chair and bell placed behind the same trellis in the episode "The Piqued Dame" give a different meaning to the semi-circular mattled wall; in the first case it becomes a bower in the orchard, in the second, the boudoir of Gourmishsky.[26]

On this neutral stage the actor created the explicitness of each moment; he did this not as a biomechanical gymnast but through stylized characterization. When the biomechanical acrobat used the stage apparatus it remained apparatus, but as individual characters (or caricatures) in Ostrovsky's drama the actors transformed, Midas-like, the otherwise neutral set pieces and stage.

This manner of staging freed the actor from having to conform to explicitly predetermined environments. Instead of the philosophical implications of Zolaesque naturalism in which the environment shapes the character, the actor-character created the scenic environment through his presence on and use of the stage. Furthermore, this manner of staging allowed Meyerhold to circumvent the physical limitations of a stage and arrange the episodes in whatever spatial or temporal sequence he desired. This was very important for him at this time for it allowed him to take yet another step in the direction of theatrical montage—the concept which his student Eisenstein introduced to film art.

The montage idea, firmly rooted in his concept of the grotesque, espoused the cause of freeing the theatre from strict adherence to the linear and sequential cause-effect progression so typical of nineteenth-century realistic drama. In a sense, what he was attempting to do in the theatre in his adaptation and production of *The Forest* was very similar to what Joyce did in terms of the novel with *Ulysses*. And this concept of montage rather than linear cause-effect composition related to his idea of the grotesque in that he sought to communicate the idea of the play through the effect of scenic and episodic *contrasts* rather than through a consistent cause-effect progression of events. Consequently, it could be said that he sought to communicate a conclusion through an inductive rather than a deductive process.

In the theatre—at least the theatre of the 1920s—this kind of presentation inherently denied literature's hold on the stage. It was the linear nature of nineteenth-century literature, including drama, that had imposed a similar linear scheme on the stage. The opponents of this kind of literary and theatrical structure had only to point to Shakespeare and the Elizabethan stage to prove that it need not be this way.

But Meyerhold, with his Bolshevik revolutionary disregard for things past, didn't revert to Shakespearean plays but took instead Ostrovsky's essentially linear drama and brazenly adapted it to fit a nonlinear concept of stage production. By reordering the sequence of some scenes, by playing some episodes simultaneously in different areas of the stage, and by changing the locale of some episodes, Meyerhold sought to sharpen the satire of *The Forest*. The result was a contrapuntal effect of contrasting manners, morals, motives, actions, and reactions.

By most accounts the acting in *The Forest* was the best ever achieved in a Meyerhold production. Many of his most talented young students, some of whom had been with him since 1920, were soon to go out on their own. But as of the production of *The Forest* the company was still intact and some of the members were becoming very accomplished performers: Igor Ilinsky, Mikhail Mukhin, Boris Zakhava, Varvara Remizova, and Maria Babanova were already well on their way to individual prominence.

The bare stage and nondescript set pieces called for virtuoso acting. It was only through the performances of the actors that the drama, the setting, and the theatre as a whole could be brought to life. It is perhaps worth recalling that nearly twenty years earlier, in "On the History and Technique of the Theatre" (1906), Meyerhold stated, without qualification that "Theatre is acting."[27] * It is one of the major contentions of this present study that with the exception of occasional excursions into the realm of scenic symbolism in his pre-Revolution period and agitprop productions in his post-Revolution period, Meyerhold's productions consistently evinced his conviction that "theatre is acting," and that the theatre becomes art only when acting is an art and not just a replica of actuality. In other words, the virtuosity of the theatre must begin and end with the virtuosity of the actor. And insofar as this is true, *The Forest* may very well have been Meyerhold's most successful achievement. Although he first worked out an effective compromise with biomechanics in *A Lucrative Post,* it was in *The Forest* that this compromised form of biomechanics reached its full bloom.

By Rostotsky's account (see p. 106), Meyerhold's production of *A Lucrative Post* suggested a shift in his concern from innovating via external forms to vivifying the contents of the drama and the psychological states of the characters. Of course, in order to accomplish such vivification Meyerhold continued to direct his actors in such a way that the results were innovative, or at least surprising, in their external form. After having transformed the two traveling actors in *The Forest* into Don Quixote and Sancho Panza, Meyerhold, according to Marc Slonim, "presented the rest of the cast as grotesques: they wore multicolor wigs, and behaved like clowns."[28] Gorchakov recalls that Meyerhold accompanied the virtuoso acting with real props and "effects": "A single phrase in Ostrovsky's text recalls that Neschastlivtsev had once performed some tricks, so a good number of them were shown on the stage. Aksiusha recalls, 'Day and night, since I was six, I have helped my mother work,' and so Meyerhold had her constantly working on stage. When the merchant declares, 'I shall give up everything,' a

---

*In the article's subsequent inclusion in *O teatre*—in which it was the leading article—this statement was italicized.

flood of furs, shoes, and hats drops down on the stage from above."[29]

This should suggest that in leaving purely acrobatic biomechanics behind Meyerhold certainly did not convert to representational acting. Rather, his temporary infatuation with the machine aesthetic of Futurism seems to have revealed to him a means of adapting the concepts and methods of commedia to the modern stage. This adaptation and transformation was primarily concerned with the relationship between the actor and the character he portrayed, and secondarily the relationship between this actor-character and his theatrical materials—costume, makeup, props, and setting. The result was an approach to production which was more tendentious and script-oriented than commedia and at the same time more humanized and realistic than biomechanics. It was, in fact, the closest Meyerhold ever came to the full realization of his long-held dream of a contemporary form of cabotinage.

Aesthetic Implications of *The Forest*

The Forest was a very popular and successful production—it continued to run in the repertoire for several years and in 1934 the Meyerhold Theatre celebrated the fifteen-hundredth performance of this "revitalized" classic.* By Boris Zakhava's account [30] the success came none too soon. Although *The Magnificent Cuckold, The Death of Tarelkin,* and *The Earth Rebellious* had created a great deal of excitement and enhanced Meyerhold's reputation, they were not the kind of productions designed for long runs in repertoire and consequently did little to relieve the financial strain of Meyerhold's company and theatre. *The Forest,* on the other hand, was just the kind of production that could—and in fact did—provide the theatre with some regular income.

*By Meyerhold's own account (*Pages from Tarusa,* p. 316), the original production had to be modified when it went into regular repertoire. The original staging ran over four hours and "when the performance was over, it was very late and the audience was missing its streetcars." So Meyerhold reduced the original thirty-three episodes to twenty-six and the running time was reduced to three and a half hours. But this was still too much and eventually only sixteen episodes were left and the running time was down to two and a half hours.

This suggests a meaningful comparison between *The Forest* and its predecessors at the theatre on Sadovaya Street. Both *The Magnificent Cuckold* and *The Death of Tarelkin* were very much in the nature of classroom exercises. Keeping in mind that the theatre at Twenty Sadovaya Street was then regarded as a kind of showcase for the work being done at the State Workshop, we can see more clearly the relationship between the extreme nature of biomechanics and scenic constructivism in *The Magnificent Cuckold* and *The Death of Tarelkin* and their seemingly modified forms in *The Forest*.

The two earlier productions should be regarded as examples of working techniques displayed pretty much as an end in themselves. *The Forest,* on the other hand, was the implementation of such techniques as a means toward the goal of the effective theatrical realization of a drama for the entertainment and enlightenment of the general public.

Once this is understood a common misconception about Meyerhold's work can be eliminated: he never intended the "pure" biomechanics and scenic constructivism of *The Magnificent Cuckold* and *The Death of Tarelkin* as an aesthetic end in themselves—anymore than Stanislavsky intended emotional recall to be employed in the course of a finished production. They were, instead, means to a particular end. Meyerhold himself referred to them as "stylistic extremes."[31] And just as Stanislavsky's method of emotional recall produced performances of high emotional involvement, so Meyerhold's biomechanics and scenic constructivism produced in both actors and audience a sense of emotional detachment from the characters and their environment. Thus, insofar as Meyerhold directed attention to the physical and external *how* of something rather than the psychological and internal *why*, it follows that he excelled in the comical and satirical while the Moscow Art Theatre was best known for sentimental drama and tragedy.

Meyerhold's production of *The Forest* became a model for numerous imitators in the years following. With an eye to becoming something like a second Meyerhold, many an aspiring young director made a practice of manhandling classic dramas and rewriting them into virtual parodies of themselves. This was one of the aspects of "Meyerholdism" from which Meyerhold tried in vain to disassociate himself. But his critics insisted on labeling him as the leader of a "plot" to destroy the classics of Russian drama. One writer suggested that the next offering at the Meyerhold Theatre might read,

> *The Marriage* by N. V. Gogol
> Text by Schershelyafamova
> Verses and prose by Antiokhiskovo
> Author of the show, Nikolai Sestrin [32]

Meyerhold's difficulty in denying such charges arose from the fact that he was not entirely guiltless. When he wrote in 1912, "words in the theatre are only a design on the canvas of motion,"[33] he made it clear that in his idea of theatre there was nothing sacrosanct about the work of the playwright. The only "sacred" thing in the theatre was the physical dynamism of the actor. And the script should never be allowed to compromise it. In fact, the best way to most effectively communicate the essence of a script was to make sure that its verbiage did not interfere with the actor's virtuosity. If this necessitated some surgery on the script, then it was ultimately in the best interest of the drama itself: "Any re-creation of a work justifies its existence if it springs from an inner necessity."[34]

This attitude sometimes resulted in a final product that was radically different from the original material. According to Yuri Jelagin, "A tragedy he would turn into a farce, a drama into an eccentric comedy, a play of revolutionary content into a brilliant review with jazz and dancing girls."[35] But *The Forest* was no such radical transformation. Meyerhold took a satirical comedy, reorganized its sequence of events and added a great deal of "business," but he didn't tamper with the dialogue and the final result was still a satirical comedy. His next production, however, was the one Jelagin had in mind when he spoke of a play of revolutionary content "with jazz and dancing girls": *D.E. (Dayesh Europu*—Give Us Europe!).

Single Story Agitprop: *D.E.*

D.E.—an "agit-sketch in three parts"[36] —represents another

Meyerhold production designed specifically for political purposes. Like *The Dawns* and *The Earth Rebellious* it was in the nature of an offering by Soviet artists to the cause of Communism and the Soviet state. It was first presented on 15 June 1924 in Leningrad for the delegates to the Fifth Congress of Comintern (International Communism). Three weeks later, on July 3, it opened at the Meyerhold Theatre in Moscow.

Like *The Dawns* and *The Earth Rebellious, D.E.* was a severe adaptation of an original work. In fact, Nikolai Gorchakov speaks of the text as having been "compiled"[37] by Mikhail Podgayetsky from novels by Ehrenburg, Hamp, Kellerman, and Upton Sinclair. The main source, though, was Ilya Ehrenburg's novel, *The Give-Us-Europe Trust.*

The Trust, in Ehrenburg's novel, was a Soviet radio trust which rose up to challenge American capitalist millionaires for control of postwar Europe. In 1924 the radio was looked upon as a tool of great, perhaps even awesome, potential for influencing the world. Thus, it heightened the significance of the novel's depiction of a struggle between the forces of capitalist exploitation (America) and the organized proletariat (Soviet Russia).

But in Meyerhold's free adaptation of Ehrenburg's party line novel the general agitprop theme became so embossed with theatrical devices that party critics wondered aloud whether Meyerhold really cared about the "message." Especially grating was the fact that the scenes depicting capitalist decadency—sexy dancing girls in black mesh hose and tights moving to a pulsating jazz accompaniment—were more exciting and "real" than the scenes depicting the good, clean, upright proletarian man. Of course no one suggested publicly that this was intentional on Meyerhold's part, and quite certainly it wasn't; nevertheless, he once again found his efforts in behalf of Communist agitprop more criticized than praised by party authorities.

Aside from its agitprop nature the production form of *D.E.* was in one important aspect very similar to the form of Meyerhold's two preceding productions, *Lake Lyul* and *The Forest*: its distinctly episodic quality. It was, if anything, even more fragmented than the previous two productions. The seventeen episodes in which forty-five performers played more than ninety-five roles—none of the characters appeared in more than two or three episodes—comprised more of a political review than a drama. The fact that Meyerhold called it an "agit-sketch" would seem to suggest that this was not to be looked upon as a production of a drama. Nevertheless, the episodic, montage quality of *Lake Lyul* and *The Forest* makes it clear that the fragmented nature of *D.E.* was not just an idea peculiar to it, but was a production concept which interested Meyerhold at this time regardless of the material at hand.

Just as he had striven for the ultimate in actor mobility through biomechanics and the ultimate in mobility of stage action through scenic constructivism, so now he sought to "mobilize" the entire production through the device of episodic progression, slide projections,* highly selective spotlighting, an infinitely flexible setting—ten nine-by-twelve wooden screens on casters which were moved about the bare stage floor by hidden stagehands in order to shape the playing area of each individual episode—and equally flexible actors such as Ernst Garin who appeared as seven different characters in one fifteen minute scene.

If nothing else, the Meyerhold stage was an active one— constantly. Gorchakov says that the production was of interest not for its "coarse and deliberate" propaganda, but because of new devices that Meyerhold introduced to the Soviet theatre. "He gave stage action a quality of almost motion-picturelike impetuosity by his rapid change of scenes, and he created tremendous and dynamic tension." As for the acting, "Pantomime came to the fore in this production even more than in Meyerhold's earlier efforts. There were a number of episodes that lasted altogether about ten or fifteen minutes and contained an insignificant amount of speech but much pantomime."[38]

According to Boris Zakhava, who played an English lord and a French parliamentarian in the production, the personages in the sketch (he too says that it was not really a play but more on the order of a review) were clearly and simply divided into two groups—the good guys and the bad guys: "Those belonging to the bourgeois world were treated in the manner of sharp social grotesque—the theatre of masks; the Soviet personages—people of

*He first used projections in *The Earth Rebellious*.

the socialist world—were played simply and naturally, strictly according to real life."[39] The surprising thing is that neither Zakhava (even in retrospect) nor Meyerhold realized the potential for trouble and misunderstanding that such an approach was bound to entail.

It would take considerable naiveté—as well as ignorance of the medieval public's great fascination with and fondness for the devil and his henchmen in their drama—for a theatre-of-masks proponent like Meyerhold to believe that in such a division of characters the dull and naturalistic Soviet heroes would be of anything more than secondary interest. For years Meyerhold had been proclaiming that the real excitement of theatre art was in the concept of the grotesque—i.e., the theatre of masks. When the American and European bourgeoisie are played in this manner and the Soviet characters are played naturalistically, why, if his dictum was true, should not the former be the most interesting part of the production?

Perhaps to his own chagrin—and certainly to that of party authorities—the truth of his theatre concept (at least in the context of a Meyerhold production) was proven all too clearly. The grotesqueries of the bourgeois caricatures stole the show from the exemplary Soviets. This, as much as anything, gives substance to the idea that Meyerhold was more concerned with effective theatre than effective propaganda. Only a director whose abiding concern for theatrical effectiveness had created a propaganda blindspot could have failed to anticipate the reaction of the audience and party critics. Despite the antipathy of some of the stricter party critics, *D.E.* was an undeniable success with the general public. The Meyerhold Theatre was gaining fame and popularity, and something resembling a "Meyerhold system" was beginning to emerge—or so people thought.

But just as critics and theatregoers began to form some idea of what to expect from a new Meyerhold production, he seemed to pull the rug from under them. Boris Alpers recalls the situation:

Nothing presaged any serious change in the Meyerhold Theatre. Only a year earlier *The Forest* was produced—the most joyous work of the revolutionary theatre. It was only half a year after the premiere of *D.E.*, which completed the series of agitational productions of Meyerhold, in which many devices of the revolutionary theatre were brought to their full perfection. Never did the precipitancy of the tempo, the dynamic saturatedness reach such limits in the theatre of Meyerhold as it did in the case of *D.E.* True, even then some of the episodes—the Versailles episode for instance, struck one by its slackened tempo. Likewise, the pantomime performances in a few places were distinguished by an excessive detailization . . . but all that seemed at the time but mere chance occurrence, unfinished touches of a grand whole. In reality, these details presaged . . . a new turn in the creative work of Meyerhold and his theatre.[40]

The production which came as such a surprise, for Boris Alpers at least, was Meyerhold's production of Faiko's *The Teacher Bubus*—premiere, 29 January 1925.

Meyerhold, age 26, at the beginning of his third season with the Moscow
Art Theatre. 1900.

The Dawns. Inaugural production of the First Theatre of the R.S.F.S.R. 1920.

Meyerhold at the time of his campaign for a "Theatrical October." 1920.

The Magnificent Cuckold. A scene from Act III. 1922.

A Lucrative Post. The production in which Meyerhold found a balance between the extremes of scenic constructivism and biomechanics employed in *The Magnificent Cuckold* and *The Death of Tarelkin.* 1923.

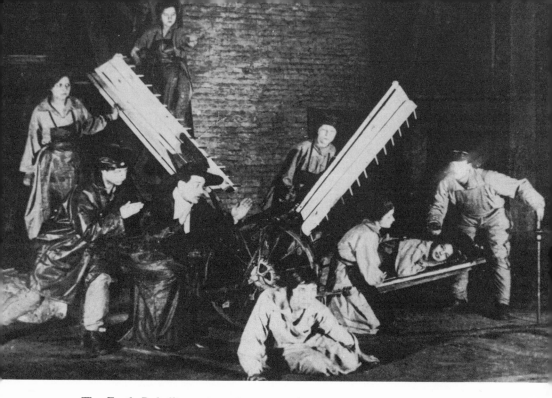

The Earth Rebellious. An agitprop production in honor of the fifth anniversary of the founding of the Red Army. 1923.

The Forest. Z. Raikh as Aksyusha and K. Samborsky as Pyotr. 1924.

The Forest. M. Mukhin as Neschatlivtsev and E. Tyankina as Turmvizh-skaya. 1924.

The Forest. Final episode from one of Meyerhold's most popular productions. 1924.

The Inspector General. An episode entitled "A Festive Occasion!" 1926.

The Inspector General. Seated at left, E. Garin as Khlestakov; leaning over the couch, Z. Raikh as Anna Andreyevna. 1926.

Meyerhold and his production associates for *The Bedbug:* seated, D. Shostakovich and Meyerhold; standing, V. Mayakovsky (behind Meyerhold) and A.
Rodchenko. 1929.

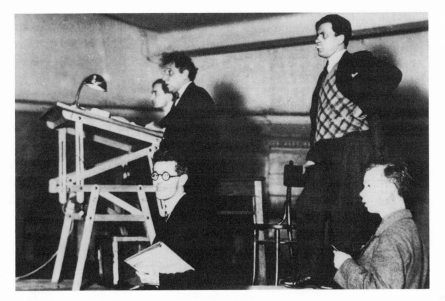

At a rehearsal of *The Bathhouse:* Meyerhold (at desk), Mayakovsky (in plaid vest), and composer V. Shebalin (with glasses). 1930.

The Bathhouse. Impromptu ballet parody from Act III. 1930.

The Bathhouse. Final scene: Pobedonosikov the bureaucrat is left behind as the proletarian heroes (in time-travelers' suits) depart for the future Golden Age of Communism. 1930.

6

A Pause for Aim

Acting and Pre-Acting

In 1935 Meyerhold told Alexander Gladkov,

> I have often been reproached to the effect that I do not develop my
> own finds and discoveries, I always hurry on to new labors: after one
> play, I do another, completely different as to style. But in the first
> place, human life is short, and in repeating yourself there are many
> things you won't have time to do; in the second place, where a
> superficial glance sees a chaos of different manners and styles, my
> colleagues and I see the application of the same general principles to a
> different material, a variant treatment of it in relation to the style of
> the author and the problems of the present day.[1]

Meyerhold's seemingly consistent inconsistency was at no time
more startlingly in evidence than when his productions of *The
Forest* and *D.E.* were followed by *The Teacher Bubus.* It is as
close as we come to a real anomaly in Meyerhold's major work,
and it is one of the rare instances of a radical Meyerhold
experiment seeming to spring from nothing but a sudden impulse.

The production is not totally without explanation in terms of his previous work and concepts, but it is such a surprising departure that one cannot help but ponder the possibility of motives beyond those of theatrical experimentation. But as tempting as it is to see in this production a grandiose slap in the face to his critics by an abrupt reversal, there is no evidence that such was his intention.

Whatever his intentions, his production of *The Teacher Bubus* was absurdly pedantic, and the internal, psychological method of acting was extended to the point of the ridiculous. He called it "pre-acting:"*

> The actor's work consists in the artful juxtaposing of acting and pre-acting. . . .
>   Pre-acting prepares the spectator's perception in such a way that he comprehends the scenic situation fully resolved in advance and so has no need to make any effort to grasp the underlying message of the scene. This was a favorite device in the old Japanese and Chinese theatres. Nowadays, when the theatre is once more being employed as a platform for agitation, an acting system in which special stress is laid on pre-acting is indispensable to the actor-tribune.[2]

If Meyerhold was serious about this justification of propagandistic pre-acting on the basis of Oriental theatre conventions, it must stand as his sloppiest bit of theatrical reasoning. Had this article ("Acting and Teaching") appeared ten years later—it appeared in a brochure entitled *"The Teacher Bubus"* the same year as the production (1925)—it would be tempting to doubt the validity of Meyerhold's authorship. But in 1925 there was still considerable freedom of expression and Meyerhold himself was influential enough to prevent anyone from misrepresenting him. Either he was laughing up his sleeve or he was guilty of propagating some half-baked ideas.

As an example of the contradiction between the actor-tribune idea which he promoted at the time of *The Teacher Bubus* and the concept of theatre which he espoused both before and after *The Teacher Bubus,* consider the following statements: (a) from "Acting and Teaching," "The actor-tribune created his art not for

---

*In Russian, *predigroi: pred* (before) and *ingrat* (to act).

art's sake; it is not even by means of "art" that he desires to work;"[3] (b) from Jelagin's notes of Meyerhold's final speech in June, 1939, "The pitiful and wretched thing that pretends to the title of the theatre of socialist realism has nothing in common with art. But the theatre is art! And without art, there is no theatre! "[4] Or, if one holds Jelagin's stenographic notes suspect, consider the following from one of Meyerhold's best known essays,* "Reconstruction of the Theatre," written in 1930:

> Since a dramatic performance depends on laws peculiar to the theatre, it is not enough for it to appeal purely to the spectators' intellect. A play must do more than prompt some idea or depict events in such a way as to invite automatic conclusions.
>
> Actors do not perform simply to demonstrate the idea of the author, the director, or themselves; their struggles, the whole dramatic conflict has a far higher aim than the mere exposition of thesis and antithesis. It is not for that that the public goes to the theatre.[5]

And of course numerous examples could be culled from his writings in the pre-Revolution period that clearly contradict his statements about pre-acting and the actor-tribune in the brochure *"The Teacher Bubus."*

Both the production of *The Teacher Bubus* and Meyerhold's expressed concepts regarding it verge on being anomalous to everything else he did and wrote both before and after 1925. If the notion that it was just a big hoax is discarded—and discarded it must be for want of any supporting evidence—then we must regard *Bubus* as the experimental manifestation of a new Meyerhold approach to propaganda theatre. And in spite of the unsuccessful oddities of the production, it would appear that it was not without some positive influence on later, much more successful shows.

The Teacher Bubus

Alexy Faiko's *The Teacher Bubus* was the first original play from the modern Soviet repertoire to be presented at the Meyerhold Theatre, and only the second such presentation by

*Based on three public lectures he delivered in 1929.

Meyerhold since *Mystery-Bouffe* in 1921—the other was also a play by Faiko, *Lake Lyul,* presented at the Theatre of the Revolution in 1923.* *The Teacher Bubus* is generally regarded as one of Meyerhold's weaker selections. Marc Slonim refers to it as "an inferior play,"[6] and Edward Braun says that Faiko's play "was so insubstantial that it presented no intellectual challenge whatsoever to Meyerhold."[7]

Essentially, the play depicted the dilemma of the old, effete, nineteenth-century European intellectuals who were caught in the vortex of a radically changing twentieth-century world. The embodiment of such people and their dilemma was the old teacher, Bubus. The old intellectual, clinging to the refined manners and life-style of a rapidly disappearing era, hesitates to accept the Revolution unconditionally because of its cruelty and intransigence. But in his efforts to compromise with both the bourgeoisie and the proletariat, he ends up being the dupe and tool of the former.

The play was therefore but a variation on the theme which absorbed the interest of nearly all educated Russians in the 1920s: the proletariat versus the capitalists. The twist to this particular play was its focus on the pitiful plight of noncombatant "former people" caught in the middle. The purpose was not, however, to arouse pity for a man like Bubus—except of the most condescending nature—but to emphasize the futility of compromise and the necessity of total commitment to the cause of communism. But if this propaganda message was the point and purpose of the play it was soon lost, as usual, amid the controversial theatrical innovations of Meyerhold.

There were three major aspects of the production which caused surprise and consternation: the enclosed stage, the continuous use of music to the extent of turning the production into a dramatized symphony, and the laborious technique of pre-acting.

---

*An interesting pattern of productions appears if we look over the sequence of Meyerhold productions from 1923 through *Bubus* in 1925: agitprop (*The Earth Rebellious*), Ostrovsky (*A Lucrative Post*), Faiko (*Lake Lyul*), Ostrovsky (*The Forest*), agitprop (*D.E.*), and Faiko (*The Teacher Bubus*). Over the two-year span from 1923 to 1925 Meyerhold staged six productions, alternating between agitprop, Ostrovsky, and Faiko. However, there is no reason to believe that this little pattern was anything more than coincidence.

Starting with the constructivist productions of *The Magnificent Cuckold* and *The Death of Tarelkin* in 1922, Meyerhold increasingly emphasized vertical movement in his staging, culminating in the myriad of graduated platforms used for *Lake Lyul* in 1924. But in *The Forest,* which immediately followed *Lake Lyul,* his stage contained only one vertical element: the long, winding stairway. Although this stairway was used extensively and allowed for considerable vertical movement in the staging, there was also a great deal of action which took place on the level of the stage floor. In the following production, *D.E.,* Meyerhold worked almost entirely in the horizontal plane via his various arrangements of wooden screens.

Finally, in *The Teacher Bubus,* he covered the stage floor with a huge, round, luxurious carpet and backed this with a continuous semicircle from one side of the stage to the other of dangling bamboo strips. Thus an enclosed horizontal circle constituted the playing area for *The Teacher Bubus*—a far cry from the construction of ramps, stairs, and levels amid a denuded stage that typified his earlier work. As a result, the "Meyerholdism" of virtually continuous stage movement—either by means of vertical constructions or the movable wooden screens—was noticeably absent from the production of *The Teacher Bubus.* Instead, the production became at times more physically static than even the Moscow Art Theatre productions of Chekhov.

The one exception to the horizontal plan of the production was a large platform which overlooked the stage from a height of about twenty feet at a position all the way upstage center. But there was no acting on this platform; instead, it contained a concert Bechstein piano and a prominent Moscow pianist who played Chopin and Liszt almost continuously throughout the production. In all, he played forty-six excerpts from the two romantic composers, both as background to the spoken dialogue and as accompaniment for the extensive pauses and miming that constituted such a large part of the acting.

As described in the brochure which has handed out at the premiere of *The Teacher Bubus,* the work of the actor in this production consisted in "the artful juxtaposition of acting and pre-acting."[8] In an attempt to prepare the audience for what was to come and to justify the concept, the brochure quoted at length a description of the famous actor Lensky's performance in *Much Ado About Nothing* as recounted in a 1908 article from the *Russkie vedomosty* [Russian register]:

> Benedict emerges from his hiding-place behind a bush, where he has just overheard the conversation about his love for Beatrice which had been contrived especially for his ears. For a long time he stands staring at the audience, his face frozen in amazement. Then suddenly his lips move very slightly. Now watch his eyes closely: they are still fixed in concentration, but from beneath the brows imperceptibly, gradually, there begins to creep a triumphant happy smile; the actor doesn't say a word, but you can see that a great irrepressible wave of joy is welling up inside Benedict; his face muscles, his cheeks begin to laugh and a smile spreads uncontrollably over his quivering face; suddenly a thought penetrates his uncomprehending joy and in a final mimetic chord the eyes which until now have been frozen with astonishment light up with delight. Now Benedict's whole body is one transport of wild rapture and the auditorium thunders with applause, although *the actor has yet to say a single word and only now begins his speech.* 9

This, ostensibly, was the historical precedent in the Russian theatre for the experiment in pre-acting which Meyerhold conducted in his production of *The Teacher Bubus.*

Meyerhold, a committed maximalist, was disinclined to consider the possibility of too much of a good thing until he had given it a good practical application—e.g., biomechanics, scenic constructivism, Theatrical October, denuded stage, bas-relief staging, and Symbolism. In his hands this device of Lensky's, employed at a particularly climactic moment in the play when Benedict is momentarily alone and on the verge of delivering a soliloquy to the audience, became the basis of performance for an entire cast throughout an entire play.

Meyerhold's intention, however, was not just to go Lensky one better. He had never been inclined to follow anyone else's lead. By invoking the precedent of Lensky he was undoubtedly seeking merely to forearm himself against the critics of pre-acting who were bound to charge him with senseless experimentation, dilletantism, aestheticism, and so forth.

Such criticism did follow, but these charges to the contrary notwithstanding, Meyerhold's purpose and motive in the matter of pre-acting appear to have been quite serious and not at all divorced from his previous concepts and methods of acting. Nikolai Gorchakov, then a student at the Moscow Advanced Theatre School, recalls that pre-acting "was constructed on the same principle that he [Meyerhold] used for staging the dances in the play—not on a 'legato' but rather on short rhythmic bits."[10] He goes on to say, "After performing these bits, the dancers would pause motionlessly. The characters in the play would also freeze into the numbness of pre-acting before moving or uttering a word, as if they were trying first to listen for something before moving. The text merely furnished the sense of the pantomime to follow."[11]

Thus pre-acting was, in a sense, a continuation of Meyerhold's abiding interest in the art of the mime. This time, however, instead of concentrating on external physical dynamics—a kind of *gestalt* characterization—he was primarily concerned with revealing the internal thought processes and emotions which precede and underlie speech.

But unlike Stanislavsky, who was interested in the same thing, he did not seek to reveal this *through* speech (the dialogue) but through the physical expressions of gesture, movement, and pose. Consequently, his new concern for the internal* did not result in a contradiction of his belief that "words in the theatre are only a design on the canvas of motion."[12]

He was still very much committed to a physical and visual theatre in his production of *The Teacher Bubus;* but in this production the tempo was slowed so drastically to allow for the effect of internal processes at work that it must have seemed that he was practically renouncing physicalness altogether—as if retreating from his original ideas all the way back to and beyond the quiet subtleties of the Moscow Art Theatre. It was as if one of Charlie Chaplin's early, herky-jerky films was suddenly turned down to the super slow-motion and stop-action of television football coverage. In fact, Meyerhold was at this time a great admirer of Chaplin. Several years later, in 1936, he delivered a

---

*Such an interest was not entirely new: see Rostotsky's comments about Meyerhold's approach to *A Lucrative Post* on pages 104-107.

lecture entitled "Chaplin and Chaplinism," in which he related Chaplin to his productions of the 1920s; it may suggest what he had in mind for the experiment in pre-acting:

> As a young man, Eisenstein studied a number of works on the movement and behavior of man in space in order to consolidate his theoretical knowledge. This helped him to formulate a coherent system based on his work in our biomechanics studio between 1922 and 1924, the period of *The Magnificent Cuckold, Tarelkin's Death,* and *The Forest.* The object of our experiments was the maximum exploitation of the expressive power of movement.
>
> This skill can be acquired from a study of Chaplin. His so-called "momentary pauses for aim," that peculiarly static style of acting, the freeze—it all comes down to the expedient concentration of action.[13]

It was probably just such "momentary pauses for aim" that Meyerhold had in mind with his idea of pre-acting. Although it need not be didactic or propagandistic—certainly the Chaplin films of the 1920s were not designed for such purposes—such a method could be assigned a propagandistic function or interpretation as Meyerhold sought, not very convincingly, to do in the "Acting and Teaching" article.

The concept of pre-acting, contrary as it appears at first glance to Meyerhold's previous instructions to actors, is not really inconsistent with his earlier ideas of acting. Not only is it still in line with a fundamentally visual, physical, and mimetic approach to acting, but it is also closely connected with one of Meyerhold's most basic concerns as a theatricalist: the integration of music and drama. Along with such pioneers as Appia, Craig, and Fuchs, Meyerhold had always insisted that music was as much a part of the theatre as literature, if not more. At a time when Stanislavsky was considered an innovator for having removed the orchestra from the theatre, Meyerhold insisted on retaining it and sought to employ it not only for mood and intermission entertainment but also to involve it directly in the production.

The tempo and brassiness of American popular music and jazz in particular had great appeal for him in the 1920s, as evidenced by his frequent use of it in *Lake Lyul* and *D.E.* (although ostensibly with negative connotations). In the pre-acting of *The*

Teacher Bubus music and musical tempos played a very important part. Not only were there several scenes of actual dancing (highly stylized), but each major character was assigned a particular rhythm and tempo of speech and movement which served—like the symbolic costume colors in several of his earliest productions—to identify a character and his nature through theatricalist devices. Gorchakov called it "a system of 'rhythmic masks,' "[14] and Lunacharsky termed the feature "sociomechanics"[15] as opposed to biomechanics.

In other words, the strangeness of the acting in *The Teacher Bubus* resulted from two experiments by Meyerhold: the pre-acting "pauses for aim," and the "rhythmic masks." As a consequence of this unusual acting style, the flat stage, the interminable piano numbers, and the overall deliberateness of the production, *The Teacher Bubus* was—since the days of his pre-Revolution productions—Meyerhold's first major failure with critics, friends, and the general audience alike.

Consistency Through Eclecticism

In his memoirs Boris Zakhava, who performed in *Bubus,* recalls: "*The Teacher Bubus* was an unsuccessful Meyerhold production. But everyone who worked on the production benefited from it. This was a laboratory experiment in staging."[16] He goes on to say that one critic seemed to correctly characterize the situation in pointing out that by inviting the general, uninitiated public—"in full dress"—to see what was essentially a laboratory experiment, Meyerhold was courting failure.[17]

But of course Meyerhold had been working this way for several years. Even his pre-Revolution productions at the Imperial Theatres from 1910 to 1917 challenged audiences with theatrical innovations. And starting with his productions at the First Theatre of the R.S.F.S.R. in 1920 he became totally dedicated to theatrical experimentation—not just within the confines of the Workshop, but on the public stage as well.

As did many artists and planners of the early 1920s, Meyerhold accepted the Revolution as an invitation to experiment openly in any direction for the sake of building a new and better society.

Since the old was out and there were consequently no established criteria, the very idea of artistic success or failure was, for the time being, irrelevant.

But in actual practice it didn't work out quite this way. There were still influential critics who felt justified in passing judgment on something as being artistically sound or unsound, good political intentions notwithstanding. And Meyerhold himself had no qualms about dismissing the experiments of Tairov as the work of a dilettante.* But whether or not Meyerhold always respected the rights of others to experiment, it is important to remember that in his own work he was primarily concerned with experimentation in new directions of theatre art and was disinclined to polish and refine a successful formula.

On the other hand, Meyerhold was not an impulsive innovator. As the preceding discussion should suggest, even the apparently impulsive approach to *The Teacher Bubus* was actually very much in line with his basic concerns and beliefs regarding theatrical art. And when in subsequent productions like *The Inspector General* and *Woe to Wit*** they were combined with other earlier innovations the result did not appear to be full of contradictions but resulted in a synthesis.

The synthesis of theatrical modes and methods is one of the most characteristic aspects of Meyerhold's mature work. Each subsequent production contained experimental elements and influences from previous productions. Unlike Stanislavsky or Tairov, Meyerhold was not inclined to work out a unique experimental approach which would be confined to a particular production. Instead, each production seemed to synthesize and build upon the experiments and innovations of previous productions. As a result, his later productions were generally richer and more complex than their predecessors. In this respect, although Meyerhold's discussion of the grotesque in 1912 was with regard

*In his 1922 review of Tairov's book, *Notes of a Director,* Meyerhold stated, "Tairov, a dilettante, fails to offer any insight into the theatre's most complex area: into the art of the actor, the system of his playing, and theoretical matters such as the material of the actor's form" ("Observations on A. Y. Tairov's Book, *Notes of a Director,*" *V. E. Meyerhold,* 2:37).

** Meyerhold's reworking of Griboyedov's script in the general direction of its original, uncensored version included changing the title from *Gore ot uma* [Woe from Wit] to Griboyedov's first-draft title, *Gore umu* [Woe to wit].

to individual productions, it also suggests the nature of the relationship between his various productions: "The grotesque . . . is the method of synthesizing rather than analyzing. . . . In reducing the riches of the empirical world to a typical unity, stylization impoverishes life, whereas the grotesque refuses to recognize but one aspect, *only* the vulgar or *only* the elevated. It mixes the opposites and by design accents the contradictions."[18]

Whereas directors such as Tairov and Reinhardt are thought of as eclectic due to the variety in the types of drama which they staged, Meyerhold's eclecticism resulted not from a heterogeneous repertoire—in fact, there was considerable similarity between the plays in his repertoire, especially in the 1920s—but from the accumulated diversity of theatrical elements, methods, and devices in each production. Each show was in itself the manifestation of an eclectic approach to production. And as his "repertoire" of theatrically effective devices grew, it follows that his productions became more and more montagelike.

This matter of the consistent evolution of Meyerhold's thought is brought up at this point because it is with *The Teacher Bubus* that such an idea is most strained. It is not difficult to perceive consistency from, say, *The Magnificent Cuckold* to *The Earth Rebellious,* or from *A Lucrative Post* to *The Forest;* but that there is continuity between such rough and bold productions as these and the solemn deliberateness of *The Teacher Bubus* or between *The Teacher Bubus* and later productions is, at first glance, a difficult proposition to sustain.*

Nevertheless, the production approach to *The Teacher Bubus* was not wholly inconsistent with the ideas fundamental to Meyerhold's previous work. In the productions subsequent to *The Teacher Bubus* the new elements in *Bubus* (aspects of pre-acting, the enclosed stage, the musical fundament, the pauses for aim, and sociomechanics) were not discarded as impulsive ideas that didn't work out, but were added to Meyerhold's increasingly complex synthesis of theatrical devices. Consequently, it seems that, circumscribing Meyerhold's eclecticism and apparent impulsive-

*In *Theatre of the Social Mask* Boris Alpers charges that with *The Teacher Bubus* Meyerhold violated all the theatrical principles he previously held and henceforth life came to a standstill on the Meyerhold stage (Alpers, p. 57 and passim).

ness, was an idea of theatre which gave a unity and consistency to the whole of his directorial career—*The Teacher Bubus* included.

The Warrant

The Teacher Bubus premiered at the end of January 1925; three months later, on April 20, Meyerhold presented Nikolai Erdman's *The Warrant* (or, *The Credentials*). For once at the Meyerhold Theatre what was said attracted more attention than how it was said.

This was an interregnum period in Russia: Lenin died in January 1924 and Stalin succeeded him—but it wasn't quite that simple. There was no established line of succession and power went to the man who could grab it. In 1924 Stalin had sufficient power to replace Lenin but not sole power. Men such as Trotsky, Kamenyev, Bukharin, and Zinovyev still had considerable personal influence and forced Stalin to move cautiously. And so long as there was a balance of power within the Kremlin, there was considerable freedom of expression without. Nevertheless, the idea of satirizing any aspect of the young Communist society was very daring, if not heretical, and Erdman's *The Warrant* was just such a satire.

In Russian literature, dramatic and otherwise, there are two archetypal male characters. One is the Superfluous Man. Characters such as Chatsky in *Woe from Wit,* Oblomov in *Oblomov,* Chulkaturin in *Diary of a Superfluous Man,* Pierre in *War and Peace,* Verkovensky, Sr. in *The Possessed,* and several characters in the plays and stories of Chekhov are representative of this character type. The other archetypal character, the comedy counterpart of the Superfluous Man, is the conniving scoundrel—a kind of Russian con man. Of course he has his European predecessors and counterparts—Figaro being one of the best examples—but in Russian literature Khlestakov, Gogol's fraudulent Inspector General, is probably the best known of this type. In *The Warrant,* Nikolai Erdman presented a latter-day version of *The Inspector General* in which the Communist society and bureaucracy rather than the Tsarist of Gogol's time became the butt of a latter-day Khlestakov named Pavlusha Guliachkin.

Like Khlestakov, the rogue Guliachkin decides to impersonate a government official and in Soviet society the veritable icon of authority is a warrant or special credentials duly affixed, with a gaggle of seals, stamps, and signatures. If Tsarist officials were typified by being surrounded by sycophants and servants, the Soviet official was likewise ensconced by decrees, manifestos, warrants, and credentials. Soviet officialdom in the 1920s—like any participatory democracy, ostensible or actual—was virtually awash in a sea of paperwork. And in focusing the deception in the play on the iconic Soviet warrant, Erdman was effectually satirizing the methods of the Communist bureaucracy even though the people duped by Guliachkin were mostly non-Communist "former people" like Bubus.

With the forged warrant as evidence, Guliachkin spreads the rumor that he has been granted special powers that would allow him to imprison half of Russia. As a result, the fearful "former people" flock to him and are ever so eager to do his bidding. In addition, the profiteering Nepmen bend over backward to curry his favor. As in *The Inspector General,* a man who has gotten rich through something less than honest means eagerly offers his daughter in marriage to this "important official."

In the end, however, everything falls apart when Guliachkin is revealed as the son of a middle-class bourgeoisie and his warrant a fake. And as he is taken away by the secret police the laugh is on him as much as the "former people" and the Nepman, while the goodness and honesty of the state remains intact. Thus, since Guliachkin, unlike Khlestakov, is prevented by the real authorities from getting away with his fraud, the satire of *The Warrant* is presumably limited to rogues like Guliachkin and the people taken in by him rather than extending into the circles of power and authority as Gogol's comedy had done. In the setting of Gogol's play, not only is it possible for a rogue like Khlestakov to get away with his ruse, but it is government officialdom itself (albeit on the provincial level) which is outwitted by him.

But this nice distinction was not enough to obscure the fact that *The Warrant* was a satire on contemporary Soviet life which rubbed very close to the bone of the Soviet bureaucracy and officialdom. Yuri Jelagin recounts that in the spring of 1925 there was more than passing interest among the party elite in the April premiere of Erdman's play at the Meyerhold Theatre. Rumors spread that anti-Stalin demonstrations were being planned to take place at the theatre on opening night.

At the April 20 opening there was no riot, but by Jelagin's account it was a wild affair. At one point, he says, many in the audience rose to scream, "Down with Stalin, the swindler. Down with Stalin!"[19] At the end of the show Meyerhold, Erdman, and Znaida Raikh were greeted by enthusiastic applause and more shouts of *Proch Stalina!*"

Whether Jelagin has exaggerated the audience response and official concern or whether the balance of power during this interregnum was such that outbursts of this sort had to be tolerated, the fact is that not only did Meyerhold and Erdman get away with such a production but some high officials actually professed admiration for it. Kamenyev said of the production, "Very good. Very merry. Very serious. Very perceptive."[20] (Kamenyev was not by trade a theatre critic.) Critic Pavel Markov wrote, "The production makes you think. It questions premises and proceeds by deduction."[21] And in general, according to Jelagin, the party critics were amused. Nikolai Gorchakov puts it this way:

> The Bolshevik critics considered that Meyerhold's treatment of *The Warrant* depicted the tragedy of "former people" unsparingly. These were individuals who had "slept through the Revolution" and "lost their last pitiful ideological baggage and their final illusions." The Bolsheviks felt that the play seemed to be limited only because it dwelt on the middle-class, dreaming of restoring the monarchy and living in the ready expectation that their lands and factories would be returned to them.[22]

But Gorchakov, like Jelagin, believed that the satirical aim of Erdman and Meyerhold was broader and of a much more serious nature than the party critics realized or cared to acknowledge. He says that men such as Meyerhold, Erdman, and Mayakovsky were concerned that during the period of the NEP the idea behind the Communist Revolution was being threatened from within by pettiness, greed, and an increasingly parasitic bureaucracy: "Guliachkin, with a Soviet "warrant" in his pocket, personified the petty and roguish philistine against whom Meyerhold was in revolt. The director's unsparing struggle through satire against this "Soviet trash" began with *The Warrant* and continued with Erdman's *The Suicide,* a play that the censors forbade [in 1931]."[23]

It is important to note, however, that Meyerhold's "revolt," as Gorchakov calls it, was clearly not anti-Communist or even anti-Stalinist. It should be recalled, as mentioned earlier, that even as late as 1937, according to Ilya Ehrenburg, Meyerhold believed that the terror and atrocities of the 1930s were being carried out without the knowledge of Stalin. If only Stalin could be made aware of the situation, thought Meyerhold (according to Ehrenburg), he would put an immediate stop to it. So it was not likely that the anti-Stalin reaction of the opening night audience in 1925 was what Meyerhold was seeking to produce. The very fact that not until 1929—four years after *The Warrant*—did Meyerhold stage another contemporary satire (Mayakovsky's *The Bedbug*) would seem to suggest that *The Warrant* was something less than the opening salvo of a satirical attack by Meyerhold on corruption in the Soviet bureaucracy.

The political hoopla aroused by *The Warrant* tended to overshadow the production aesthetics. However, by putting aside the political nature of the play for a moment one can see some important production aspects which indicate the continuing evolution of Meyerhold's theatrical concepts. The staging of *The Warrant* was similar in many respects to the staging of *The Teacher Bubus.* The stage was not built up vertically and the natural flat horizontal plane of the stage floor accommodated nearly all of the action (there was some playing in the pit). Where there had been a large, circular rug in *The Teacher Bubus* there was a turntable consisting of a center circular platform (about fifteen feet in diameter) enclosed by two concentric rings (each about four feet wide) which could rotate with the inner platform or in the opposite direction. Thus Meyerhold was experimenting with yet another means of stage mobility, this time in the horizontal plane, just as scenic constructivism had explored the possibilities in the vertical plane.

By mobilizing the stage floor in this way Meyerhold could employ some of the methods and effects of pre-acting, e.g., pauses for aim and tableaux, while at the same time avoiding a static stage. There is no indication in his writings that his interest in films led him to this idea, but the principle is essentially the same: early film-makers discovered a source of dynamism in shifting from a moving actor before a fixed camera to a fixed actor before a moving camera. With his rotating rings and turntable Meyerhold could operate on the same principle: "These circles 'drove' persons and things from the rear of the stage to the foreground. Groups in frozen poses would use them to disappear in the fog. The circles often split groups of characters in two: some of them would remain downstage, while others—no longer needed for the plot—would be carried off into the wings."[24]

As in *The Forest* and *The Teacher Bubus,* Meyerhold's basically bare stage was often cluttered with realistic props: a large gramaphone, a tripod camera, a wardrobe trunk, a fully decorated dining table, a sewing machine, occasional chairs, and so forth. Likewise, the costumes and makeup were realistic rather than stylized.* But these realistic props, costumes, and makeup were placed upon a frankly nonillusionistic stage.

There was no act curtain and the set design eliminated the proscenium distinction between stage and auditorium. The scenic backdrop consisted of nine wooden panels (about six feet wide and fifteen feet high), each painted in a pattern resembling a patchwork quilt. These panels were arranged around the sides and back of the triple turntable in a modified wing-and-shutter manner. But unlike the panels in *Lake Lyul,* these did not move. Instead the panels were stationary and the stage moved. Thus through the stationary construction of a machine for acting in *The Magnificent Cuckold* and *D.E.,* the movable construction devices in *The Death of Tarelkin* and *The Earth Rebellious,* the contrast of flat stage floor with a broad, sweeping stairway in *A Lucrative Post* and *The Forest,* the moving panels on a fixed floor in *Lake Lyul,* and the moving floor with fixed panels in *The Warrant,* we

_____

*Marc Slonim writes that the makeup was highly stylized; but photographs do not bear this out. Perhaps there was some stylization, something like Chaplin's film makeup.

see the relentlessly experimental Meyerhold virtually attacking the stage in his efforts to find ever new and different forms of production movement and dynamics. Only in *The Teacher Bubus,* a kind of quietus in Meyerhold's otherwise ceaseless efforts to mobilize the stage, had the Meyerhold stage been flat and fixed.

In many respects *The Warrant* was a modification of *The Teacher Bubus.* Like *Bubus,* it was a play about the "former people"; but this time the central character was a child of the NEP period rather than one of the "former people" themselves. Like *Bubus,* it was also staged on a flat stage floor with a neutral backing, but this time the stage floor moved. And like *Bubus,* it also featured a kind of pre-acting, but the pauses were diminished, and the actors in fixed poses were set into motion on the revolving stage.

The workshop nature of the Meyerhold Theatre is again evident. As a legitimate experimenter he seemed to have no qualms about tacitly admitting the shortcomings and failures of an experiment. But if he was convinced that the basic idea had merit he would pursue it in a following production with appropriate modifications and adjustments.

This method of theatrical experimentation usually followed a two-step procedure: *The Magnificent Cuckold* was followed by *The Death of Tarelkin, A Lucrative Post* by *The Forest, Lake Lyul* by *D.E.,* and *The Teacher Bubus* by *The Warrant.* The two productions which comprise each of these pairs have a great deal in common with each other and yet each pair is so distinctive that the impression given is that of an experimental idea manifesting itself, being modified, and then put aside in order to move on to a new experimental idea.

Of course the ideas were not completely put aside and there are no grounds for proposing that Meyerhold was consciously following precisely this procedure. But it does suggest what might be called a workshop or studio approach: an idea is put forth and then worked on, rather than continually repeating a successful idea or quickly dismissing an unsuccessful one, as in the case of the Moscow Art Theatre—or, as in the case of the Kamerny Theatre, one new idea following another regardless of success or failure and with no apparent connection between them.

At the Vakhtangov Studio

Not much has been mentioned thus far regarding the antipathy with which some people viewed Meyerhold. Even such admirers as Boris Alpers and Yuri Jelagin imply in their studies that as the decade of the twenties wore on, Meyerhold became more dogmatic, subjective, and aesthetically myopic:

> The part of the actor . . . becomes of secondary importance requiring at the same time so much precision in the execution of a definitive technical task that we can rightly consider the performer but a picturesque vehicle in the hands of the artist-director.
>
> In such a show, the actor turns from a performer into a mechanical executor of an extraneous assignment. Quite a considerable distance separates the actor of this type from the mobile and jovial cabotines who enacted before the guffawing audiences the fascinating farces of *The Magnanimous* [sic] *Cuckold* and *Tarelkin, The Forest, The World at an End* [*The Earth Rebellious*].[25]

But some of his activities during the mid-twenties tend to contradict this impression of Meyerhold as an increasingly self-indulgent and dictatorial director. They concern his interest in the Vakhtangov Theatre—or as it was known until 1926, the Third Studio of the Moscow Art Theatre.

Meyerhold's reputed egocentricity in matters of theatre is challenged by his relationship with the Vakhtangov company. This relationship is rarely touched upon by Meyerhold commentators (it is not discussed by Houghton, Slonim, Carter, Braun, Alpers, or even Gorchakov), but it offers some insight into the kind of man Meyerhold was.

Soon after his most successful production, *Princess Turandot,** Vakhtangov died at the age of thirty-nine. At the Third Studio he left behind a dedicated group of talented young actors and actresses, but without his inspiring leadership they soon fell into difficulties. In 1923 the troup toured Scandinavia and Germany but returned in worse financial condition than before. The parent theatre, the Moscow Art Theatre, was itself on the financial ropes

---

*Turandot premiered 28 February 1922—just two months before the premiere of *The Magnificent Cuckold.*

and had taken an American tour for the purpose of acquiring some financial security.

Like everyone else in the Russian theatre Meyerhold had greatly admired his young competitor. Vakhtangov had studied briefly with Meyerhold but was much more Stanislavsky's protégé, even though most critics regarded his productions as a balanced synthesis of the two opposite approaches. In 1923, however, Meyerhold was in a much better position than Stanislavsky to help the floundering Third Studio, and when it was on the verge of being liquidated he convinced government authorities to keep it in operation. According to Yuri Jelagin, who was a musician at the Third Studio and devoted to the memory of Vakhtangov, "the present Vakhtangov Theatre owes its existence to Meyerhold."[26]

Not only did Meyerhold come to the aid of Vakhtangov's theatre, he also became a virtual godfather to Vakhtangov's son, Sergei, who was fourteen when his father died. Meyerhold looked after the young man, helped him through his studies in architecture, and then employed him as a designer at the Meyerhold Theatre in 1930. Finally, he worked closely with him in the 1930s on the planning and construction of the magnificent new Meyerhold Theatre. In their turn, the Vakhtangov family, like Stanislavsky, stood by Meyerhold in the late 1930s when it was neither wise nor particularly safe to do so.

When the Third Studio was having its most serious problems— from 1923 to 1926—Meyerhold was a frequent visitor and adviser. In 1924 they invited him to direct a new production of *Boris Godunov,* and in spite of the fact that he was then working on *The Forest* and *D.E.* at his own theatre, he accepted. Production plans got under way with S. P. Osakov as designer and Boris Zakhava as Meyerhold's chief assistant.*

The production was never realized, but in the preparations and rehearsals, which continued until 1926, there is revealed a side of Meyerhold's personality and artistic nature that is never mentioned in regard to his work with his own company at his own theatre. In a phrase, it is the personal quality of adaptability and artistic objectivity.

*It is Zakhava's memoirs which contain most of the information about this venture (*Sovremniki,* pp. 364-385).

Such qualities are rarely attributed to the Meyerhold of 1925. Instead, he is most often described as a man at the height of his fame and influence, justifiably confident in his own theatrical perspicacity, and not the least inclined to worry about anyone else's methods or ideas. At his own theatre this may have been quite true, but according to Zakhava—who worked with Meyerhold after the death of Vakhtangov but eventually became known as Vakhtangov's most famous disciple and a director of the Vakhtangov Theatre—when Meyerhold set to work with the actors of the Third Studio he adapted his approach to suit the Vakhtangov method of working.

> It is interesting to note that at the Vakhtangov studio Meyerhold worked in a much different manner than in his own theatre. He seemed to consider himself as Vakhtangov's deputy and therefore sought to work not in the Meyerhold manner, but in the Vakhtangov manner. And he was successful in this. He rarely went onto the stage. He did very little demonstrating. Sitting on a director's stool in the back of the auditorium, he would from there toss up to the performers his ideas and advice.
>
> In his own theatre Meyerhold could not work this way—his actors were not trained in this method. And it was quite evident to me that Meyerhold thoroughly enjoyed the chance to work in what was for him such an unusual manner.[27]

Zakhava goes on to say that Meyerhold's willingness to work in the spirit of Vakhtangov's "collective" theatre surprised the company and soon resulted in a warm working relationship. In the end, however, a series of developments—financial and managerial as well as a disagreement between Meyerhold and the actor playing Boris—coupled with pressing demands from Meyerhold's own theatre caused an indefinite postponement of the production.

The upshot of all this was not hostility between Meyerhold and the members of the Third Studio, but quite the contrary. They were well aware of the fact that it was through Meyerhold's efforts that liquidation of the company was prevented. But after it was reconstituted as the independent Vakhtangov Theatre in 1926 Meyerhold was no longer involved as adviser and unofficial guardian. Then, on an evening in 1930 when he was in attendance at a sweetly sentimental production of *Craftiness and Love* under the direction of N. P. Akimov, Meyerhold shouted his disgust from the audience and during the intermission went backstage to reprimand the actors and the director for indulging in such sentimental claptrap. From then on, according to Yuri Jelagin, [28] diplomatic relations between Meyerhold's theatre and the Vakhtangov Theatre were severed.

Keeping Authorities at Bay: *Roar China*

During what was for Meyerhold an uncommonly long period of time between productions—between *The Warrant* and *The Inspector General*—he was involved not only with the Third Studio production of *Boris Godunov* but also with supervising a student-directed production of Sergei Tretyakov's *Roar China* at the Meyerhold Theatre. This was the first time that he had entrusted one of his theatre's productions to someone else—although it should be noted that Vasily Fedorov, the "student" director, was, at thirty-five, certainly no neophyte.

Fedorov had joined Meyerhold in 1922 as a student at GVIRM and for the following four years worked primarily as a production assistant. His production of *Roar China* was not antithetical to the production style of Meyerhold—in fact, it accurately reflected the situation: the efforts of a devoted disciple working under the supervision of his master. The chronicler of the first years of the Meyerhold Theatre, Alexy Gvozdyev, writes:

> In his first independent work, *Roar China,* V. Fedorov made use of the methods and theories from *Bubus.* He employed them to reveal the psychology of poor Chinese who were awakened to conscientious battle with European imperialists. For working up a Chinese atmosphere, especially in the last acts, he employed a slow tempo, chanting voices to musical accompaniment concealed in the background, with suffering groans and gestures intensifying the tragic torment of the masses. . . .
>
> Before the audience passed believable Chinese poor in masks which were cleverly outlined with a few ethnographic characteristics rather than individualized.[29]

Gvozdyev goes on to say that only in the "European episodes" were the characters treated individually and realistically.

The production of *Roar China* (premiere, 23 January 1926) was both a fortunate and an unfortunate event. It was fortunate in that it succeeded very well with party critics and officials at a time when the Meyerhold Theatre's ideological commitment was becoming somewhat suspect. But it was unfortunate because it came to be regarded in the West as representative of productions and repertoire at the Meyerhold Theatre. It was the first of Meyerhold's modern repertoire to be done in the United States— by the Theatre Guild in 1927—and in the 1930s it toured Europe, along with *The Magnificent Cuckold, The Forest,* and *The Inspector General,* as an example of Meyerhold's contemporary repertoire.

It is not surprising that Tretyakov's "coarse . . . propaganda piece," as Marc Slonim calls it,[30] with its depiction of innocent Chinese coolies being brought to the point of revolution by the torturous exploitation of American and British "imperialist vampires,"[31] would be the choice of Soviet authorities for foreign exportation and tours, rather than *The Teacher Bubus, The Warrant,* or even worse, *The Bedbug* or *The Bathhouse.* But to pass it off as representative of the work and repertoire of Meyerhold was a deception. Although it was done at the Meyerhold Theatre and he did supervise (to whatever extent) Fedorov's production, it was not Meyerhold's personal work nor was it at all typical of the kind of play he was doing.

There were increasing pressures at this time on all Soviet theatres and directors to stage modern, Soviet plays—i.e., propaganda drama. (Stanislavsky did his only party presentation in 1927: *Armored Train 14-69.*) Although Meyerhold certainly had no aversion to doing propaganda drama, he was uninterested in doing dull, unimaginative plays. And most of the party line plays were just that. Furthermore, due to their ideological purity such plays were expected to be staged faithfully, as written. And this, of course, was the kind of harnessing that Meyerhold had never been able to accept.

Consequently, it might be surmised that Meyerhold recognized the necessity of accommodating the demands of the authorities and thus offered Tretyakov's *Roar China,* but excused himself from the dull task of directing it.* Or, perhaps he was just too busy with his own plans—specifically, plans for his finest directing achievement, *The Inspector General.*

*Not everyone considered Tretyakov's play a coarse bit of propaganda. Bertolt Brecht reportedly said in an interview in 1934, "In Russia there's one man who's working along the right lines, Tretyakov; a play like *Roar China* shows him to have found quite new means of expression" (*Brecht on Theatre,* ed. J. Willett, p. 65). Tretyakov was arrested and executed in the same year as Meyerhold's arrest—1939. In 1955 Brecht proudly accepted the Stalin Peace Prize.

7

Meyerhold's "Song of Songs"

The Inspector General

His production of *The Inspector General* is to the art of Meyerhold what the production of *The Cherry Orchard* or *The Three Sisters* is to the art of Stanislavsky: the highest achievement of one man's personal vision of theatre art. Few historians of the Soviet theatre would disagree with Nikolai Gorchakov's evaluation: "On December 9, 1926, Meyerhold offered Nikolai Gogol's *The Inspector-General* at the Vsevolod Meyerhold State Theatre. This production was his "Song of Songs" as a director. If a description of this masterpiece alone is preserved of all his presentations, it would be quite enough to permit one to understand his creative personality. The production was the key to all the secrets of his work."[1]

Meyerhold had been experimenting with methods of realizing his concept of the theatre of the grotesque for many years; now, at the age of fifty-two, it was as if he was ready to polish and synthesize all of the best that his years of tireless experimentation had produced. To do so he chose what is probably the finest Russian comedy ever written—and with characteristic audacity he immediately set about rewriting it. For those critics who thought it presumptuous of him to reorganize the scenes of an Ostrovsky play, the idea of rewriting *The Inspector General* verged on the heretical. But to such critics he would quote Mounet-Sully: *"Chaque texte n'est qu'un pretexte"*[2] and for him that applied to the texts of Gogol and Ostrovsky just as it did to the work of contemporaries like Faiko and Erdman.

There is no way of knowing just how much time and thought Meyerhold had been giving *The Inspector General* prior to its production in the winter of 1926. Yuri Jelagin may be a bit expansive in suggesting that he had been ruminating on it since 1908;[3] on the other hand, there would be nothing particularly unusual or even significant about this. It is most likely that every Russian director, past and present, has occasionally given thought to how he would handle Gogol's classic—in the same way that every French director thinks about his approach to Molière.

But it is uncertain just how soon after the premiere of *The Warrant* in April 1925 Meyerhold began serious preparation on the production that would not open for another twenty months. Without a diary or extensive private correspondence for reference, the student of Meyerhold's work can only draw inferences from circumstantial evidence. From this, one must conclude that he set to work immediately after *The Warrant* on what was to be one of his most carefully planned productions.

Was he consciously planning a *chef d'oeuvre*—a monumental synthesis of all the best his years of experimentation had taught him? Although consideration in retrospect would seem to give validity to this idea, there is no reason to believe that Meyerhold in 1925-1926 sensed that his career was at its apogee. Nevertheless, he devoted an inordinate amount of time to the preparation of *The Inspector General:* from his first productions with the "Comrades of the New Drama" in 1902 until after the advent of official Socialist Realism in 1932, the twenty-month period between *The Warrant* and *The Inspector General* is by far the longest stretch of time in his career without a production opening. This was due not to circumstances of health or travel but, apparently, a decision to enter into extensively detailed and careful preparations of Gogol's comedy.*

*As early as 20 October 1925—more than a year before opening—he was delivering to his company a lengthy "production explanation" of *The Inspector General*. Whether rehearsals had already started is unclear; within four months, however, they were definitely in progress (*V. E. Meyerhold*, 2:108, 123).

With few exceptions the theatre of Meyerhold should be regarded as an experimental workshop rather than a professional enterprise striving for polished professionalism. The production of *The Inspector General* is one such exception. We may never know exactly what prompted Meyerhold to concentrate at this time on mounting a very polished production, but whatever the motivation, the result was a production which, more than any other, has come to be regarded as the epitome of his theatrical art. And in Edward Braun's opinion, it represented "the clearest and most coherent realization of the style which in his crucial essay, 'The Fairground Booth' (1912), Meyerhold defined as the 'tragic grotesque.' "[4]

However, before examining the details of the production we should note that *The Inspector General* was not an unqualified success. Despite its appeal to the general public* and the publicly-stated support and admiration of such men as Lunacharsky and Andrey Biely, the production provoked a swarm of indignant reviews and letters to the press charging Meyerhold with making a mockery of one of the great treasures of Russian literature. In Marc Slonim's opinion, "It probably had more detractors than defenders; but," he continues, "its impact on dozens of directors was prodigious."[5] Thus in the true spirit of Meyerhold the innovator, his greatest success came not with his most widely accepted production but with his most controversial and outrageous one.

The Inspector General is one of the few Russian plays that needs little or no introduction. The story of how the greediness and culpability of a group of smalltown civil servants is exposed as the rogue Khlestakov makes the most of having been mistaken for a government inspector is a tale familiar to many Western as well as nearly all Russian theatregoers. But as with *The Misanthrope* or *The Merchant of Venice,* there has never been unanimity on how to interpret the play.

The question is whether it is simply innocent amusement or serious social satire. Of course, this question may arise with regard to almost any comedy, and in the hands of Meyerhold especially,

---

*The production was still in the regular repertoire when the Meyerhold Theatre was liquidated in 1938.

comedies tended to become serious just as tragedies became farcical. But *The Inspector General,* even before the 1926 Meyerhold production, was a particularly noteworthy example of conflicting interpretations.

The original Petersburg production of *The Inspector General* resulted in an oversimplified polarization of opinion because the cast played the drama as a trivial farce and conservative critics attacked Gogol for what seemed to them an outrageous satire on government officialdom. The political climate being what it was in 1836, Gogol was at pains to deny the critics' charges—although the critics were probably closer to the truth than the players had been. And when the comedy was presented a month later in Moscow with a much better cast (including the great Shchepkin) but with the same approach as the Petersburg cast, Gogol left the country in disgust.

Gogol's final version, published in 1842, contained numerous changes of the text used in the premieres six years earlier. But in spite of his attempt to sharpen the serious satire and reduce the burlesque elements, this finished version—which was not performed until 1870—was still treated in production as a rather simple, rib-tickling comedy. When D. S. Mirsky writes, "in the great oppositional movement against the depotism of Nicholas I and the system of bureaucratic irresponsibility, its influence was greater than that of any other single literary work,"[6] he is talking about the drama's reception by the reading public and not as it was played in the theatre.

This was not so much a matter of stupidity on the part of theatrical producers as it was a natural result of the character of nineteenth-century Russian theatre. It was a reservoir of sentimentality, heroic bombast, and burlesque. Not until the late nineteenth-century works of Ostrovsky, Sukhovo-Kobylin, Tolstoy, and Turgenev did the theatre begin to think of itself in terms of social relevance.

By the beginning of the twentieth century the efforts of such men as Ostrovsky, Davidov, Lensky, Stanislavsky, Nemirovich-Danchenko, Suvorin, Korsh, Chekhov, Komissarzhevsky, and the "first lady" of the Russian stage, Maria Yermolova, had prodded the theatre into asserting itself as a serious art form. In the process, Gogol's dramatic style was claimed by two emerging schools of opinion: the Realists, who would interpret him as a generic forerunner of Ostrovsky and Chekhov, and the Symbolists, who would interpret *The Inspector General* in the light of Gogol's late "mystical" period in which Khlestakov becomes the personification of man's "venal, treacherous conscience."[7] Reflecting something of a compromise of these interpretations, Mirsky states, "*Revizor* [*The Inspector General*] was intended as a *moral* satire against bad officials, not a social satire against the *system* of corruption and irresponsible despotism. But quite apart from the author's intention, it was received as a social satire."[8]

While going through his own "Symbolist period" in 1908, Meyerhold was attracted to such an interpretation of *The Inspector General.* But by 1926 Meyerhold was no longer interested in imposing on the play either a Symbolist or Realist approach; rather, he was concerned with realizing the peculiar nature of Gogol's paradoxical comedy and then allowing it to determine its own form or genre. In March of 1926 he said to the cast of *The Inspector General:*

> What is most amazing about *The Inspector General* is that although it contains all the elements of those plays written before it, although it was constructed according to various established dramatic premises, there can be no doubt—at least for me—that far from being the culmination of a tradition, it is the start of a new one. Although Gogol employs a number of familiar devices in the play, we suddenly realize that his treatment of them is new. . . .
>
> The question arises of the nature of Gogol's comedy, which I would venture to describe as not so much "comedy of the absurd" as "comedy of the absurd situation." One needs to be as tentative as this because of the further question: Is it comic at all? I suspect that it is not. When Gogol read the first chapters of *Dead Souls* to Pushkin, Pushkin—who, after all, loved a good laugh—"gradually became more and more gloomy, and finally was absolutely miserable." When Gogol finished reading, Pushkin said in a grief-stricken voice: "My God, how sad our Russia is! " Gogol had achieved the desired effect: although the treatment was comic, Pushkin understood at once that the intention was something more than comic.[9]

But this respect for Gogol's intentions rather than production traditions did not mean that Meyerhold had any intention of treating the script as sacrosanct.

Quite the contrary. Rarely had Meyerhold taken such freedoms with a text as he did with that of *The Inspector General,* and never had he been so bold with a classic. Even in his scandalous production of *The Forest* in which he reordered the sequence of scenes and events, he had tampered but little with the dialogue. But with *The Inspector General* his reworking went so far that the program acknowledged that the production which premiered on 9 December 1926 was an adaptation of Gogol's play by Meyerhold and Mikhail Korenyev. Unfortunately this script, to the best of my knowledge, was never published; and if an unpublished prompt script exists it has not been made available. Consequently, comparisons of Gogol's script with Meyerhold's adaptation of it must rely on accounts of the production by eyewitnesses.

Gogol had said, "In *The Inspector General* I decided to gather into one heap everything rotten in Russia as I then saw it . . . ; I decided to hold up everything to ridicule at once."[10] In effect, what Meyerhold attempted was to allow such ridicule the posthumous advantages of the Revolution's overthrow of Tsarist authority and censorship. Not only did he go back to Gogol's original 1836 script, but he took the action out of its provincial setting, plopped it down in the midst of Petersburg-like aristocracy, and promoted the minor civil servants to high-ranking authorities in Tsarist officialdom. As a result, the "distancing" of the tale which Gogol had found necessary and which allowed even the Tsar himself to enjoy the play's satire was eliminated and the ridicule fell on the heads of the most authoritative and "respectable" persons in nineteenth-century Russia.

Furthermore, Meyerhold added some particularly caustic moments and characters from Gogol's notebooks and his novel, *Dead Souls.* All in all, the provincial setting and subtleties which cloaked the serious nature of Gogol's satire were brusquely removed by Meyerhold as he turned the play into a nonhumorous satirical condemnation of the greed, corruption, and fatuousness which the Communists associated with nineteenth-century Russian aristocracy. According to Norris Houghton,

He has tried to show what he believes to be Gogol's disgust at the hypocrisy of the time, Gogol's ridicule of the provincial government of early nineteenth-century Russia [as noted above, Meyerhold actually took it out of its provincial setting], Gogol's condemnation of the middle class's watery morality. Whether he has succeeded, or whether Gogol even intended these things, no one but Gogol, dead these hundred years, could say; but that Meyerhold has definitely succeeded in expressing his own thought through *The Inspector General* there can be no doubt.[11]

Houghton thus brings up the point which perhaps more than any other determines whether a person sides with or against Meyerhold's idea of the theatre: does the director have the right to use (or exploit) the script in whatever way he sees fit, or is he obliged—once having made his choice of a script—to faithfully stage the drama essentially as written?

Meyerhold never left any doubt as to where he stood in regard to this question: "The director's art is the author's art, and not the performer's. But you must have [earned] a right to it." [12] Although he studied scripts and authors' intentions with great care, and although he was severely critical of directors who changed scripts just to be different or to create a hubbub (his reworking of *The Forest* and *The Inspector General* inspired many novices to drastically rewrite classics in the name of "Meyerholdism"), he constantly insisted that with regard to the script in production, the director's prerogatives were no less than those of the playwright.

> In the good director, there potentially sits a dramatist. You see, once these were one profession; only afterwards did they separate. . . . This is not a division in principle, but it is technically necessary, for the art of the theatre has become complicated, and one would have to be a second Leonardo da Vinci in order both to write dialogue with sparkle, and to cope with the world (I am, of course, simplifying a bit).[13]

And in no production did Meyerhold assert his directorial prerogatives with greater insistence or to the greater chagrin of conservatives than in *The Inspector General.*

Meyerhold's production scheme for *The Inspector General* is in a direct line of development from *A Lucrative Post* in 1923 and, more specifically, from *The Teacher Bubus* in 1925. It has already been noted how, with *A Lucrative Post,* Meyerhold began to modify his earlier emphasis on vertical movement and proliferation of levels. With *The Teacher Bubus* came the stop-action tableaux in a singular horizontal plane of action and a production that was virtually scored to music. In *The Warrant* the stylized stop-action tableaux were, in a sense, activated by the revolving stage. Now, in *The Inspector General,* Meyerhold continued to work in the horizontal plane with frequent tableaux, ambient music, and highly selective lighting, but this time he "activated" his stage not by turntables but by means of a fourteen-foot by twelve-foot platform which functioned like a modified wagon stage.

The permanent stage setting consisted of a series of ten imitation mahogany panels—each containing a double door—which enclosed the stage in a shallow semicircle. Rising above this to mask the flies was a green cloth valance. Hanging directly over the playing area, at the same height as the tops of the mahogany panels (about eighteen feet), were three large spotlights encased in shiny black cylinders. It was as if Gogol's characters and their society—and perhaps even the drama itself—were being revealed and examined under the harsh, unrelenting glare of the modern electrical age.

Out onto this bare stage, backed by the mahogany panels and overhung with the green valance and the three black spotlight housings, would emerge the twelve-by-fourteen platform bearing characters and paraphernalia frozen in a scene from an age gone by. Emmanuel Kaplan describes the effect:

> Somewhere, slow quiet music begins to play. In the center of the stage massive doors swing silently wide open of their own accord and a platform moves slowly forward towards the spectator, out of the gloom, out of the distance, out of the past—one senses this immediately, because it is contained in the music. The music swells and comes nearer, then suddenly on an abrupt chord—*sforzando*—the platform is flooded with light in unison with the music.
>
> On the platform stand a table and a few chairs; candles burn; officials sit. The audience seems to crane forward towards the dark and gloomy age of Nicholas in order to see better what it was like in those days. . . .
>
> There they sit, wreathed in a haze with only the shadows of their

pipes flickering on their faces; and the music plays on, slower and quieter as though flickering too, bearing them away from us, further and further into the irretrievable "then." A pause—*fermata.* And then a voice: "Gentlemen, I have invited you here to give you some most unpleasant news. . . ."

Then suddenly, as though on a word of command, at a stroke of the conductor's baton, everyone stirs in agitation, pipes jump from lips, fists clench, heads swivel. The last syllable of "revizor" [inspector] seems to tweak everybody. Now the word is hissed in a whisper: the whole word by some, just the consonants by others, and somewhere even a softly rolled "r". The word "revizor" is divided musically into every conceivable intonation. The ensemble of suddenly startled officials blows up and dies away like a squall. Every one freezes and falls silent; the guilty conscience rises in alarm, then hides its poisonous head again, like a serpent lying motionless and saving its deadly venom.[14]

Kaplan's splendidly evocative description is of the opening of the first episode—first of the fifteen into which Meyerhold divided Gogol's five-act script. All but four of these episodes were played on the platform. Presumably, Meyerhold employed two of these platforms, setting up one backstage while the other was onstage. When an episode concluded the characters would freeze into tableau, the platform would slowly retreat upstage and out of sight as the lights went out, then emerge (the other platform?) containing a different set and tableau.

As Kaplan recounts, all of this took place to almost constant atmospheric music. But the musical element was much more than just atmospheric; according to Alexy Gvozdyev's account, "The show was divided into fifteen episodes, each of which became part of a large symphonic suite—a stage symphony of Gogolian themes. Meyerhold defined his production of *The Inspector General* as musical realism. The production was, in fact, based on the principles of musical composition."[15]

What in *The Teacher Bubus* was often the blatant and arbitrary use of a musical basis for the production in general and the acting in particular was now subtly synthesized with Gogol's drama by Meyerhold and his composer, Mikhail Gnessin. The moment-by-moment orchestration of actors' voices, movements, and gestures which in turn was coordinated with the lighting and the actual orchestral accompaniment could only be compared, in Gvozdyev's phrase, with the orchestration of "the instruments of a large symphony orchestra."[16] It was in this way that Meyerhold produced, in *The Inspector General,* a sense of mystery without resorting to theatrical illusion, and a sense of verisimilitude without resorting to actualism. This he called musical realism: theatre based on reality, but conventionalized in the direction of musical abstraction.

The musical basis of a production is particular evidence of Meyerhold's interest in the classical theatres of Japan and China. Much has been said about his interest in the conventions of the commedia dell'arte, but it is also true that he was interested in and influenced by the Oriental theatre. His subordination of language and gesture to musical themes and rhythms suggests the integration of this influence with that of the commedia. But not too much should be made of this since his interest in music and the resultant musical realism may have followed as much from his own musical background—his music training in his youth, his opera productions at the Marinsky, and his reading of such music-oriented theorists as Appia, Craig, and Fuchs—as from his study of Oriental theatre conventions.*

But from whatever commingling of influences, it is true that music and musical concepts played a much larger part in the Meyerhold theories and methods than is generally acknowledged. Unlike such innovators as Stanislavsky, Tairov, Craig, and Brecht, he had several years of music training in his youth and was deeply interested throughout his life in the theories and accomplishments of serious composers—e.g., Prokofiev, Scriabin, and Shostakovich—not to mention his fascination with American jazz. Furthermore, during his years with the Imperial Theatres he became an accomplished director of opera.

Odd as it may seem, Meyerhold—the Bolshevik materialist—was probably as close to the letter if not the spirit of Wagner's music-drama synthesis as any director in the first quarter of the

---

*Although some writers have suggested the Oriental theatre as a primary influence on Meyerhold, I am inclined to believe that his knowledge of and interest in it was superficial. Not until the Chinese opera performances of Mei-Lan-Fang's troupe in Moscow in 1935 did Russian directors and actors become seriously interested in Oriental practices.

twentieth century. His antiromantic, antisentimental bias notwith-standing, Meyerhold was profoundly concerned with forming a synthesis of musical and dramatic conventions. In 1907 he wrote: "The theatre is constantly revealing a lack of harmony amongst those engaged in presenting their collective creative work to the public. One never sees an ideal blend of author, director, actor, designer, composer and property-master. For this reason, Wagner's notion of a synthesis of the arts seems to me impossible."[17] But in 1910, in an article discussing his production of *Tristan and Isolde,* he wrote: "The artistic synthesis which Wagner adopted as the basis for his reform of the music drama will continue to evolve. Great architects, designers, conductors and directors will combine their innovations to realize it in the theatre of the future."[18]

In 1910, however, he still had reservations in that "there can be no complete synthesis before the advent of *the new actor.*"[19] But by 1930 this "new actor" was virtually a reality at the Meyerhold Theatre. Having evolved through the experiments with commedia dell'arte, Oriental conventions, and biomechanics, this new actor was not, in Meyerhold's eyes, an *über*-marionette or a diminution of the Stanislavsky actor. He was instead practically the embodi-ment of Wagnerian synthesis, although in the manner of a satirical revue rather than a romantic opera: "The actor appears now as a dramatic artist, now as an opera singer, now as a gymnast, now as a clown."[20] And it is through this multifarious performer that Meyerhold in 1930 saw Wagner's idea coming to fruition:

> There was a time when Wagner's idea of a new theatre which would be a dramatic synthesis of words, music, lighting, rhythmical movement and all the magic of the plastic arts was regarded as purely utopian. Now we can see that this is exactly what a production should be: we should employ all the elements which the other arts have to offer and fuse them to produce a concerted effect on the audience.[21]

And finally, in a nutshell: "You must regard the dramatic theatre as a musical theatre as well."[22]

The point is that Meyerhold's abiding interest in music and his efforts to synthesize elements of music and drama—i.e., *The Inspector General* as "a stage symphony on Gogolian themes"[23] —

suggests a pertinent relationship between the ideas of Meyerhold and those of Wagner. And it is a relationship which is more than just speculative or coincidental. Meyerhold frequently invoked the name of Wagner when discussing his own ideas of total theatre—in both his pre-Revolution and post-Revolution theorizing.

Furthermore, his Wagnerian sense of theatre's affinity to music is an important indicator of aesthetic consistency in Meyerhold's work both before and after the Revolution. In a lecture—"The Art of Directing"—delivered in 1927, one year after the premiere of *The Inspector General,* he said: "If I were asked, what is the artistic challenge of the regisseur, I would say, 'He has to comprehend the uncomprehended.' The difficulty in the art of directing consists in that the regisseur must first of all be a musician; that is, he is concerned with one of the most difficult areas of musical art: he is always creating contrapuntal stage movement. This is a very difficult business."[24]

His use of the term "contrapuntal," which is frequently employed in this lecture, is noteworthy. For Meyerhold, the dramatic action of both the script and the stage movement proceeded according to point and counterpoint—a contrapuntal effect. In a truly Marxist didactic presentation the action is regarded as proceeding from thesis to antithesis and finally to synthesis—a dialectic effect. Although Meyerhold often spoke of a theatrical synthesis, it was a Wagnerian rather than a dialectical synthesis which he had in mind. And although his point-counterpoint movement may have resembled a kind of theatrical dialectic of thesis-antithesis, his idea of the contrapuntal was an artistic concept and not a political one. As a result his productions, which often seemed at first glance to be truly Marxist and dialectical, usually left party line critics and officials dissatisfied and suspicious. And the main reason was that his "dialectic" produced no believably healthy and inspirational synthesis. According to a disgruntled Boris Alpers:

> The insulated, suffocating, sinking world was placed alongside the fresh full-blooded world of new self-confident men. The appearance of the Red Army men in *D.E.* and *Bubus* voided the import of all the events and personages shown upon the stage before the finale. The outcome of

the strife of steel bayonets in the hands of strong and robust men ... against the effeminate, refined representatives of a dying culture, was too obvious. The whole aesthetic conception of the theatre was built upon sand. . . .

The conflict disappears from the stage of the Meyerhold theatre. Scenic action is circumscribed by the boundaries of a decaying social milieu. . . .In *The Inspector General* and *The Trouble from Reason* [premiere, March 1928] the director's field of vision embraces only the dark and hopeless aspects of the historical epoch which is taken up by these works.[25]

For a true Marxist critic like Alpers the significance of a drama like *The Inspector General* or *Woe from Wit (The Trouble from Reason)* lies in its relationship to the historical process. But Meyerhold, for all his sincere support of the Revolution and the Soviet state, thought like an artist and not like a political dialectician. He could, of course, put himself at the service of the state and dramatize the appropriate propaganda—*The Dawns* and *The Earth Rebellious*—but such productions were hastily, albeit energetically, prepared, whereas his more considered productions would not qualify as dialectical thesis pieces and were political only in the broad sense of social satire.

To say that Meyerhold thought as an artist rather than as a political dialectician is a bit difficult to explain and substantiate. But the distinction is an important one for an understanding of Meyerhold's work, especially *The Inspector General.* In the first place, the dark satire of Meyerhold's theatre of the grotesque failed to communicate the idea or the feeling that the suffering and foolishness of man's existence was due solely or even primarily to social conditions that could and would be eradicated. In productions such as *The Inspector General, The Forest, The Teacher Bubus, The Warrant,* and others, the angle of vision on man's existence was not so very different from that in *Masquerade, The Life of Man, The Puppet Booth,* or *The Death of Tintagelles.* That vision, which we now label Existentialist, sees man imbued with and surrounded by dark, mysterious forces which never have and never will be explained or eradicated; and it is a view which regards most of what is foolish and laughable about the social man as constant, however such societies change.

Such beliefs were and are contradictory to the Marxist concept of historical process. To the extent that such ideas were suggested in Meyerhold's productions, however subconsciously on his part, such productions struck party critics like Alpers as reactionary. And in the arts reactionaries were labeled "formalists" or "aesthetes"—titles which before long would be applied to Meyerhold. For the devoted political activist—especially a Marxist—the idea of sociopolitical constancy and permanence is anathema. To regard the historical process as cyclical rather than lineal ("the more things change the more they remain the same") is to undercut the whole motivation to dedicated political activism.

On the other hand, it is probably legitimate to say that artistic thinking imposes consistency on that which is inexplicable and nondiscursive in the affairs of men. The business of the artist is to illuminate this penumbral area wherein resides the wellspring of human motives and emotions. Hence Meyerhold's statement: "If I were asked, what is the artistic challenge of the regisseur, I would say, 'He has to comprehend the uncomprehended.' "[26]

It is important to remember that he made this statement not in his pre-Revolution period of Symbolist theatre but in 1927. And it can be said that with but few exceptions (possibly only *The Dawns* and *The Earth Rebellious*—each of which was designed specifically as a production in celebration of a political anniversary), Meyerhold was always more interested in the artistic challenge—"to comprehend the uncomprehended"—than the political-educational function of the theatre.

A specific and striking example of this occurred in *The Inspector General*. To the central character of Khlestakov Meyerhold added something like a shadow or alter ego in the form of an "officer in transit."[27] He followed Khlestakov throughout the production as a silent accomplice and companion who performed in pantomime an action parallel or in counterpoint to Khlestakov's. He was not a ghost figure since other characters acknowledged his presence (at one point the two of them danced a suggestive quadrille with the Mayor's wife and daughter); but aside from being ostensibly identified as an officer in transit in the company of Khlestakov, his identity and purpose were of no concern to the other characters and had no immediate bearing on the developing situation. So he was, in effect, the kind of twilight zone figure which in the plays of such dramatists as Blok, Andreyev, and Maeterlinck serve as a connecting link between the worlds of the known and the unknown.

Furthermore, the character of Khlestakov himself was, in Meyerhold's production, something more than the portrait of a clever nineteenth-century rogue: "He appears onstage, a character from some tale by Hoffmann, slender, clad in black with a stiff mannered gait, strange spectacles, a sinister old-fashioned tall hat, a rug and a cane, apparently tormented by some private vision. He is a flâneur from the Nevsky Prospect, a native of Gogol's own Petersburg."[28] He was, in fact, something of an amalgam of Don Juan, Harlequin, Man (*Life of Man,* Andreyev, 1907), Tarelkin (Alexandrinsky production, 1917), Arbenin *(Masquerade),* and many other characters out of Meyerhold productions who were similarly "tormented by some private vision." It was as if Meyerhold was adding a new, twentieth-century character type to the commedia roster. Or perhaps it was still the bemused Harlequin, now suffering in the twentieth-century mode of metaphysical *angst.*

In any event, such a character and the kind of drama from which he emerges certainly had little to do with agitprop or Socialist Realism. It is not surprising that angry Soviet critics accused Meyerhold of "no longer hearing the music of revolution," and charged that he had turned from clear and purposeful didacticism to a "romantic Gogolian-Hoffmannesque, and fantastic" mode of production.[29]

His famous staging of the finale would seem to give credence to the critics' charge. The characters, upon hearing the news that Khlestakov was an imposter and that the real Inspector General is at the station, were shocked into frozen, distorted poses. The lights then went out for a few seconds and when they came up again the audience saw not the actors but mannequins in the same ridiculous poses. Of this climax Nikolai Gorchakov writes, "Meyerhold for the first time revealed his secret to the audience. For him, the world still possessed the young passions of symbolism. Even in the 'proletarian dictatorship' the world struck him as merely an exhibit, a collection of benumbed puppets who were the playthings and victims of Fate."[30]

Even though Gorchakov may be overstating the case somewhat—Meyerhold's writings, lectures, and productions do not suggest a cynical pessimism that would most certainly possess a man who saw the world as "merely an exhibit, a collection of benumbed puppets"—it is nonetheless true that the production of *The Inspector General* made it unmistakably clear that Meyerhold's concept of theatrical characterization was imbedded in the traditions of the commedia and that his theatre was a consistent development of the grotesque and the theatre of masks.

Beginning of the End

The Inspector General premiered 9 December 1926. But rather than inaugurating a period of success, it was destined to be the climax of Meyerhold's career. What followed may be regarded as the beginning of the end. During the next two years his work at his theatre—which was nationalized prior to *The Inspector General* and consequently renamed the Meyerhold State Theatre—was erratic, generally unsuccessful, and clearly struggling under the increasing pressures and demands from Stalinist authorities. From the end of 1926 to the beginning of 1929 Meyerhold's activities included a film, *The White Eagle* (based on Andreyev's *The Governor*), in which Meyerhold played the leading role; a political review called *Window Into a Village* which was directed by a student-collective and supervised by Meyerhold; an unsuccessful struggle with government censors for permission to do Sergei Tretyakov's *I Want a Child* (a documentarylike examination—with audience participation—of the proper attitudes toward love and sex for the Soviet man and woman); a revival of *The Magnificent Cuckold* with Znaida Raikh noticeably miscast as the female lead; another attempt at revitalizing a classic, this time Griboyedov's *Woe from Wit* which Meyerhold retitled *Woe to Wit*; and finally, a five-month stay in France—ostensibly on tour—from which he reluctantly returned when his theatre was threatened with liquidation.

There is little of artistic significance in his work on *I Want a*

Child, Window Into a Village, the revival of *The Magnificent Cuckold,* or *Woe to Wit.* Personal, political, and financial matters during these two years began to occupy more and more of his time and energies. According to Yuri Jelagin, "Soon after the premier of *The Inspector General* a whole series of various causes and unpleasantly complex circumstances began to form serious and chronic crises in his creative work."[31]

In the first place, Meyerhold was increasingly frustrated by the lack of good Soviet plays—especially in light of the increasing pressure from government authorities to do such dramas. In an urgent telegram to Mayakovsky in the spring of 1928 he implored: "For the last time we turn to your good sense. The theatre is dying. There are no plays. We are forced to repudiate the classics. I do not wish to degrade the repertoire. You must soon give me a serious answer: can we count on receiving your play during the summer? "[32]

All during the decade of the twenties there had been strong encouragement by government authorities for the theatres to favor the work of "positive" Soviet dramatists—even if the artistic suitability of such dramas lagged far behind their ideological suitability. But by 1927 such encouragements were beginning to sound like demands. This was due in part to a political development which was particularly noteworthy and ominous for Meyerhold personally.

At the Fifteenth All-Union Congress of the Communist Party in late 1927 Stalin and his followers scored a decisive victory over the Trotskyites; Trotsky and his allies—among whom were Meyerhold's friends-in-high-places—were subsequently expelled from the party and banished to the provinces.* Thus four years after the death of Lenin, Stalin was in absolute control. He immediately set about tightening his grip on the country by silencing or eliminating the voices of dissent, doubt, or even mild criticism. It now became, even more than before, a matter of policy that anyone who was not foursquare for the party and anything it did was, *ipso facto,* an enemy of the state.

---

*The three party leaders purged by Stalin were Zinovyev, Kamenev, and Trotsky. All three were on friendly terms with Meyerhold; the fact that all three were of Jewish ancestry may also have been noted by Meyerhold.

In 1928 Stalin replaced the quasi freedom of the NEP with the first of the five-year plans. In the same year all the private art groups, schools, and organizations were dissolved by government fiat. As Hilton Kramer says in his essay on the history of Soviet art, "The experiment was over."[33] And if such innovators as Alexander Rodchenko and Vladimir Tatlin were being silenced one can well imagine how thin the ice was becoming beneath the feet of such a prominent and, by the very nature of the theatre, such a public experimenter as Meyerhold. It was in this same year, 1928, that the director of the Second Studio and one of Russia's most prominent young actors, Mikhail Chekhov, emigrated from Russia to the United States. In fact, Chekhov's departure may have had some bearing on the government's insistence that Meyerhold return immediately from France rather than continue on an extended tour.

Given Meyerhold's fascination with Europe and "jazzy" America it is hard to believe that he was not tempted to join the growing number of expatriate Russian writers and artists in France and the United States. His wife was with him, many of his best performers had recently left his theatre (Babanova, Okhlopkov, Orlov, Sverdlin, Zakhava, Yakontov, and others), and he was sorely frustrated with the quality of plays available for production in the Soviet Union. On top of all this, his theatre had fallen into serious financial trouble. The continuing popularity of *The Forest* and *The Inspector General* was not enough to offset his extravagant use of funds for such financially unsuccessful experiments as *The Teacher Bubus, The Warrant,* and *Woe to Wit.*

Ostensibly, it was due to the financial crisis at the Meyerhold State Theatre that he was refused permission to develop an extended tour of Europe. He was given the ultimatum of returning to Moscow to set his house in financial order or of suffering the loss of the Meyerhold State Theatre.

Considering all this, one wonders why Meyerhold bothered to return—except that he must have been deeply committed to his theatre. Perhaps somewhere there is private correspondence or a diary in which his thoughts and feelings at this time are recorded. But for the present such material, if it exists, remains out of reach. All of the archive material which has recently been released and published deals with Meyerhold's artistic theories and methods and virtually none of it deals directly with the personal and political complications of his life.

There is one further matter, according to Yuri Jelagin,* that was hindering Meyerhold's work at this time. He says that there was growing dissension and bitterness among the members of the company at the Meyerhold State Theatre due to favoritism, Meyerhold's egocentricity, and Znaida Raikh's domineering influence on her husband. Allowing for the distortions due to jealousy and backbiting that are common in the theatre, it is worth noting—in passing at least—that workers in the Meyerhold Theatre were beginning to feel that his renowned artistic integrity did have one blind spot: Raikh. Unlike Tairov's wife and helpmate, Alice Koonen, Znaida Raikh was regarded less as a fine actress and valuable asset to her husband than as one of the last of the big time party girls in the Russian theatre. She was reputedly quite vain about her looks, her sex appeal, and her acting ability—a vanity which critics and photographs fail to justify. But Meyerhold seems to have found her charms irresistible, and after considerable padding of her role as Anna in *The Inspector General*, he dedicated his revival of *The Magnificent Cuckold* to her and gave her the lead role of Stella. But according to Jelagin, it was not so much the parts which she was given that disturbed the rest of the company as it was their suspicion that she had undue influence with her husband regarding the fortunes of other members of the company, particularly the nonstars.

How much truth there is in Jelagin's gossipy account of Raikh's backstage shenanigans is open to question. It is true, however, that after *The Inspector General* many of Meyerhold's best performers—some of whom had been with him since the original *Magnificent Cuckold* in 1922—left the company. Only Igor Ilinsky, of those who were most prominent, stayed with him well into the 1930s. Thus, along with financial and political difficulties, the waning twenties brought personal problems as well.

---

*As noted earlier, the accuracy of Jelagin's biography is questionable. He rarely gives sources, is at times obviously relying on hearsay, and is sometimes wrong. But since he now lives, writes (in Russian), and publishes in the U.S., he is free to recount some things that Soviet writers cannot.

Woe to Wit

Before taking up what might justifiably be considered the final vestiges of Meyerhold's uncompromised audacity—the productions of Mayakovsky's *The Bedbug* and *The Bathhouse*—some notice must be taken of his last production in the "series" of revised Russian classics: Griboyedov's *Woe from Wit*. Meyerhold's productions seemed to run in pairs: *The Dawns* and *Mystery-Bouffe* (Futuristic agitprop); *The Magnificent Cuckold* and *The Death of Tarelkin* (scenic constructivism and biomechanics); *A Lucrative Post* and *The Forest* (presentational Ostrovsky); *Lake Lyul* and *D.E.* (satire of the West); *The Teacher Bubus* and *The Warrant* (satire of "former people").* And now a treatment similar to that given Gogol's early nineteenth-century satire is applied to Griboyedov's.

Much of what has been said about Meyerhold's irreverent approach to *The Inspector General* can be repeated with respect to *Woe to Wit*. In order to sharpen the satirical thrust of Griboyedov's comedy he included sketches and first drafts that the author had thrown out, shuffled the order of the scenes, shifted the locales, and inserted revolutionary verses by Pushkin and K. N. Ryleyev. In fact, while the playbill acknowledged *Woe to Wit* as "a comedy by A. S. Griboyedov," it also listed Meyerhold as "author of the spectacle."[34]

The play would seem to be a nearly perfect vehicle for the style of the Meyerhold State Theatre at this time. It is basically a plotless play which derives its interest mainly from splendidly comical characterizations and terse, epigrammatic dialogue. As D. S. Mirsky states,

> In the art of character-drawing Griboyedov is . . . unique. [His characters] are persons, but they are also *types*—archetypes or quintessences of humanity, endowed with all we have of life and individuality, but endowed also with a super-individual existence. . . . This is not to say

---

*This pairing accounts for all of Meyerhold's major productions between 1920 and 1929 except *The Earth Rebellious*. In fact, when we look at his secondary work it still holds true: the two low-budget Ibsen productions in 1921, his two Toller productions at the Theatre of the Revolution, and his supervision of two student-directed productions in 1926 and 1927 (*Roar China* and *A Window Into a Village*).

that his characters are not alive; they are, and very lively too, but they have a life more durable and universal than our own. They are stamped in the really common clay of humanity.[35]

Such a description of characterization might well apply to the work of Meyerhold-trained actors at its best. It was just this idea of characterization—characterization which refelcted "archetypes and quintessences of humanity," and characters "stamped in the really common clay of humanity"—that was compatible with Meyerhold's efforts in the direction of a more conventionalized and universal theatre.

The play is built around the confrontation of Chatsky—a young, romantic, and intellectual aristocrat who has just returned from completing his education in Paris—and the boorishly inane world of Moscow's "high society" in the 1820s. The action is set at the home of a prominent civil servant, Famusov, whose daughter Sophia was Chatsky's sweetheart before he went abroad. As preparations are made for an evening gala we follow Chatsky in his disillusioning reacquaintance with Russian aristocratic society and his attempts to reestablish his claim to Sophia who has become enamored of her father's secretary, Molchalin. By the time Chatsky has exposed Molchalin and the rest of the guests for the pretentious and petty opportunists they are, he finds that he has talked himself out of upper-class society but knows that he is unprepared to lead any other kind of life. As F. D. Reeve sums it up, "He knows he is right, but he does not know where he is, except when with those who are wrong."[36]

A comparison of Chatsky with Gogol's Khlestakov is interesting and illustrative. Like Khlestakov, Chatsky is an outsider-protagonist in conflict with the "vegetably selfish"[37] aristocratic society of early nineteenth-century Russia. But Chatsky is the obverse of Khlestakov: Khlestakov is a lower-class rogue who gets the best of a vulnerable aristocracy by cleverly insinuating himself into their hypocritical society and making off with the loot; Chatsky, on the other hand, is himself a member of the upper-class and when he, like Khlestakov, sees through the pseudosophisti-cated machinations of society he becomes an obstreperous idealist rather than an insinuating con man and ends up bemoaning his self-imposed ostracism rather than chuckling over a juicy bit of successful chicanery.

In both plays the central object of satire is the same: the stuffy aristocracy (full of commedia types). But the *agents provocateur* are, in certain essential respects, almost opposites. It is worth noting that the same actor, twenty-four year old Ernst Garin, originated both roles for the Meyerhold productions. (Raikh, of course, played Sophia in *Woe to Wit* and Famusov was played by Ilinsky.)

As he had done with *The Forest* and *The Inspector General,* Meyerhold loosened the general structure of Griboyedov's play by replacing the act divisions with a series of brief episodes—seventeen of them. This not only diluted the condensed cause-effect progression resulting from Griboyedov's adherence to "classic unities" (a dilution which, as has been previously noted, Meyerhold felt was essential to the revitalization of the theatre), but it also allowed him necessary elbowroom for the theatrical interpolations through which he sought to revitalize such a literary classic.

For example, the opening of the show was a pantomime episode depicting young gallants and society girls having a bash in a fashionable night cabaret. There is no such scene in Griboyedov's play, which takes place entirely in Famusov's house. On the other hand, this opening was not just a bit of theatrical color for its own sake—like an extra "number" added to take up slack in a Broadway musical. Rather, Meyerhold was setting the scene and establishing the production tone through visual means instead of relying entirely on dialogue.

Throughout the production Meyerhold remained true, as usual, to his 1912 maxim that words in the theatre are only a design on the canvas of motion.[38] After the opening pantomime episode, as Boris Alpers expresses it, "all the succeeding acts [were] enveloped by a series of such 'ceremonious' local color pantomimes; the billiard-play, the dressing behind the curtains, piano play, the ceremonial of a society day visit—all these fragments move[d] in a continuous chain."[39]

And as the production proceeded through this series of ceremonial pantomimes Meyerhold again employed his idea of theatrical dynamics using the contrapuntal effect: Chatsky sat at a

grand piano playing romantic compositions while lecturing Famusov on the principles of free thought and democracy; while a
sumptuous ball was in progress Chatsky could be seen in the
adjoining room lecturing vociferously to a group of young men
about revolutionary Decembrist ideas.

The show reached its climax both in terms of scenic conception
and plot when, in the penultimate episode, the almost totally
ostracized Chatsky confronts Fumasov, Sophia, and two dozen
guests seated shoulder to shoulder at a long banquet table
stretching across the stage in a line parallel to the edge of the
apron. And as they greedily consume the delicacies before them,
they "chew up with their hard jaws not only the food but Chatsky
himself."[40] When Chatsky approaches and seeks to confront them
one more time, they raise large white napkins to cover their faces
from the "insane" young man as he delivers the famous closing
monologue:

> The scales have fallen from my eyes, the dreams are gone!
>   It would not be a bad thing now
>   To vent my spleen and all
>   My spite on both the daughter
> And the father, the stupid love and the world together!
>
>   Whom was I with? Where did my fate land me?
> Everybody shoves and shouts! A crowd of torturers,
>   Of traitors in their love, endless in their hate,
>   Indomitable storytellers,
>   Incoherent wits, conniving simpletons,
>   Sinister old hags, old men
>   Growing decrepit over lies and nonsense!
> All of you in chorus glorified my madness—
> And you are right: he will pass through fire unharmed
>   Who manages a day with you,
>   Who breathes the same air that you breathe
>   And whose intelligence stays whole.
>   Away from Moscow! I will not come back again.
> I'm off, I won't look back, I'll go search through the world
>   To find a little corner for a wounded heart!
>   My carriage, now, my carriage! [41]

As might be expected, this monologue was traditionally delivered with great denunciatory pathos. But in the Meyerhold production it was spoken by Garin in a barely audible whisper as he was finally "consumed" by the omniverous decadency of nineteenth-century Russian aristocracy. Thus "the comedy of Griboyedov is transferred into the plane of tragedy."[42]

It is unclear just how much Meyerhold had to do with the design of the setting. In his five previous productions the playbill credited the "plan" of the setting to Meyerhold and listed a second person as "assistant." But for *Woe to Wit* the set credits consist of V. A. Shestakov for "construction," and N. P. Ulyanov for "costumes and makeup."[43] But as usual, it is safe to assume that Meyerhold had more than a little to do with the setting. Shestakov's previous association with Meyerhold, it will be recalled, had been as designer for *A Lucrative Post* and *Lake Lyul* at the Theatre of the Revolution in 1923. That had also been the last time that Meyerhold had yielded the design credit to someone other than himself.

The design of the setting—which most critics felt was unsuccessful (e.g., certain large elements were obstructive rather than useful)—was something of a throwback to his earlier productions. The flies, wings, and rear wall were haphazardly masked by enormous blank curtains. Against the curtain at the back wall was a kind of constructivist widow's walk at about twenty feet from the stage floor. At each side of the stage, running from each upstage corner down to the apron, was a catwalk at about fifteen feet which was underhung with masking panels and which terminated in a stairway (again) curving down to the apron at stage level. In the midst of this was the bare stage onto which pastel-colored screens would be rolled to form the shape of the interior for a given episode. These rolling screens were last employed by Meyerhold in Shestakov's design for *Lake Lyul.*

This flexible and comparatively bare stage was complemented by selective but realistic props, furnishings, and costumes. The makeup was generally stylized to the same extent as the characterizations: the two-dimensional caricature which Ilinsky made of Fumasov was accompanied by a modified fright wig, large glasses, and an extended proboscis; Garin's makeup for Chatsky, on the other hand, was basically realistic and handsome (as was Raikh's for Sophia, although this may have been motivated by something other than characterization).

Concerning the significance of *Woe to Wit* in relation to the rest of Meyerhold's work, the critic was undoubtedly correct who, two weeks after the premiere, stated in *Pravda,* "With regard to [theatrical] form the production added nothing to [Meyerhold's] already prominent position in the theatre."[44] There is nothing in the concept or method of staging *Woe to Wit* that hadn't already been seen on the Meyerhold stage, nor was there an example of a previous experiment being worked out more successfully.

Without the diversion of theatrical innovation which tended to qualify the critics' abhorrence of Meyerhold's treatment of the classics, the critical reaction was predictably unmitigated. According to Boleslav Rostotsky:

> Portentously, *Woe to Wit* called forth a greater wave of sharply critical reaction than even *The Inspector General.* Refusing to accept the obvious violence of the regisseur on a literary classic, especially as graphically as it appeared in this instance, the critics demanded that the producer revise his position. Concurrently, there was particular emphasis on the necessity of working on Soviet plays, plays relevant to the times.[45]

In a sense then, Meyerhold was getting it from both sides: the literary critics were harping about his disfigurement of the classics, and the cultural "authorities" for the State were pressing him to do more up-to-date, Soviet plays extolling the virtues of Communism, hard work, patriotism, the New Soviet Man, and so forth.

In his next production, which opened eleven months after the premiere of *Woe to Wit,* he did leave off the classics and set about staging a contemporary play by a contemporary Soviet writer; however, Vladimir Mayakovsky's *The Bedbug*—a stinging satire on the pettinesses in Soviet life—was hardly what the authorities wanted or expected.

8

The Incident Is Closed

Other Hands at Work: *The Bedbug*

It has been suggested that in the history of the Russian theatre the twenties might appropriately be labeled "The Meyerhold Decade." Although Meyerhold had become a prominent theatre figure long before 1920 and even though his activities were to continue—at a reduced level—throughout the 1930s, he was the kind of man and artist who was both a product of and a contributor to the style and spirit peculiar to the 1920s.

From 1929 to 1931 this combination of style and spirit, and Meyerhold's contribution to it, draws to a conclusion. Outside Russia the Depression of 1929 becomes the unmistakable line of demarcation between the 1920s and all that will come after. In Russia it is not so much the effect of Wall Street's collapse which distinguishes the twenties from subsequent decades as it is the final consolidation of absolute power by Stalin. But whether due to Stalin or the Depression, the results were similar: the raucous joie de vivre which marked the beginning of the 1920s did not continue into the 1930s.

There were six Meyerhold productions in this period of transition, starting with the premiere of *The Bedbug* on 13

February 1929 and concluding with the premiere of *The List of Good Deeds* on 4 June 1931. This series of productions constitutes the conclusion of this study and in a very real sense also marks the end of Meyerhold's freedom to innovate and experiment—although he would continue to work in the theatre for eight more years. The sad fact is that if radio productions, revisions of earlier productions, and productions which were prepared but never opened to the public are discounted, there are only four Meyerhold productions between *The List of Good Deeds* in 1931 and his disappearance in 1939: Yuri German's *Prelude* in 1933, Dumas-fils' *Lady of the Camelias* in 1934, and in 1935 Tchaikovsky's *Queen of Spades* and a dramatization of three short stories by Chekhov which Meyerhold titled *Thirty-three Fainting Spells*. (Meyerhold's work with Stanislavsky on Verdi's *Rigoletto* and his staging of their combined effort in March 1939, after Stanislavsky's death seven months earlier, could be considered a fifth production.)

Sadder still is the fact that none of these four (or five) productions from 1932 to 1939 was very successful, exceptional, or even noteworthy. It was as if Meyerhold was biding his time—making the best of a bad situation until such time as creative freedom returned to the arts. Unfortunately, he was running out of time, since the forces of political intimidation were settling into the arts for quite a long stay.

The play Meyerhold was referring to in his urgent telegram to Mayakovsky in the spring of 1928 (see p. 165), asking "can we count on receiving your play during the summer? " turned out to be *The Bedbug*. Not until December was Mayakovsky ready to turn it over to Meyerhold; on 28 December 1928 Mayakovsky read it to the company and rehearsals began immediately. Less than two months later, on 13 February 1929, the production opened at the Meyerhold State Theatre.

The Bedbug was quite unlike anything previously seen at the Meyerhold Theatre. Not since his production of *The Warrant* in 1925 had the content of a Meyerhold production raised such a stir that it precluded any concern for the manner in which the play was staged. In this production, which was codirected by Meyerhold and Mayakovsky, concern for aesthetic and artistic effects was clearly subordinated to the desire to drive home the satirical point of the play: that the Revolution was in danger of losing its human vitality and idealism to the lazy self-indulgence of uninspired citizens on the one hand and a sterile, inhuman scientism on the other.

The play was divided into two parts. The first half, smacking of all the pettiness, self-indulgence, and general indolence of the NEP period, depicted the efforts of Prisypkin—a simpleminded version of *The Inspector General*'s Khlestakov and *The Warrant*'s Guli-achkin—to procure a life of refinement, ease, and plenty by marrying the daughter of a well-to-do barber. In the midst of a vulgar, tasteless wedding feast a fire breaks out and everyone at the vodka-soaked party dies. The scene ends with the firemen marching down the aisle of the theatre reciting:

> Citizens and comrades,
>
> > vodka is poisonous!
>
> Drunkards
>
> > are setting
> >
> > > the republic aflame!
>
> Beware of fireplaces
>
> > beware of primuses—
>
> If your house catches fire,
>
> > you may well do the same! [1]

Up to this point the play is a rather simple, black comedy satirizing indolence and ideological irresponsibility. But in the second half, scenes five through nine, the play changes from a comparatively innocent piece of didactic comedy to an ominous and thought-provoking satire.

After the fire a period of fifty years elapses and scene five opens in 1979. It happens that during the fire the unconscious Prisypkin was covered by the firemen's water which quickly froze around him and preserved him in a block of ice. He is now defrosted and brought to life in "The Federation"—a sterile, "perfected" society of the future. Before long, Prisypkin has both frightened and fascinated the new people: frightened them with his Soviet jargon, vulgar tastes, and ideas; fascinated them with his passion for beer, vodka, and singing of little ditties. Fearing that he might infect society with such passions, the authorities of The Federation decide to cage Prisypkin—and along with him the bedbug which had been frozen onto him and thawed out with him—in a zoo with the labels, "Bugus Normalis" and "Philistinus Vulgaris."

Suddenly, Prisypkin becomes aware of the audience in the theatre and yells through the bars of his cage to them:

> Citizens! My people! My own people! Dear ones! How did you get here? So many of you! When did they unfreeze you? Why am I alone in this cage? Dear ones, my people! Come in with me! Why am I suffering? Citizens! —

The visitors at the zoo begin to panic and the Zoo Director hurries out to calm them:

> I beg your pardon, Comrades. I apologize. . . . The insect was tired. The noise and bright lights brought on hallucinations. Please be calm. It was just a fantasy. The creature will calm down tomorrow. . . . Leave quietly, citizens. See you tomorrow! Band leader, play a march!
> CURTAIN[2]

Thus ended Mayakovsky's "Fantastic Comedy"[3] — a grim prediction of the future. *The Bedbug* was staged through the joint efforts of five of the most diverse and notable talents in Soviet Russia. In addition to Meyerhold and Mayakovsky were the actor Ilinsky, the artist A. M. Rodchenko, and a young composer named Dimitri Shostakovich.

As Meyerhold's production assistant, Mayakovsky probably asserted greater influence on the production scheme than anyone who had ever worked as Meyerhold's assistant or codirector (with the possible exception of Golovin in the pre-Revolution productions at the Alexandrinsky and Marinsky). It was Mayakovsky's idea that Shostakovich's score be a raucous cacophony based on the strident marches of fire brigade bands; it was Mayakovsky's idea that a group of young graphic satirists known as the Kukriniksy* cartoonists be invited to design the settings, cos-

---

*The derivation of their name is probably from the Russian word for "doll"—*kukla*. A *teatr kukol* is a "puppet show."

tumes, and makeup for the first half of the show (before the leap into the future)—which they did in what today might be called Pop Art by purchasing all the costumes and props right across the counter in Moscow department stores in order to show just how vulgar and pretentious the contemporary tastes were. And finally, it was Mayakovsky who urged Ilinsky to use him—Mayakovsky—as an explicit model for the character of Prisypkin.[4]

The setting for *The Bedbug* was worked out between Meyerhold, the Kukriniksy group, and Rodchenko. For the first four scenes—those in the present—Meyerhold supervised the planning which was then carried out by the young cartoonists. It consisted of a few set pieces and façade screens on an otherwise bare stage representing first a department store, then a dormitory apartment, and finally a hairdressing salon (the fourth scene—the firemen fighting the fire—was very brief and played mostly on the bare stage in darkness).

For the second half of the show the constructivist sculptor and painter Rodchenko devised a suggestively futuristic setting of bright metals, plastics, and glass in streamlined, nondescript forms. When accented with flashing lights, blaring public-address speakers, sliding glass doors, and a movie screen, it represented successively an amphitheatre, a laboratory, an apartment, and a city zoo (indicated by a stylized glass cage for Prisypkin). Although descriptions are vague and the photographs difficult to interpret, the impression is that all of the action took place at stage floor level and that there were no elevated platforms or levels in the designs for either the first or second part.

In the opinion of Yuri Jelagin, the Meyerhold-Mayakovsky production of *The Bedbug* stressed the contrast between the "delightfully modern cosmopolitan style of our century" and the "wretched Soviet realities."[5] Most critics at the time, however, regarded the production as a tasteless conglomeration of sights and sounds which satirized everything in general, nothing in particular, and consequently was a "comic fantasy without relevance to anything happening at the time."[6]

But there were others who knew only too well that neither Meyerhold nor Mayakovsky was likely to be frivolous about satire and for them *The Bedbug* seemed a much more serious matter— bordering, perhaps, on anarchy. These critics charged that the sterilized future depicted in the second half of the production was in fact intended as a caricature of Communism. And by Nikolai Gorchakov's account, Mayakovsky even had to take an official oath that he had not been depicting a socialist society.[7]

But as party critics and authorities stewed, the public attended and filled the Meyerhold State Theatre with laughter. Whatever the long range consequences of the production on the lives of Meyerhold and Mayakovsky, the immediate result was a much needed finanacial shot-in-the-arm for the Meyerhold State Theatre. For three months the production played to enthusiastic audiences, and for once they were attracted to Number Twenty Sadovaya Street by something other than Meyerhold's latest theatrical innovation. There were three attractive aspects of the show for Moscow audiences: satire aimed at the Soviet state—a rarity by 1929; Mayakovsky—the most exciting and popular poet of the day; and Igor Ilinsky—a popular comic actor who was giving the most brilliant performance of his career. This combination of Mayakovsky, Ilinsky, and political irreverence overshadowed the directorial contribution of Meyerhold.

Actually, there was really nothing of Meyerhold's that suffered from being overshadowed. When the contributions of the Kukriniksy group, Rodchenko, and Shostakovich are added to those of Mayakovsky and Ilinsky it becomes evident that the production of *The Bedbug* was much less the immediate product of Meyerhold's thinking than the result of several contributors whose efforts he coordinated. Rarely, if ever, had Meyerhold functioned this way—certainly not in the decade of the twenties. Although the change was neither dramatic nor irreversible, after *The Bedbug* he never again asserted quite the degree of authority which had been his trademark for years.

At least some of the reasons for this subtle but—in light of subsequent productions—conclusive change in his approach are discernible; but any attempt to measure their relative importance must be speculative and the list itself is incomplete due to ignorance of personal factors that have gone unrecorded (or are recorded but unreleased). The first and most obvious of possible explanations is that he may have been getting a bit tired. Although in good health and looking considerably younger than his fifty-five years, he had been working arduously on political and artistic matters in the theatre virtually without interruption for thirty-one years. The growing political pressure was undoubtedly another factor. Individual assertiveness in the arts, even for much younger men, was becoming increasingly dangerous and difficult. And after Stalin's purge of party liberals in 1927 and 1928 Meyerhold's position of artistic independence was becoming less and less tenable.

A third factor may have been the increasing demands on Meyerhold's time resulting from the practical business of running a state theatre. The theatre was under threat of liquidation due, at least in part, to a growing financial deficit, but it is also quite likely that a theatre closer to the party line would have found it less difficult to sustain a subsidy. The fact that *The Bedbug* initiated a sequence of six consecutive Soviet dramas at the Meyerhold State Theatre—two of which were full-blown propaganda pieces—would seem to suggest that Meyerhold was well aware of what it would take to keep the doors of his theatre open. If his creative energies were less than fully aroused by such a steady diet of Soviet drama, it would hardly be surprising.

Furthermore, his managerial responsibilities began to divert more and more of his energies to matters that were important but nonetheless once removed from actual directing: drawn-out struggles with party censors in an effort to stage Erdman's *The Suicide** and Tretyakov's *I Want a Child* (a losing struggle in each case); company tours of France and eastern Russia in 1930 and 1931; and in 1931, work on a complete renovation of his theatre—a project that absorbed much of his time until it was taken out of his hands just prior to his disappearance in 1939. Whether these extracurricular activities were cause or effect of the apparent slackening of personal authority and innovation in his productions is impossible to know. But it would stand to reason that if his theatre was in serious jeopardy and he was vitally concerned with its preservation, he would have to divide his efforts between directing productions on the one hand and handling practical matters on the other.

*In a recent article for the *New York Times* (28 June 1970) Marc Slonim reports that *The Suicide* has been recently "unearthed" in Western Europe and that national premieres, starting in Sweden in March 1969, have been highly successful.

Attempts at Mollification

After *The Bedbug* Meyerhold's next production opened in the summer of 1929 in the city of Karkovye and subsequently moved into the Meyerhold State Theatre when the Moscow theatre season resumed in the fall. This was his production of Ilya Selvinsky's *Commander of the Second Army*—a rather unconventional piece of Soviet propaganda drama insofar as the villain was neither a Tsarist reactionary nor a Western capitalist but a Red Army commander whose fanaticism resulted in the needless loss of hundreds of troops. It was also an unconventional choice of dramatic genre for Meyerhold: his first production without a strong satirical element since *The Dawns* in 1920.

Commander of the Second Army was staged by Meyerhold in a highly formalized manner suggestive of the conventions of classical Greek tragedy—or, in Gorchakov's phrase, "Red Nibelungs."[8] The stage was completely enclosed in a semicircle of bare, plywood panels which reached from the stage floor to a height of about twenty-five feet.*

Attached to these panels and descending in a long curve from a high point down left (about eighteen feet above the stage to stage floor level at the opposite side) was another of Meyerhold's long stairways. Up center, under the descending stairway, was a kind of inner-below which sometimes contained realistic props and set pieces for brief interior scenes. For the most part, however, this was a bare, shallow, and completely unadorned setting and may well represent Meyerhold's most formalistic and nonrepresentational set conception.

Although the production was suggestive of relief staging it was not, strictly speaking, in accordance with the principles of Georg Fuchs (as was the *Sister Beatrice* production with Vera Komissarzhevskaya in 1908), since the proscenium arch was masked by the panels of the extended set and could not therefore serve as a frame for stage pictures. Nevertheless, the hieratic quality and tableaux impressions common to relief staging were unmistakable. Reacting

*The height of the proscenium opening in this old opera theatre was about forty feet. The proscenium arch was never removed but Meyerhold often masked it with scenery or plain masking pieces in order to eliminate it as a psychological barrier between audience and production.

to the results of such staging techniques for Selvinsky's drama, Boris Alpers complained that it was impossible to imagine these soldiers as recently departed peers and compatriots: "While still warm and living in our memory and our life, they have been transformed under the present conditions of the class struggle into works of sculpture on the stage. . . . They stand motionless holding their tall lances; . . . they move with . . . a slow and measured tread, the imprint of some strange reverie on every face."[9]

Although Alpers meant his description as a criticism, it was probably just the effect Meyerhold wanted. Whether Meyerhold actually intended the parade of dead "knights" of Communism's Red Army as a rebuke to the banality of Soviet life in 1929 (with its new "army" of portfolio-toting bureaucrats) is a moot question. More likely, he was simply giving what was, in his view, the appropriate scenic form to the play as Selvinsky wrote it: an epic saga in strict verse form which attempted to monumentalize a portion of Soviet history.

In December of 1929, by presenting Alexander Bezimensky's *The Shot,* Meyerhold again sought to bring the Meyerhold State Theatre more in line with the demand that state theatres feature Soviet dramas and dramatists. But as with *Roar China* in 1926 and *Window Into a Village* in 1927, as supervisor Meyerhold was once removed from the production. The actual direction was in the collective hands of S. V. Kozikov, V. F. Zaichikov, and A. E. Nyesterov.

The playwright Bezimensky was quite adept at toeing the party line, but *The Shot* resulted in his one close brush with party critics.* The play's leading character, Prishletsev, was yet another of those slick operators in the manner of Khlestakov *(The Inspector General),* Guliachkin *(The Warrant),* and Prisypkin *(The Bedbug).* He was a "genius at getting along,"[10] and Bezimensky's intention was to reveal the danger to the Soviet state of such types. But the party critics—reflecting perhaps a bit of justified

---

*Most of the contemporary Russian playwrights whose plays were staged by Meyerhold in the 1920s eventually had more than a "close brush" with authorities. Mayakovsky, Erdman, Tretyakov, Selvinsky, and Olesha had serious collisions with them.

paranoia—accused the play of being a satire on party functionaries in general and accused Bezimensky of being a disguised Trotskyite.

Just as the play was about to be driven off the stage by the irate press, the following was received by Bezimensky: "I have read *The Shot* and *Day of our Life*. I have found nothing 'petty-bourgeois' or 'anti-Party' in these works. Both of them, especially *The Shot*, can be considered models of revolutionary art for the present."[11] The signature was that of Comrade Stalin. And it was just this kind of thing that led men like Meyerhold to continue to believe that honest criticism—including satire—would be permitted and even encouraged if it could surmount the pedantry of minor party officials and critics.

In the year 1929, then, Meyerhold offered three successive Soviet dramas to the audiences at the Meyerhold State Theatre. But neither *The Bedbug, Commander of the Second Army,* nor *The Shot* resulted in anything like a reconciliation between Meyerhold and the party line critics. In fact, it was much more like a tug-of-war in which Meyerhold and the critics pulled in opposite directions on the idea of Soviet dramaturgy.

For Meyerhold, to forego the classics in order to encourage contemporary Soviet playwrights was one thing, but to also forego satire and theatricalism for the sake of the shallow-minded optimism of Socialist Realism was something else again. He seems to have been trying hard to work out some kind of ideological compromise. But there were apparently some areas that were so basic to his idea of theatre, Soviet or otherwise, that for Meyerhold they were nonnegotiable. To forego the theatre of masks, of the grotesque, and of satire would have been for Meyerhold not a compromise but a capitulation. And with his production of Mayakovsky's *The Bathhouse* in the spring of 1930 the tension nearly reached the breaking point: one month after the premiere in March, Mayakovsky—the robust, outspoken, poetic voice of the proletariat and idol of young Russians everywhere—took his own life with a single bullet through his heart.

A Last Blast: *The Bathhouse*

The Bathhouse was certainly not Meyerhold's most daringly

innovative piece of theatricalism, but it was his, and Mayakovsky's, most daring bit of political satire. Never before or ever
again did the stage of the Meyerhold State Theatre ring with such
unmitigated satirical criticism of Soviet bureaucracy.

> The Soviet bureaucrats who tolerated *The Bedbug* because it was
> largely incomprehensible found little to tolerate in *The Bathhouse*. The
> cutting edge was too sharp; the parodies of bureaucratic double-talk
> were too accurate; the portrait of Pobedonosikov was too evidently
> based on the reigning dictator. Although the play was performed—for
> Mayakovsky had too much authority and renown to be rejected from
> the theatre—the literary bloodhounds were in full pursuit.[12]

As in *The Bedbug,* Mayakovsky made his satirical points in *The
Bathhouse* through a comparison of the current state of affairs
with an imaginary future. But instead of projecting the present
into the future as he did in *The Bedbug,* he brought a
representative of the future into the midst of the present.

The play depicts the efforts of an inventor and his young
assistant to inform the Chief of the Federal Bureau of Coordina-
tion, Pobedonosikov, that they are on the verge of completing a
time machine and with a little financial assistance will be able to
complete the experiments. But the maze of bureaucratic red tape
is so obstructive and Pobedonosikov's preoccupation with handing
down slogans, arguing with his wife, and planning his vacations so
unending that the frustrated inventor must follow Pobedonosikov
home in an effort to get a hearing. There, on the landing of the
stairway just as Pobedonosikov is emerging from his apartment,
the machine suddenly bursts into action and the Phosphorescent
Woman (Znaida Raikh, of course) appears—a representative from
the future age of Communism.

This Future Age of Communism is entirely different from the
one depicted by Mayakovsky in *The Bedbug.* It is a time of virtual
perfection (the year is 2030) when all the difficulties and
temporary misdirections have been overcome. But most important, in the context of *The Bathhouse,* it is an age of future
perfection from which perspective may be gained on the values of
the present (1930). The Phosphorescent Woman, as the voice of

the future, is full of praise for Soviet accomplishments:

> You yourselves can't see the greatness of what you are doing. To us it is
> more apparent: we know what has already been achieved. . . . It was
> not until today, as I looked around me on my brief survey flight, that I
> fully understood the strength of your will and the rumbling of the
> stormy upheaval here. . . . You have no time to step back from your
> work and admire both it and yourselves. But I am glad to tell you of
> your greatness.[13]

So far, so good. Then comes the rub: she has been authorized to accept as passengers with her on her return to the Future Age of Communism "those persons . . . whose names will be remembered one hundred years from now."[14]

With that the die is cast and the outcome predictable. The time machine becomes a kind of bathhouse which not only washes the dirt and grime from the real toilers, but also washes away—leaves behind—the parasitic bureaucrats and their sycophants. The destiny of Pobedonosikov and those like him is not enshrinement but oblivion. And as the machine with its passengers of workers, mathematicians, the inventor, and the Phosphorescent Woman disappears in a flash of blue light and to the tune of "The March of Time," Pobedonosikov and his underlings find themselves "knocked flat and sprawling by the devilish wheel of time." [15] Pobedonosikov, left alone on the stage at the end, finally begins to get the idea:

> She, and you, and the author—all of you! What have you been trying
> to say here? That people like me aren't of any use to Communism?

CURTAIN [16]

The political satire of *The Bathhouse* was not just a personal vendetta by two embattled artists. At the Fifteenth Congress of the Soviet Communist Party in 1927 an extensive campaign was proclaimed against wasteful bureaucracy. Thus Meyerhold and Mayakovsky could argue that they were loyally following party policy. The problem was that in the eyes of every party functionary the wasteful bureaucratic bungling was something done by others. Since *The Bathhouse* didn't allow a distinction between good and bad bureaucrats, every functionary felt himself personally indicted.

Another complicating factor in the production of *The Bathhouse* was that Mayakovsky and Meyerhold devoted about as much time to satirizing current artistic dogma as political satire. The third act, for instance, took a Pirandellian turn when it opened with a confrontation between the director of *The Bathhouse* (not played by Meyerhold himself) and Pobedonosikov who, with his retinue of sycophants, had been watching the first two acts. A discussion about the appropriateness of the production up to that point broadens into a discussion about the "correct" form of theatre in general with Pobedonosikov charging that in the two acts they have just seen it has all been laid on too thick. "Life isn't like that," he complains. "It's unnatural. Not lifelike. Not the way things are. You'll have to rewrite that part—tone it down, poeticize it, soften the contours."[17]

The director argues that they are seeking to serve the people by stirring them up and exposing whatever is bad; but Pobedonosikov replies that he is not interested in being aroused: "You should create pleasant sights and sounds for my eyes and ears."[18] So the director proceeds to stage an impromptu ballet which turns into a broad satire on the current example of "appropriateness" in the Soviet theatre, *The Red Poppy* at the Bolshoy. But Pobedonosikov completely misses the obvious parody and instead is enchanted with the dancing girls and flitting elves: "Bravo! Splendid! When you have talent like that, how can you squander it on topical trifles—on frothy tabloid satire? What we have just seen is real art. It makes sense to me . . . and to the masses."[19] Finally, after making a pass at a couple of young actresses, Pobedonosikov and his party leave the stage and the play continues.

Meyerhold and Mayakovsky must have had a great deal of fun lampooning the very criticism that had so often been directed at them. But the results were ominous. According to Robert Payne, "Mayakovsky was sternly admonished. It was hinted that he was a reactionary, a Trotskyist, or worse. Stalin, who had been keeping a watchful eye on Mayakovsky, encouraged the attacks."[20] And by Nikolai Gorchakov's account, "The Bolshevik critics reacted . . .

with fury. Stalin himself began to hate Meyerhold now that the director had satirized the dictator's bureaucracy [not to mention the dictator himself], and the tragic end to Meyerhold's career became inevitable."[21] Needless to say, *The Bathhouse* was soon removed from the boards. Neither it nor *The Bedbug* was seen again until the post-Stalin era (mid-1950s).

In several respects the staging of *The Bathhouse*, which like *The Bedbug* was a Meyerhold-Mayakovsky joint effort, resembled the freewheeling constructivist productions at the Meyerhold Theatre in the early 1920s. Once again the bare stage (with back wall and wings in plain view) was fitted out with a huge rising zigzag of nonrepresentational steps and platforms. But also employed were a set of screens representing the inventor's workshop and an enormous Venetian blindlike apparatus which could be lowered in from the flies and on the slats of which were printed progressive slogans by Mayakovsky.*

Meyerhold used this stage setting in three different forms: the construction completely masked by screens and "blinds" (Act One and probably Two); the lower half of the construction revealed and used with the upper half still masked by the "blinds" (Act Three and probably Four); and finally, the entire construction revealed—three levels with connecting steps at approximately eight, fifteen, and twenty-four feet above the stage floor (probably Act Five and definitely Act Six).

In the performances as well as the setting the production of *The Bathhouse* resembled the Meyerhold productions of the early 1920s. Pre-acting and *tableaux vivants* had no place in Mayakovsky's hustling drama. There was not the slightest hint of the Red Nibelungs who had marched about the Meyerhold stage just a few months earlier in *Commander of the Second Army*. Instead, these were actors who apparently remembered well their early training in biomechanics. Set pieces were at a mininum and the actors were free to scamper about the virtually bare stage, steps, and platforms in their stylized contemporary attire as if they were part of a gymnastic circus. Not for nothing did Mayakovsky subtitle the play "A Drama in Six Acts, with a Circus and Fireworks."[22]

---

*"On the Iron Horse One Sits With Confidence! "; "Blaze Forth on the Village Tractor! "; "Ban Psychological Realism in the Theatre! " *(Vstrechi s Meyerholdom,* p. 464).

But in spite of all the delightful fireworks of both Meyerhold and Mayakovsky (and due, in part, to some of them), the critical attacks on *The Bathhouse* were venomous, and after about a week the production's run was terminated. Meyerhold was given permission to leave the country with members of his theatre for a tour of Germany and France and on the evening of April 15 he was in Berlin. That was when he received word of Mayakovsky's suicide.

It must have hit Meyerhold very hard for there had been few men, especially in the theatre, with whom he had been so compatible—both personally and artistically. His only immediate response recorded in the two-volume collection of his writings, speeches, and correspondences is a terse, two-line telegram:

Shocked by the death of the poetic genius and dear friend with whom we championed leftist art.

Vsevolod Meyerhold[23]

The collection does not indicate to whom the wire was sent, but most likely it was addressed to those in Moscow remaining at the Meyerhold State Theatre and was probably meant to stand as his public statement on the matter. For want of more personal correspondence we can only guess at the grief, frustration, and bitterness that he undoubtedly felt. He, as much as anyone, must have been aware of the part played by vindictive critics and officials in the suicide of his friend—certainly he had been under the gun as much as Mayakovsky as a result of their combined efforts on *The Bedbug* and *The Bathhouse.* And in the little verse penned by Mayakovsky before he pulled the trigger the poet expressed feelings that must have been easily understood, if not shared, by the director. It read,

"The incident is closed."
The love boat has been
Smashed against conventions.
I don't owe life anything,
And nothing will be gained
By counting over
Mutual hurts and slights.[24]

The death of Mayakovsky and the surrounding circumstances may well have been instrumental in Meyerhold's serious consideration of going to America. After six weeks in Germany, Meyerhold's company went to Paris in June and gave ten performances from their repertoire of *The Inspector General, The Forest,* and *The Magnificent Cuckold.* The reception at the Théâtre de Montparnasse—from audiences which included Louis Jouvet, Picasso, Dullin, Baty, and Cocteau—was full of acclaim despite protests from the Russian émigré community over Meyerhold's treatment of Gogol. When the company returned to Moscow at the end of June, Meyerhold and Raikh stayed on in France for a lengthy holiday.

Just before returning to Russia Meyerhold wrote to a Paris friend, Yuri Annenkov, that he was planning to go to America: "soon to Moscow. Then to New York (November, 1930)."[25] When Annenkov met Meyerhold and Znaida the next day he asked Meyerhold why he didn't go directly to America from Paris. "Meyerhold answered, 'Znaida. She's homesick. And I can fully understand this.' Raikh gave a slight smile."[26] Meyerhold did return to Moscow in September as planned, but he was destined never to see America.

D.E. Revised and *Final and Decisive*

Upon his return to Moscow the first thing Meyerhold did was to offer an updated version of his 1924 production, *D.E.* Not only was it time for the annual celebration of the Revolution,* it was also time to try to get back on better footing with the party. In a conversation with a correspondent from the *Moscow Evening News* he said:

> Instead of the previous fantastical-detective structure of *D.E.* in this next show, *D.S.E.* [Give Us a Soviet Europe!], we will show concrete contemporary conditions: echoes of the capitalist crisis [the Depression?], contradictory capitalist systems compared to the development of

---

*November 7 had been the premiere date for three other Meyerhold agitprop productions: *Mystery-Bouffe* (first ed.) in 1918, *The Dawns* in 1920, and *Lake Lyul* in 1923.

socialism in the USSR, threats by capitalists and their social-democratic minions . . . and so forth. . . .

The new production is harmonized politically immeasurably more than the previous *D.E.* 27

This sounds like an effort on Meyerhold's part to placate the party critics after the antagonism aroused by *The Bathhouse.* It was probably just that. Meyerhold was not a willing martyr bent on challenging party dogma at every step. He was prepared to compromise and do his fair share of ideological flag-waving. But in return he wanted the right to deal honestly and openly with problems facing the Soviet man in general and the Soviet artist in particular. And of course this meant dealing with them in a manner which accorded with his own ideas of theatre art. But the degree of independence which he sought to reserve for himself was not to be allowed.

After the revised version of *D.E.* in November, Meyerhold started the year 1931 with the February 7 premiere of Vsevolod Vishnevsky's *Final and Decisive*—the fifth (or sixth if one counts *D.S.E.*) consecutive Soviet play on the stage of the Meyerhold State Theatre since *Woe to Wit* in 1928. This play and the production given it by Meyerhold resulted in a theatrical hodge-podge that sought to please nearly everyone and ended in pleasing no one. According to Meyerhold,

The play and the production, *Final and Decisive,* are imbued with one idea: the readiness of Soviet citizens to defend the genuine frontiers of socialism—the readiness of Soviet citizens to make any sacrifice in the name of victory for the proletariat in the inevitable class struggle with the imperialist West.

In Vs. Vishnevsky's play there are three plans, gradually changing from one to the other and organically linked together: the struggle of art as one of the instruments of socialist development, the struggle with corruption in our ranks, and the heroic defense of the Soviet Union. 28

In Meyerhold's production the first of these three "plans"—the struggle of art—was established at the beginning of the show when an elaborate opening production number depicting a ludicrously idealized picture of life in the Red Navy (once again the parody of *The Red Poppy* was unmistakable) was interrupted by "real" sailors in the audience who came forward, took over the stage, and told the audience that they would show them a true story of naval life.

The second "plan"—corruption in the ranks—followed with an episodic account of the shenanigans and general debauchery of a group of sailors on a jag in Odessa. Finally, the third "plan"—defense of the Soviet Union—resulted when a group of guards and sailors made a Thermopylae-like defense of a vital frontier outpost at the advent of a future war with the West. And as the last of this handful of men who had made their final and decisive sacrifice gasped away his life, he struggled to chalk out on a screen the figures,[29]

$$
\begin{array}{r}
162,000,000 \\
-27 \\
\hline
161,999,973
\end{array}
$$

Message: having finally defeated the twenty-seven men in the bunker, the enemy now faced 161,999,973 more just like them. The last sailor then died with a smile on his lips. Immediately, however, he jumped up, faced the audience, and called for everyone who was ready to join in the defense of the USSR to rise and sing the *Internationale*[30]—the proletarian hymn which ends with the words, "It is our final and decisive battle!"*

The production seemed to have everything: parody of the mawkish in theatre, satirical grotesqueries in the exploits of the debauched sailors, plenty of pathos in the heroic realism, and a jubilant call-to-arms at the finale. Unfortunately, this Meyerhold cross section was completed with the seemingly inevitable dissatisfaction of the critics: "Bolshevism does not merely teach that one must die. Bolshevism teaches that one must conquer. . . . And if the play does not teach the need for victory, then what is left of

---

*It is interesting to note that the author of this paean to the glory of steadfastness in the face of the enemy, Vsevolod Vishnevsky, was fated to live through and chronicle the Nazi siege of Leningrad in the winter of 1941-1942 (see Harrison Salisbury's *The 900 Days*).

Act IV except for an original kind of Remarqueism and anti-Bolshevism? "[31]

When party critics refused to accept even such an unabashedly superpatriotic play as *Final and Decisive* it must have been increasingly clear to Meyerhold that no matter what he did—short of a public recantation and total submission to party-defined Socialist Realism—he would be consistently judged as out of step with the times.

Hamlet Joins the Proletariat: *List of Good Deeds*

Final and Decisive was followed four months later by Yuri Olesha's *List of Good Deeds*—premiere, 4 June 1931. This play was destined to be Meyerhold's last production at Number Twenty Sadovaya Street. In theatrical terms it bore little resemblance to the tumultuous productions of earlier years or the pre-acting "statuary" of his productions in the later 1920s. Furthermore, the play's theme was of a much more subjective nature than usually seen on the Meyerhold stage. But these matters notwithstanding, the play was, in part at least, a fitting conclusion for Meyerhold's eleven-year struggle to realize new forms of theatre under the Soviet regime.

Yuri Olesha's *List of Good Deeds* bore a certain resemblance to *The Teacher Bubus*. Like Faiko's play, Olesha's focused on the dilemma of a central character who was primarily a product of Imperial Russia and who now found herself unable to make a total commitment to Communism. But unlike Bubus, who was torn between the demands of Western capitalists on one hand and Soviet Communists on the other, Olesha's character was caught between the Communist demand for total commitment and the personal desire for privacy and neutrality.

As the play opens Lola Goncharova, a famous Soviet actress, has just completed a performance in the role of Hamlet; in an after-the-show discussion with the audience she tries to defend the work of a "bourgeois decadent" like William Shakespeare. Asked why she bothered doing *Hamlet* rather than a Soviet drama, she bluntly replies, "The contemporary plays are unimaginative, sketchy, false, heavy-handed, and obvious. Doing them impairs one's acting ability."[32]   And when another audience member says, "In our era . . . when we are involved in the breathtaking whirl of national development, the slobbering, soul-searching of your Hamlet is unbearably sickening," she answers: "Esteemed Comrades, I submit that in this breathtaking, swirling era, an artist must keep thinking slowly."[33]

Finally, she repeats the recorder scene between Hamlet and Guildenstern concluding with:

> 'Sblood, do you think I am easier to be played on than a pipe? Call me what instrument you will, though you can fret me, you cannot play upon me.
>
> (Pause.)
>
> Well, that's that. No one's applauding. That's all right with me. Close the discussion, then, Comrade Orlovsky.[34]

The point could hardly be missed, either by the audience in Olesha's play or the audience at the Meyerhold State Theatre. The fictional character Goncharova was speaking, through Hamlet, of the frustrations of Soviet artists in Stalin's Russia and the determination of some that, though they be fretted, they would not pipe forth the party tune.

Whereas artists such as Mayakovsky, Meyerhold, Olesha, and numerous others must have constantly weighed in their minds the good deeds and bad deeds of Soviet Communism, the character Goncharova kept an actual diary containing two such lists: a list of crimes against the individual and a list of the regime's assets—"Now, we'll put the two halves together," she tells a friend, "and that's me, my worries, my nightmares."[35]

Up to this point Olesha's play is provocative and, compared to the usual Soviet fare, profoundly honest. But after such a thoughtful and challenging beginning the play begins to deteriorate philosophically until in the end it resembles nothing so much as a medieval French miracle play in which the heroine sins mightily in the beginning so that her conversion in the end will be all the more marvelous.

In search of artistic freedom and personal fulfillment, Goncharova goes to Paris where she unintentionally falls in with the community of Russian émigrés—the real villians of the play—and momentarily succumbs to their lures of parties, balls, and fancy gowns. In order to get some money she seeks employment at a French theatre. But instead of finding the theatre in the West more appreciative of her talents, she discovers it to be little more than a house of venery selling tawdry jokes and pornographic stage gimmicks to a snickering, debauched audience. The director of the theatre responds to her audition (the recorder speech from *Hamlet*) that he might be able to use her "act" if she could liven it up a bit by playing some catchy tunes on an actual recorder. Furthermore, as a snappy conclusion he suggests she swallow the recorder, turn her back to the audience and "start blowing into the recorder from what we might call your reverse end! "[36]

Sickened and frustrated by the experience, Goncharova runs from the theatre and into the arms of some loyal Russian Communists on their way home from a trade mission to America.* But in their presence she learns that her diary has been stolen and the list of bad deeds published in the Russian émigré press as proof that the famous actress has left Russia in disgust and for good.

Despite the willingness of the delegates to forgive and their insistence that she return with them, Goncharova is too ashamed and instead rushes out into the streets of Paris to join some striking workers. At the height of the workers' confrontation with the police she shields the French Communist leader from a bullet fired by a Russian émigré. As she is dying she asks that her body be covered with a red flag, but at that moment the mounted police are heard approaching and "the unemployed exit in formation. Lola's body remains lying in the street uncovered. There are heard the strains of a march."[37]

In giving a comparatively realistic staging to Olesh's essentially realistic play Meyerhold offered his least stylized production since his work with the "Comrades of the New Drama." Contemporary street wear for the costumes—even for the satirized émigrés and Frenchmen—was worn with realistic makeup by actors who conducted themselves in a lifelike manner on the stage. Wall flats

---

*There is only one comment about America, but compared to the grisly portrait of Paris it is interesting. The trade delegate says that it's all right in the sense that there's plenty of everything, but it seems unorganized because there are no ration cards!

and door units were used for the interior scenes, which constituted most of the play, and although they did not extend far enough to completely mask the flies or wings, the selective lighting localized the interior scenes within the flats sufficiently to give a nearly fourth-wall illusion for those in the audience who wished to see it that way.

Although it is tempting to conclude from this that in his advancing years he began to yield to the realists, it is a temptation which should be resisted. After all, just a year earlier he had staged one of his most highly stylized productions in *The Bathhouse.* But, of course, Mayakovsky's play called for such treatment. So what we actually see is Meyerhold's growing willingness to let the drama itself determine the method of staging. No longer would he take a realistically conceived drama like *The Magnificent Cuckold, A Lucrative Post,* or *The Forest* and theatricalize it almost beyond recognition.

Depending on one's concept of the director's role this change might be regarded as a welcome, if belated, artistic maturation or as a loss of creative daring. But in the context of all that Meyerhold had said, done, and represented during a career in the theatre that stretched back over thirty years, it is hard to regard it as a positive or logical development.

But more important than whether one regards it as belated maturation or a falling off of creative energy is the fact that this was simply not the kind of directing at which he was accomplished. For the director who works primarily as a faithful servant of the playwright's script, the criterion of accomplishment must be the accuracy with which he represents on the stage every detail and subtlety of the book. And Meyerhold's genius was clearly not in the direction of detail, shading, and subtlety; rather, he played the innovator, using bold strokes, audacious surprises, and at times novelty for its own sake. Creativity thus inclined, as Meyerhold's manifestly was from his first theatrical efforts in 1892, would be unlikely to flourish when required to render faithfully another artist's creative vision.

Of course Meyerhold knew well the tricks of the trade. As a journeyman director in the service of the playwright he could function professionally and competently. And from 1932 to 1939 he did just that (not, however, with reticence and obsequiousness sufficient unto the demands of the party). But his few productions during these last years would have passed without historical notice, professionally competent though they were, had they not been the work of the man who had once been the very personification of threatrical experimentation.

Number Twenty Sadovaya Street Goes Dark

The old theatre at Number Twenty Sadovaya Street—known successively since the Revolution as the First Theatre of the R.S.F.S.R., the Actors' Theatre, the Theatre of GITIS, the Meyerhold Theatre, and finally the Meyerhold State Theatre—was sorely in need of major repair by 1931. After the opening of *List of Good Deeds* in June the theatre was closed the following October for renovation. During the season of 1931-1932 the company performed productions from their repertoire in Leningrad and Tashkent, and in the summer of 1932 they "temporarily" took up new residence in Moscow at the small Passage Theatre. After the old building had been demolished, Meyerhold submitted vastly more elaborate plans for the new structure than had originally been agreed upon. His sleight-of-hand worked, and construction of a splendid new amphitheatre was begun on the site of the old Meyerhold Theatre.

But Meyerhold never saw the completion of his new theatre—a horseshoe-shaped amphitheatre seating 1,600 people with a huge pear-shaped thrust stage containing an upstage and downstage revolve with a canopy of glass covering the entire theatre. It was nearing completion when the Meyerhold State Theatre was liquidated in January 1938.

Meyerhold himself was liquidated twenty-five months later on 2 February 1940*—eight days before his sixty-sixth birthday—after

*For several years it was rumored that Meyerhold was known to be still living at the end of World War II somewhere in Siberia. Later, it was announced that he had died in 1942. But now, according to the 1961 edition of the *Teatralnaya entsiklopediya,* the date and place of death have been set at 2 February 1940 in Moscow. The cause remains unmentioned; but considering the circumstances—death only a few months after the arrest, and in Moscow rather than a distant prison camp—a death from "unnatural" causes seems likely.

having been arrested in June 1939 following his speech denouncing Socialist Realism at the All-Union Congress of Stage Directors. Two weeks after his arrest and disappearance the mutilated body of his wife Znaida was discovered in their Moscow apartment. The "burglars" were never caught. The only thing missing was a file of Meyerhold's private papers.

Thus, when Meyerhold and his company departed the old theatre at Number Twenty Sadovaya Street after *List of Good Deeds* they were destined never to return to the site of Meyerhold's greatest achievements. For eleven years it had been a public laboratory of theatrical experimentation—the cutting edge of revolutionary fervor in the Russian theatre. Nothing like it had ever been seen in the history of the Russian theatre, and nothing quite like it has appeared since.

Epilogue

Despite seemingly propitious circumstances, Meyerhold's continued search for vital theatrical conventions never culminated in a persisting idea of theatre.[1]

This statement by Helen Chinoy in *Directors on Directing* represents what has become an almost axiomatic conclusion about Meyerhold's work. But is it really true? Or does such a statement imply an idea of theatre the nature and limits of which are a priori much too narrow to accommodate Meyerhold's theatrical vision? Certainly the range and variety of Meyerhold's productions—from the cryptic symbolism of *The Puppet Booth,* through the raucous mechanicalism of *The Magnificent Cuckold,* to the static statuary of *The Teacher Bubus*—would seem to suggest the absence of a consistent idea of theatre. Even Meyerhold's own statement that "all my efforts were directed at finding an organic form for the given content,"[2] seems to imply that his only operative concept of theatre was to realize the playwright's idea. But there was more to his work than this.

Meyerhold's theatre, especially during the twenties, was essentially a public laboratory in which he pursued experiments pointing toward a theatrical alternative to realism. A concise description of that alternative—which would amount to a statement of his idea of theatre—would be a paraphrase of a section of *Ampluya aktora: The theatre is essentially an example of the grotesque insofar as it is a deliberate exaggeration and reconstruction of nature and the unification of objects that are not united by either nature or the customs of our daily life.*[3]

The functional part of this description is in "a deliberate exaggeration and reconstruction of nature." Despite their obvious differences, this applies equally to *The Puppet Booth, The Magnificent Cuckold,* and *The Teacher Bubus.* But of course much is left unsaid by such a description. Most notably, in what spirit and to what end did Meyerhold deliberately exaggerate and reconstruct nature? Here a claim cannot be made for absolute consistency on his part, but allowing for exceptions, I believe that it can be said that *his work was done in the spirit of satirical demystification, toward the end of revealing that which was bogus and fatuous, and of promoting thereby a renaissance of man's primordial joie de vivre.* As a Bolshevik his immediate audience was Russian society, but as an artist his audience included all of the Western world.

It is now forty-five years since Meyerhold's climactic production of *The Inspector General* and thirty-two years since his disappearance. But much of the Western theatre—audience and practioner alike—has yet to catch up with him. In 1970 a critic and scholar such as Leonard Pronko finds it necessary and justified to charge, "We have lost our sense of joy; we are overwhelmed by our seriousness and by our commitment to the intellect. And yet the sense of joy is fundamental not only to play, but to those extensions of play, ritual and drama."[4] And according to Peter Brook, "the time is ripe for a Meyerhold to appear."[5]

Although Pronko and Brook may not have the same idea of theatre in mind, they, along with such commentators on the modern theatre as Mordecai Gorelik,[6] Herbert Blau,[7] Jerzy Grotowski,[8] and many others of widely diverse points of view recognize in Meyerhold a prototypical practitioner of the kind of theatre which they feel bears both the main line of theatre's traditions and the distinct imprint of the twentieth century.

But if in admiration of his accomplishments we enshrine his memory in some kind of sacerdotal catafalque, we would be well advised to recall Meyerhold's own words on the subject: "If, after my death, you have to read memoirs in which I am portrayed as a priest, puffed up with my own importance and uttering eternal truths, I charge you to declare that this is all libel, that I was always a very happy person."[9]

We should sustain an image of Meyerhold as one of his beloved cabotins: a gangly figure of disproportionate features, switching abruptly from one attitude to another, audaciously confident that his fairground booth is eternal—"Its heroes do not die; they simply change their aspect and assume new forms."[10]

Appendix: Meyerhold's Productions

Author	Play	Designer	Theatre	Premiere
(From September, 1902 to April, 1905 Meyerhold worked in the provinces as an actor and director with the troupe which he organized with A. S. Kosheverov: Comrades of the New Drama. They did over 150 different scenes, one acts, and full-length plays—most of them by contemporary authors. His first directorial work in either Moscow or St. Petersburg was with the Moscow Art Theatre Studio in the summer of 1905.)				
M. Maeterlinck	*Death of Tintagiles*	S. Sudeikin (1, 2, 3 acts), N. Sapunov (4 and 5 acts)	MXAT Studio (Moscow)	Summer, 1905 (Studio never opened to public.)
G. Hauptmann	*Schluck und Jau*	N. Ulyanov	"	"
S. Przybyszewski	*Snow*	V. Denisov	"	"
H. Ibsen	*Love's Comedy*	"	"	"
(From February to August, 1906, Meyerhold worked with the Comrades of the New Drama, touring Tiflis, Rostov-on-the-Don, and Poltava.)				
H. Ibsen	*Hedda Gabler*	N. Sapunov	Theatre of V. Komissarzhevskaya (Petersburg)	11/10 1906
S. Yushkevich	*In the City*	V. Kolenda	"	11/13
M. Maeterlinck	*Sister Beatrice*	S. Sudeikin	"	11/22

1907

Author	Play	Designer	Theatre	Premiere
S. Przybyszewski	*The Eternal Story*	V. Denisov	Theatre of V. Komissarzhevskaya	12/4
H. Ibsen	*Nora (A Doll's House)*: VEM's restaging of a play already in VK's repertoire		"	12/18
A. Blok	*The Puppet Booth*	N. Sapunov	"	12/30
M. Maeterlinck	*Miracle of St. Anthony*	V. Kolenda	"	"
G. Gerberg	*Love's Tragedy*	V. Surenyants	"	1/8
H. Ibsen	*Love's Comedy*	V. Denisov	"	1/22
H. Von Hofmannsthal	*Wedding of Zobyedy*	B. Anisfeld	"	2/12
L. Andreyev	*Life of Man*	VEM (plan), B. Kolenda	"	2/22
L. Andreyev	*To the Stars*	unlisted	Casino Theatre of V. Gardina (Terioky, Finland)	5/27
	An evening of scenes and dances from Strauss' *Salome*	N. Saven	The Musical Studio (Ollila)	6/20
	"An Evening of New Art"—readings by poets and scenes from Tchaikovsky	N. Saven	"	7/13
F. Wedekind	*Spring's Awakening*	V. Denisov	Theatre of V. Komissarzhevskaya	9/15
M. Maeterlinck	*Pelleas and Melisande*	V. Denisov	"	10/10

Author	Title	Designer/Director	Theatre	Date	Year
F. Sologub	*Death's Victory*	VEM	Theatre of V. Komissarzhevskaya	11/6	
M. Maeterlinck	*Sister Beatrice*	K. Kostin	Troupe under direction of VEM and R. A. Ungerna. (Bitebsk, Kerson, and other cities)	2/17	1908
A. Blok	*The Puppet Booth*	"	"	2/19	
F. Wedekind	*Vampire*	"	"	2/20	
H. Von Hofmannsthal	*Electra*	"	"	2/21	
H. Ibsen	*Hedda Gabler*	"	"	2/22	
F. Sologub	*Death's Victory*	"	"	2/23	
L. Andreyev	*Life of Man*	"	"	2/24	
G. Hauptmann	*Prisoners of Karl the Great*	"	"	3/12	
H. Ibsen	*Builder Solness (Master Builder)*	"	"		
K. Hamsun	*At the Gates of the Kingdom*	"	"	3/13	
K. Hamsun	*At the Gates of the Kingdom*	A. Golovin	Alexandrinsky Theatre (Petersburg)	9/30	
O. Wilde	*Salome*	L. Baskt (Choreography, M. Fokine)	Mikhailovsky Theatre (Petersburg)	Public performance disallowed by censor	
P. Potemkin	*Petrushka*	M. Dobuzhinsky	"The Seashore" (Petersburg)	12/6	

Author	Play	Designer	Theatre	Premiere
V. Trakhtenburg	The Last from Waysherov	M. Dobuzhinsky	"The Seashore"	12/6
F. L. Sollogub	Welcome, Have a Seat	I. Bilibin	"	"
N. Gogol	A Lawsuit	A. Sherbashidze	Alexandrinsky	3/19 1909
R. Wagner	Tristan and Isolde	"	Marinsky Theatre (Petersburg)	10/30
D. Merezhkovsky	Pavel I (two scenes)	"	Private apt.	Jan. 1910
E. Khardt	The Jest of Tantrise	"	Alexandrinsky	3/9
P. Calderon	Adoration of the Cross	S. Sudeikin	"Tower Theatre" (Apt. of V. Ivanov, Petersburg)	4/19
A. Schnitzler (Transcribed for pantomime by "Dr. Dapertutto")	The Scarf of Columbine	N. Sapunov	Interlude House (Petersburg)	10/12
J. -B. Molière	Don Juan	A. Golovin	Alexandrinsky	11/9
E. Znosko-Borovsky	The Transfigured Prince	S. Sudeikin	Interlude House	12/3
M. Mussorgsky	Boris Godunov	A. Golovin	Marinsky	1/6 1911
Y. Belyaev	The Red Cafe	"	Alexandrinsky	3/23
L. N. Tolstoy	The Living Corpse	K. Korovin	"	9/28
V. N. Solovyev	Harlequin, The Marriage Broker	K. Yevseyev	Assembly Rooms of the Nobility (Petersburg)	11/8
C. Gluck	Orpheus	A. Golovin	Marinsky	12/21

Author	Title	Designer	Location	Date	Year
"Dr. Dapertutto"	Being in Love	V. Schukaev / A. Yakovlev	Home of O. K. and N.P. Karabchevskikh (Petersburg)	Jan.	1912
K. Balmont	Three Blossoms	unlisted	Tenishevsky Hall (Petersburg)	3/5	
"Dr. Dapertutto"	Being in Love (second version)	N. Kulbin	Fellowship of Actors, Writers, Artists, and Musicians.	6/9	
V. N. Solovyev	Harlequin, the Marriage Broker (second version)	"	(Terioky, Finland)	"	
P. Calderon	Adoration of the Cross (second version)	Y. Bondi	"	6/29	
A. Strindberg	Crimes and Crimes	"	"	7/14	
G. B. Shaw	You Never Can Tell	"	"	7/15	
F. Sologub	Hostages of Life	A. Golovin	Alexandrinsky	11/6	
R. Strauss	Electra	"	Marinsky	2/18	1913
G. D'Annunzio	Pisanelle	L. Bakst	Châtelet Theatre (Paris)	6/11	
F. Nozarre and G. Muller	Seville Cafe	K. Veshilov	Suvorin Theatre (Petersburg)	12/16	
A. Pinero	Halfway (Mid-Channel)	A. Golovin	Alexandrinsky	1/30	1914
A. Blok	The Unknown Woman	Y. Bondi	Tenishevsky	4/7	
A. Blok	The Puppet Booth	"	"	"	
G. de Maupassant	Mademoiselle Fifi	S. Sudeikin	Suvorin	8/15	
E. Wolf-Ferrari	Secret Susan (comic opera)	"	Marinsky	9/20	
A. Bobrishchev-Pushkin	A World Festival	"	"	10/11	

Author	Play	Designer	Theatre	Premiere
M. Lermontov	Two Brothers	A. Golovin	Alexandrinsky	1/10 1915
	"An Evening at the Studio of Vs. Meyerhold"	A. Rykov	Meyerhold Studio (Petersburg)	2/12
Z. Hippius	The Green Ring	A. Golovin	Alexandrinsky	2/18
P. Calderon	The Constant Prince	"	"	4/23
G. B. Shaw	Pygmalion	P. Lambin	"	4/26
O. Wilde (scenario by VEM)	Portrait of Dorian Gray (film)	V. Egorov	Thiemann and Reinhardt Film Co. (Moscow)	Completed, July; premiere, 12/1
A. Ostrovsky	The Storm	A. Golovin	Alexandrinsky	1/9 1916
M. Glinka	Argonsky's Desire (ballet)	" (Choreography, M. Fokine)	Marinsky	1/29
A. Schnitzler (transcribed for pantomime by "Dr. Dapertutto")	The Scarf of Columbine (second version)	S. Sudeikin	"The Comedians' Rest" (Petersburg)	4/18
S. Przybyszewski (scenario by V. Akhramovich)	The Strong Man (film)	V. Egorov	Thiemann and Reinhardt Film Co.	Completed, Aug.: premiere, 12/9, 1917
D. Merezhkovsky	The Romantics	A. Golovin	Alexandrinsky	10/21
A. Sukhovo-Kobylin	Krechinsky's Wedding	B. Almedingen	"	1/25 1917
A. Dargomyzhsky	The Stone Guest	A. Golovin	Marinsky	1/27

Author	Title	Designer	Theatre	Date	Year
M. Mussorgsky	A Marriage	unlisted	Hall on Petrovsky St. (Petrograd)	2/24	
M. Lermontov	Masquerade	A. Golovin	Alexandrinsky	2/25	
O. Wilde	An Ideal Husband	"	The School of Scenic Art (Mikhailovsky Theatre)	4/24	
A. Sukhovo-Kobylin	The Case	B. Almedingen	Alexandrinsky	8/30	1918
A. Sukhovo-Kobylin	The Death of Tarelkin	"	"	10/23	
N. Rimsky-Korsakov	The Snow Maiden	K. Korovin	Marinsky	12/14	
H. Ibsen	Lady from the Sea	A. Golovin	Alexandrinsky	12/15	
L. N. Tolstoy	Peter the Baker	"	"	4/8	
I. Stravinsky	The Nightingale	VEM (plan)	Marinsky	5/30	
H. Ibsen	Nora (A Doll's House)	V. Dimitriev	Workers' Theatre (Petrograd)	6/7	
D. Ober	Fenella	P. Lambin	Marinsky	11/7	
V. Mayakovsky	Mystery-Bouffe	K. Malevich	Theatre of Musical Drama (Petrograd)	11/7	
H. Ibsen	Nora (A Doll's House) (revised version)	unlisted	The First Soviet Theatre of Lenin (Novorossisk)	8/6	1920
E. Verhaeren (adapted by VEM and V. Bebutov)	The Dawns	V. Dimitriev	First Theatre of the R.S.F.S.R. (Moscow)	11/7	

Author	Play	Designer	Theatre	Premiere	
V. Mayakovsky	*Mystery-Bouffe* (second version)	V. Kiselev, A. Lavinsky, V. Khrakovsky	First Theatre of the R.S.F.S.R. (Moscow)	5/1	1921
H. Ibsen (adapted by VEM and V. Bebutov)	*League of Youth*	VEM, V. Bebutov, O. Zhdanov	"	8/7	
H. Ibsen (adapted by VEM)	*Nora (A Doll's House)* (revised version)	VEM	The Actors' Theatre (Moscow)	4/20	1922
F. Crommelynck	*The Magnificent Cuckold*	L. Popova	"	4/25	
A. Sukhovo-Kobylin	*The Death of Tarelkin* (revised version)	V. Stepanova	Theatre of GITIS (Moscow)	11/24	
"AsGoTret" (N. Aseyev, S. Gorodyetsky, and S. Tretyakov)	*Verturnaf*	V. Palnov	Theatre of the Revolution (Moscow)	Dec.; no public performance	
M. Martinet (adapted by S. Tretyakov)	*The Earth Rebellious (Night)*	L. Popova	Meyerhold	3/4	1923
A. Ostrovsky	*A Lucrative Post*	V. Shestakov	Theatre of the Revolution	5/15	
A. Faiko	*Lake Lyul*	"	"	11/7	
A. Ostrovsky (adapted by VEM)	*The Forest*	VEM (plan), V. Fedorov	Meyerhold	1/19	1924
I. Ehrenburg (dramatized by M. Podgayets and others)	*D. E. (Give Us Europe!)*	VEM (plan), I. Shlepyanov	"	6/15	

Author	Title	Designer	Theater	Date	Year
A. Faiko	The Teacher Bubus	VEM (plan) / I. Shlepyanov	Meyerhold	1/29	1925
N. Erdman	The Warrant	VEM (plan) / I. Shlepyanov	"	4/20	
N. Gogol (adapted by VEM and M. Korenyev)	The Inspector General	VEM (plan) / V. Kiselyev	Meyerhold State	12/9	1926
F. Crommelynck	The Magnificent Cuckold (revised version)	L. Popova	"	1/26	1928
A. Griboyedov (adapted by VEM and M. Korenyev)	Woe to Wit (Woe from Wit)	V. Shestakov	"	3/12	
V. Mayakovsky	The Bedbug	VEM (plan) / Kukryniksy Group / A. Rodchenko	"	2/13	1929
I. Selvinsky	Commander of the Second Army	VEM (plan) / S. Vaktangov	" / "	12/24 (premiere in Karkovye)	1930
V. Mayakovsky	The Bathhouse	VEM (plan) / S. Vakhtangov	"	3/16	1930
I. Ehrenburg and B. Kellerman	D.S.E. (revision of D. E.)	VEM (plan) / I. Shlepyanov	"	11/7	
Vs. Vishnevsky	Final and Decisive	VEM (plan) / S. Vakhtangov	"	2/7	1931
Y. Olesha	List of Good Deeds	VEM (plan) / S. Vakhtangov	"	6/4	

Author	Play	Designer	Theatre	Premiere
J.-B. Molière	Don Juan (restaging of 1910 production)	A. Golovin	State Drama Theatre (Leningrad)	12/26 1932
Y. German	Prelude	I. Leystikov	Meyerhold State*	1/28 1933
A. Sukhovo-Kobylin	Krechinsky's Wedding (revised version)	V. Shestakov	"	4/14 (premiere in Leningrad)
M. Lermontov	Masquerade (restaging of 1917 production)	A. Golovin	State Drama	12/25
A. Dumas-fils	Lady of the Camellias	VEM (plan) I. Leystikov	Meyerhold State	3/19 1934
P. Tchaikovsky (from Pushkin)	Queen of Spades	L. Chupyatov	Maly Theatre (Leningrad)	1/25 1935
A. Chekhov (three short stories dramatized by VEM)	Thirty-three Fainting Spells	VEM (plan) V. Shestakov	Meyerhold State	3/25
A. Pushkin	The Stone Guest (radio production)	—	All-Union Network (Moscow)	4/17
A. Griboyedov	Woe to Wit (revised version)	VEM (plan) V. Shestakov	Meyerhold State	9/25 (premiere in Leningrad)
A. Pushkin	The Stone Guest (concert version)	—	"	2/10 1937

Author	Title	Designer	Theatre/Company	Date
A. Pushkin	Rusalka (radio production)	—	All-Union Network	3/24
L. Seyfullina	Natasha	F. Antonov	Meyerhold State	April; no public performance
N. Ostrovsky (dramatization by Gabrilovich)	One Life (from How the Steel Was Tempered)	V. Stenberg	"	Nov.; no public performance
M. Lermontov	Masquerade (revised version)	A. Golovin	Pushkin Theatre (Leningrad)	12/29 1938
	Unfinished Productions			
A. K. Tolstoy	Tsar Fedor Ivanovich	D. Strelletsky	Alexandrinsky	1908-1909
K.-B. Gluk	Queen of May	A. Golovin	"	1913
F. Sologub	Witchcraft (film)	V. Tatlin	Thiemann and Reinhardt Film Co.	1917
W. Shakespeare	Hamlet			1920-1938
I. Aksenov	Battles and Victories (mass spectacle)	L. Popova	Moscow	1921
G. B. Shaw	Heartbreak House	S. Eisenstein	Actors'	1922
P. Merimee	Jaquerie		Meyerhold	1923
J. Bizet	Carmen		"	1925
A. Pushkin	Boris Godunov	S. Isakov	Vakhtangov Studio (Moscow)	1925-1926

*Starting with the production of *Prelude* the Meyerhold State Theatre was relocated into the former Passage Theatre while the old building on Sadovaya Street was remodeled. The remodeling was finally nearing completion in the summer of 1939 when Meyerhold was purged.

Author	Play	Designer	Theatre	Premiere
S. Tretyakov	I Want A Child	VEM L. Lisitsky	Meyerhold State	1927-1930
P. Hindemith	Day's Tidings	VEM (plan) S. Koskov I. Leystikov	Maly	1931-1932
N. Erdman	The Suicide		Meyerhold State	1932
V. Mayakovsky	The Bedbug (revised version)	VEM	"	1936
A. Pushkin	Boris Godunov	V. Shestakov	"	1936
S. Prokofiev	The Kotko Family	A. Tishler	Stanislavsky Opera Theatre (Moscow)	1939

Supervised or Co-directed productions

Author	Play	Designer	Theatre	Premiere
P. Claudel	Exchange	G. Yakulov	Kamerny Theatre (with Tairov)	1918
R. Wagner	Rienzi	"	First Theatre of the R.S.F.S.R.	1921
GVIRM Students	The Paris Commune	GVIRM Students	Workers' Factory (Moscow)	1922
E. Toller	The Machine Wreckers	V. Komardenkov	Theatre of the Revolution	11/3 1922
E. Toller	Man and the Masses	V. Shestakov	"	1/26 1923

S. Tretyakov	*Roar China*	S. Efrimenko	Meyerhold (directed by V. Fedorov)	1/23	1926
VEM and R. Akulshin	*Window Onto a Village*	V. Shestakov	Meyerhold State	11/8	1927
A. Bezymensky	*The Shot*	V. Kalinin L. Pavlov	"	12/19	1929
G. Verdi	*Rigoletto*	M. Bobyshov	Stanislavsky Opera (with Stanislavsky —the last show for both men)	3/10	1939

Notes

Preface

1. Quoted in "The Emergence of the Director," by Helen Krich Chinoy in *Directors on Directing,* ed. Toby Cole and Helen Krich Chinoy (New York, 1953), p. 57.
2. Norris Houghton, "Theory Into Practice: A Reappraisal of Meierhold," *ETJ,* 20 (October 1968), 438.
3. From Meyerhold's last speech to the All-Union Congress of Directors in June 1939 as quoted by Nikolai A. Gorchakov, *The Theatre in Soviet Russia,* trans. Edgar Lehrman (New York, 1957), p. 363.

Chapter 1

1. Alexander Gladkov, "Meyerhold Speaks," trans. Karen Black, in *Pages from Tarusa,* ed. Andrew Field (Boston, 1963), p. 321.
2. Gorchakov, *The Theatre in Soviet Russia,* p. 364.
3. Harrison Salisbury, "Theatre: The Naked Truth," *The Soviet Union: The Fifty Years,* ed. Harrison Salisbury (New York, 1967), p. 191.
4. Nikolai Volkov, *Meyerhold,* 2 vols. (Moscow, 1929), 1:31.
5. Yuri Jelagin, *Temny geny* (New York, 1955), p. 68.
6. Ibid., p. 83.
7. Gladkov, "Meyerhold Speaks," *Pages from Tarusa,* p. 311.
8. Konstantin Stanislavsky, *My Life in Art,* trans. J. J. Robbins (New York, 1957), p. 429.
9. Ibid., pp. 437, 438.
10. Feodor Komissarzhevsky, *Myself and the Theatre* (New York, 1930), p. 78.
11. Vsevolod E. Meyerhold, *O teatr* (St. Petersburg, 1913), p. 199.
12. Vsevlod E. Meyerhold, "Notes on Productions," *Meyerhold on Theatre,* trans. Edward Braun (New York, 1969), p. 72.

13. Ibid., p. 70.
14. Quoted in *An Anthology of Russian Plays,* ed. and trans. F. D. Reeve, 2 vols. (New York, 1963), 2:164.
15. Meyerhold, "The Fairground Booth," *Meyerhold on Theatre,* p. 127.
15. Meyerhold, "Inaugural Speech to the Company of the R.S.F.S.R. I," *Meyerhold on Theatre,* p. 170.
17. Gladkov, "Meyerhold Speaks," *Pages from Tarusa,* p. 312.
18. Volkov, *Meyerhold,* 1:342; Jelagin, *Temny geny,* p. 135.
19. Volkov, *Meyerhold,* 1:346.
20. Quoted in Marc Slonim, *Russian Theatre from the Empire to the Soviets* (New York, 1962), p. 218.
21. Ibid.
22. Jelagin, *Temny geny,* p. 141.
23. Slonim, *Russian Theatre,* p. 218.
24. Ibid.
25. Meyerhold, "The Fairground Booth," *Meyerhold on Theatre,* pp. 130-134.
26. Stanislavsky, *My Life in Art,* p. 437.

Chapter 2

1. Huntley Carter, *The New Theatre and Cinema of Soviet Russia* (London, 1924), p. 13.
2. Slonim, *Russian Theatre,* p. 260.
3. Carter, *New Theatre of Russia,* p. 31.
4. Gorchakov, *Theatre in Soviet Russia,* p. 134.
5. Ibid., p. 137.
6. Meyerhold, *V. E. Meyerhold: statyi, pisma, rechi, besedy,* 2 vols. (Moscow, 1968), 2:18.
7. Gorchakov, *Theatre in Soviet Russia,* p. 420.
8. Ibid., p. 138.
9. Meyerhold, *V. E. Meyerhold,* 2:17.
10. Meyerhold, *O teatr,* p. 40.
11. Meyerhold, *V. E. Meyerhold,* 2:17.
12. Ibid., 2:515.
13. Gorchakov, *Theatre in Soviet Russia,* p. 114.
14. Meyerhold, *V. E. Meyerhold,* 2:514.
15. Gorchakov, *Theatre in Soviet Russia,* p. 113.
16. Jelagin, *Temny geny,* p. 233.
17. Gorchakov, *Theatre in Soviet Russia,* p. 137.
18. Carter, *New Theatre of Russia,* p. 73.
19. Meyerhold, *V. E. Meyerhold,* 2:145.
20. Vladimir Mayakovsky, *The Complete Plays of Vladimir Mayakovsky,* trans. Guy Daniels (New York, 1968), pp. 45-47.
21. Ibid., p. 44.
22. Alexander Fevralsky, "Vnachale dvadtsatikh godov i pozhe," *Vetrechi s Meyerholdom* (Moscow, 1967), p. 183.
23. Slonim, *Russian Theatre,* p. 267.
24. Fevralsky, "Nvachale dvadtsatikh godov i pozhe," *Vstrechi s Meyerholdom,* p. 183.
25. *Sovietsky teatr-dokumenty i materialy, 1917-1967,* ed. A. E. Yufit (Leningrad, 1968), 1:142.

Chapter 3

1. Meyerhold, "The Fairground Booth," *Meyerhold on Theatre,* p. 122.
2. Ibid., p. 123.

3. Arthur Miller, "In Russia," *Harper's Magazine* 239 (September 1969), 60.
4. Ibid.
5. Meyerhold, "The Fairground Booth," *Meyerhold on Theatre*, p. 122.
6. Ibid., p. 123.
7. Alexy Gripich, "Uchitel steny," *Vstrechi s Meyerholdom*, p. 122.
8. Ibid.
9. Ibid.
10. Ibid.
11. Ibid.
12. Ibid., p. 123.
13. Ibid.
14. Ibid., p. 125.
15. Volkov, *Meyerhold*, 2:363.
16. Alexandra Smirnova, "V studii na borodinskoy," *Vstrechi s Meyerholdom*, p. 92.
17. Vsevolod E. Meyerhold, *Le théâtre théâtral*, trans. Nina Gourfinkel (Paris, 1963), p. 104.
18. Ibid., p. 108.
19. Gladkov, "Meyerhold Speaks," *Pages from Tarusa*, p. 321.
20. Meyerhold, *Le théâtre théâtral*, p. 104.
21. Ibid.
22. Gorchakov, *Theatre in Soviet Russia*, p. 69.
23. Jelagin, *Temny geny*, p. 188.
24. Fevralsky, "Vnachale Dvadtsatikh godov i pozhe," *Vstrechi s Meyerholdom*, p. 185.
25. Ibid.
26. Sergei Yutkevtch, "Doktor Dapertutto, ili sorok let spustya," *Vstrechi s Meyerholdom*, p. 211.
27. Fevralsky, "Vnachale dvadtsatikh godov i pozhe," *Vstrechi s Meyerholdom*, p. 185.
28. Gorchakov, *Theatre in Soviet Russia*, p. 202.
29. Ibid.
30. Ibid., p. 203.
31. Ibid., p. 202.
32. Ibid., p. 204.
33. Ibid., p. 204.
34. Meyerhold, "Tristan and Isolde," *Meyerhold on Theatre*, p. 92.
35. Meyerhold, "Velikodushnii rodonosets," *V. E. Meyerhold*, 2:47.
36. Ibid., 2:604.
37. Ibid., 2:592-610.
38. Yutkevich, "Doktor Dapertutto, ili sorok let spustya," *Vstrechi s Meyerholdom*, p. 211.
39. Ibid., p. 212.
40. Gorchakov, *Theatre in Soviet Russia*, p. 199.

Chapter 4

1. Meyerhold, "The Magnanimous Cuckold," *Meyerhold on Theatre*, p. 205.
2. Quoted by Jan-Albert Goris in his introduction to *Two Great Belgian Plays, About Love*, trans. Marnix Gijsen (New York, 1966), p. xi.
3. Gorchakov, *Theatre in Soviet Russia*, p. 199.
4. Boris Alpers, *Theatre of the Social Mask*, trans. Mark Schmidt (New York, 1934), p. 29.
5. Meyerhold, *V. E. Meyerhold*, 2:523.
6. Meyerhold, "The Magnanimous Cuckold," *Meyerhold on Theatre*, p. 204.
7. Gorchakov, *Theatre in Soviet Russia*, p. 363.
8. Jan Kott, "Theatre and Literature," *Theatre Notebook: 1947-1967*, trans. Boleslaw Taborski (New York, 1968), p. 264.

9. Ibid., p. 265.
10. Ibid., p. 266.
11. Ibid., p. 268.
12. Meyerhold, "The Magnanimous Cuckold," *Meyerhold on Theatre*, p. 204.
13. Alexander Sukhovo-Kobylin, *The Death of Tarelkin*, in *The Trilogy of Alexander Sukhovo-Kobylin*, trans. Harold B. Segel (New York, 1969), p. 261.
14. Alexy Gvozdyev, *Teatr imeni Vsevolod Meyerhold, 1920-1926* (Leningrad, 1927), p. 33.
15. Ibid.
16. Braun, *Meyerhold on Theatre*, p. 187.
17. Meyerhold, "The Magnanimous Cuckold," *Meyerhold on Theatre*, p. 204.
18. Yuri Annenkov, *Dnevnik moikh vstrech* (New York, 1966), 2:61.
19. Gorchakov, *Theatre in Soviet Russia*, p. 73.
20. Slonim, *Russian Theatre*, p. 268.
21. Ilya Ehrenburg, *Memoirs: 1921-1941*, trans. Tatania Shebunina (New York, 1964), p. 426.

Chapter 5

1. *Vstrechi s Meyerholdom*, illus., p. 240.
2. Gorchakov, *Theatre in Soviet Russia*, p. 428.
3. Braun, *Meyerhold on Theatre*, p. 187.
4. Gorchakov, *Theatre in Soviet Russia*, p. 449.
5. Bolislav Rostotsky, *O rezhissorskom tvorchestve V. E. Meyerholda* (Moscow, 1960), p. 44.
6. Ibid.
7. Ibid., p. 43.
8. Ibid.
9. Ibid.
10. Alexy Faiko, "Ozero Lyul," *Vstrechi s Meyerholdom*, p. 298.
11. Ibid., p. 299.
12. Ibid.
13. Ibid.
14. Ibid.
15. Ibid.
16. Ibid.
17. Alexy Faiko, "Ozero lyul," *Vstrechi s Meyerholdom*, as quoted in Braun, *Meyerhold on Theatre*, p. 190.
18. D. S. Mirsky, *A History of Russian Literature from Its Beginning to 1900*, ed. Francis Whitfield (New York, 1958), p. 250.
19. Alexander Ostrovsky, *Five Plays of Alexander Ostrovsky*, trans. E. K. Bristow (New York, 1969), p. 360.
20. Meyerhold, *V. E. Meyerhold*, 2:56.
21. Gorchakov, *Theatre in Soviet Russia*, p. 207.
22. Slonim, *Russian Theatre*, p. 270.
23. Alpers, *Theatre of the Social Mask*, p. 34, and Norris Houghton, *Moscow Rehearsals* (New York, 1936), p. 93.
24. Slonim, *Russian Theatre*, p. 270.
25. Braun, *Meyerhold on Theatre*, p. 192.
26. Alpers, *Theatre of the Social Mask*, p. 34.
27. Meyerhold, *O teatr*, p. 40.
28. Slonim, *Russian Theatre*, p. 270.
29. Gorchakov, *Theatre in Soviet Russia*, p. 207.
30. Boris Zakhava, *Sovremniki* (Moscow, 1969), p. 340.

31. Meyerhold, "The Magnanimous Cuckold," *Meyerhold on Theatre*, p. 204.
32. Jelagin, *Temny geny*, p. 275.
33. Meyerhold, *O teatr*, p. 149.
34. Alexander Gladkov, "Meyerhold Speaks," *Pages from Tarusa*, ed. Andrew Field (New York, 1967), p. 317.
35. Jelagin, *Temny geny*, p. 274.
36. *Vstrechi s Meyerholdom*, illus. facing p. 357.
37. Gorchakov, *Theatre in Soviet Russia*, p. 208.
38. Ibid., p. 209.
39. Zakhava, *Sovremniki*, p. 355.
40. Alpers, *Theatre of the Social Mask*, p. 49.

Chapter 6

1. Gladkov, "Meyerhold Speaks," *Pages from Tarusa*, p. 318.
2. Meyerhold, "Pre-acting," *Meyerhold on Theatre*, p. 206.
3. Ibid.
4. Gorchakov, *Theatre in Soviet Russia*, p. 364.
5. Meyerhold, *Meyerhold on Theatre*, p. 253.
6. Slonim, *Russian Theatre*, p. 271.
7. Meyerhold, *Meyerhold on Theatre*, p. 194.
8. Ibid., p. 205.
9. Ibid.
10. Gorchakov, *Theatre in Soviet Russia*, p. 210.
11. Ibid.
12. Meyerhold, *O teatr*, p. 149.
13. Meyerhold, *Meyerhold on Theatre*, p. 321.
14. Gorchakov, *Theatre in Soviet Russia*, p. 211.
15. Ibid.
16. Zakhava, *Sovremniki*, p. 363.
17. Ibid.
18. Meyerhold, *Le théâtre théâtral*, p. 105.
19. Jelagin, *Temny geny*, p. 283.
20. Ibid., p. 285.
21. Meyerhold, *Meyerhold on Theatre*, p. 196.
22. Gorchakov, *Theatre in Soviet Russia*, p. 212.
23. Ibid.
24. Ibid., p. 211.
25. Alpers, *Theatre of the Social Mask*, p. 66.
26. Jelagin, *Temny geny*, p. 295.
27. Zakhava, *Sovremniki*, p. 365.
28. Jelagin, *Temny geny*, p. 297.
29. Gvozdyev, *Teatr imeni Vsevolod Meyerhold, 1920-1926*, p. 47.
30. Slonim, *Russian Theatre*, p. 273.
31. Gorchakov, *Theatre in Soviet Russia*, p. 194.

Chapter 7

1. Gorchakov, *Theatre in Soviet Russia*, p. 212.
2. Valery Bebutov, "Neutomimy novator," *Vstrechi s Meyerholdom*, p. 77.
3. Jelagin, *Temny geny*, p. 298.
4. Braun, *Meyerhold on Theatre*, p. 211.
5. Slonim, *Russian Theatre*, p. 274.

6. Mirsky, *History of Russian Literature*, p. 161.
7. Braun, *Meyerhold on Theatre*, p. 210.
8. Mirsky, *History of Russian Literature*, p. 116.
9. Meyerhold, "Observations on the Play," *Meyerhold on Theatre*, p. 220.
10. Quoted in Braun, *Meyerhold on Theatre*, p. 209.
11. Houghton, *Moscow Rehearsals*, p. 102.
12. Gladkov, "Meyerhold Speaks," *Pages from Tarusa*, p. 209.
13. Ibid.
14. Kaplan, *Meyerhold on Theatre*, p. 217.
15. Gvozdyev, *Teatr imeni Vsevolod Meyerhold, 1920-1926*, p. 52.
16. Ibid.
17. Meyerhold, "First Attempts at a Stylized Theatre," *Meyerhold on Theatre*, p. 49.
18. Meyerhold, "Tristan and Isolde," *Meyerhold on Theatre*, p. 82.
19. Ibid.
20. Meyerhold, "Reconstruction of the Theatre," *Meyerhold on Theatre*, p. 254.
21. Ibid.
22. Ibid.
23. Gvozdyev, *Teatr imeni Vsevolod Meyerhold, 1920-1926*, p. 52.
24. Meyerhold, "Iskusstvo rezhissero," *V. E. Meyerhold*, 2:156.
25. Alpers, *Theatre of the Social Mask*, pp. 56-57.
26. Meyerhold, "The Art of Directing," *V. E. Meyerhold*, 2:156.
27. Braun, *Meyerhold on Theatre*, p. 213.
28. Leonid Grossman, *Gogol i Meyerhold*, quoted by Braun, *Meyerhold on Theatre*, p. 213.
29. Gorchakov, *Theatre in Soviet Russia*, p. 215.
30. Ibid., p. 214.
31. Jelagin, *Temny geny*, p. 304.
32. Meyerhold, *V. E. Meyerhold*, p. 174.
33. Hilton Kramer, "Art: A Return to Modernism," *The Soviet Union: The Fifty Years*, p. 208.
34. Illus. of playbill for *Gore Umu, Vstrechi s Meyerholdom*, p. 493.
35. Mirsky, *History of Russian Literature*, p. 116.
36. Reeve, *An Anthology of Russian Plays*, 1:13.
37. Mirsky, *History of Russian Literature*, p. 116.
38. Meyerhold, *O teatr*, p. 149.
39. Alpers, *Theatre of the Social Mask*, p. 84.
40. Ibid.
41. Reeve, *An Anthology of Russian Plays*, 1:163.
42. Alpers, *Theatre of the Social Mask*, p. 85.
43. Playbill for *Gore Umu, Vstrechi s Meyerholdom*, p. 493.
44. Rostotsky, *O rezhissorskom tvorchestve V. E. Meyerholda*, p. 76.
45. Ibid., p. 77.

Chapter 8

1. Daniels, *The Complete Plays of Vladimir Mayakovsky*, p. 166.
2. Ibid., p. 195.
3. Ibid., p. 130.
4. Robert Payne, "Introduction," *Complete Plays of Vladimir Mayakovsky*, p. 12.
5. Jelagin, *Temny geny*, p. 315.
6. Ibid.
7. Gorchakov, *Theatre in Soviet Russia*, p. 218.
8. Ibid., p. 308.
9. Alpers, *Theatre of the Social Mask*, p. 58.

10. Gorchakov, *Theatre in Soviet Russia*, p. 306.
11. Ibid., p. 307.
12. Payne, "Introduction," *Complete Plays*, p. 15.
13. *Complete Plays*, p. 243.
14. Ibid., p. 244.
15. Ibid., p. 263.
16. Ibid., p. 264.
17. Ibid., p. 226.
18. Ibid.
19. Ibid., p. 232.
20. Payne, "Introduction," *Complete Plays*, p. 15.
21. Gorchakov, *Theatre in Soviet Russia*, p. 220.
22. *Complete Plays of Vladimir Mayakovsky* p. 197.
23. Meyerhold *V. E. Meyerhold*, p. 221.
24. Payne, "Introduction," *Complete Plays*, p. 16.
25. Annenkov, *Dnevnik moik vstrech*, 2:85.
26. Ibid., 87.
27. *V. E. Meyerhold*, p. 228.
28. Ibid., p. 241.
29. *Vstrechi s Meyerholdom*, illus. pp. 464-465.
30. Gorchakov, *Theatre in Soviet Russia*, p. 306.
31. Ibid., p. 446.
32. Yuri Olesha, *"List of Assets," Envy and Other Works*, trans. Andrew MacAndrew (Garden City, 1967), p. 223.
33. Ibid., p. 224.
34. Ibid., p. 225.
35. Ibid., p. 226.
36. Ibid., p. 259.
37. Ibid., p. 288.

Epilogue

1. Helen Chinoy, "The Emergence of the Director," *Directors on Directing*, p. 57.
2. Gorchakov, *Theatre in Soviet Russia*, p. 363.
3. Ibid., p. 69.
4. Leonard Pronko, *Theatre East and West* (New York, 1969), p. 179.
5. Peter Brook, *The Empty Space* (New York, 1969), p. 25.
6. "Meyerhold was essentially . . . a restless destroyer of mouldy tradition." Mordecai Gorelik, *New Theatres for Old* (New York, 1940), p. 347.
7. " . . . Vsevolod Meyerhold [is] perhaps the greatest, surely the most courageous director of our century." Herbert Blau, *The Impossible Theatre* (New York, 1964), p. 23.
8. " . . . the idea of an autonomous theatre came to us much earlier [than Artaud] from Meyerhold in Russia." Jerzy Grotowski, *Towards a Poor Theatre* (New York, 1969), p. 119.
9. Gladkov, "Meyerhold Speaks," *Pages from Tarusa*, p. 321.
10. Meyerhold, "The Fairground Booth," *Meyerhold on Theatre*, p. 135.

Bibliography

Selected Bibliography

Alpers, Boris. *The Theatre of the Social Mask.* Trans. Mark Schmidt. New York: Group Theatre, 1934.

Annenkov, Sergei. *Dnevnik moikh vstrech.* 2 vols. New York: International Literary Society, 1966.

Bakshy, Alexander. *The Path of the Modern Russian Stage.* Boston: J. W. Luce and Co., 1918.

Beeson, Nora Beate. "Vsevold Meyerhold and the Experimental Pre–revolutionary Theatre in Russia (1900-1917)." Unpublished Ph.D. dissertation, Columbia University, 1961.

Bilington, James H. *The Icon and the Axe.* New York: Random House, 1966.

Bradshaw, Martha (ed.). *Soviet Theatres 1917-1941.* New York: Research Program on U.S.S.R., 1954.

Carter, Huntley. *The New Theatre and Cinema of Soviet Russia.* London: International Publishers, 1924.

Cole, Toby and Chinoy, Helen Krich (ed.). *Directors on Directing.* New York: Bobbs-Merrill, 1953.

Duchartre, Pierre Louis. *The Italian Comedy.* Trans. Randolph T. Weaver. London: George G. Harrap and Co., 1929.

Ehrenburg, Ilya. *Memoirs: 1921-1941.* Trans. Tatania Shebunina. Cleveland: World Pub. Co., 1964

Freeman, Joseph, Kunitz J., and Lozowick, L. *Voices of October.* New York: Vanguard Press, 1930.

Fuchs, Georg. *Revolution in the Theatre.* Trans. Constance C. Kuhn. Ithaca: Cornell University Press, 1959.

Fuerst, Walter René and Hume, Samuel J. *Twentieth-Century State Decoration.* 2 vols. New York: Alfred A. Knopf, 1928.

Gorchakov, Nikolai A. *The Theatre in Soviet Russia.* Trans. Edgar Lehrman. New York: Columbia Univ. Press, 1957.

Gorelik, Mordecai. *New Theatres for Old.* New York: Samuel French, 1940.

Gray, Camilla. *The Great Experiment: Russian Art, 1863-1922.* New York: Harry N. Abrams, 1962.

Gregor, Joseph and Fulop-Miller, Rene. *The Russian Theatre.* Trans. Paul England. Philadelphia: Lippincott, 1930.

Gvozdyev, Alexy A. *Teatr imeni Vsevolod Meyerhold, 1920-1926.* Leningrad: Akademiya, 1927.

Gyseghen, Andre Van. *Theatre in Soviet Russia.* London: Faber and Faber, 1943.

Harkins, William (ed.). *Dictionary of Russian Literature.* New York: Philosophical Library, 1956.

Hoover, Marjorie. "V. E. Meyerhold: A Russian Predecessor of Avant-Garde Theatre." *Comparative Literature,* 17 (1965), 234-50.

Houghton, Norris. *Moscow Rehearsals.* New York: Harcourt, Brace, 1936.

Houghton, Norris. "Theory Into Practice: A Reappraisal of Meierhold." *ETJ,* 20 (October 1968), 437-43.

Houghton, Norris. *Return Engagement.* New York: Holt, Rinehart, and Winston, 1962.

Jelagin, Yuri. *Taming of the Arts.* Trans. Nicholas Wreden. New York: Dutton, 1951.

Jelagin, Yuri. *Temny geny.* New York: M. A. Chekhov, 1955.

Jennings, Lee Byron. *The Ludicrous Demon: Aspects of the Grotesque in German Post-Romantic Prose.* Univ. of California Publications in Modern Philology, LXXI. Berkeley: Univ. of California Press, 1963.

Kayser, Wolfgang. *The Grotesque in Art and Literature.* Trans. Ulrich Weisstein. Bloomington, Indiana: Univ. of Indiana Press, 1963.

Kisch, Cecil. *Alexander Blok: Prophet of Revolution.* London: Weidenfeld and Nicolson, 1960.

Komissarzhevsky, Feodor. *Myself and the Theatre.* New York: Dutton, 1930.

Komissarzhevsky, Vasily. *Moscow Theatres.* Trans. Vic Schneirson and W. Perelman. Moscow: Foreign Languages Pub., 1959.

Komissarzhevskaya, Vera. *Komissarzhevskaya.* Ed. A. Y. Altshuler. Leningrad: Iskusstvo, 1964.

Kott, Jan. *Theatre Notebook: 1947-1967.* Trans. Boleslaw Taborski. Garden City: Doubleday, 1968.

Kramer, Hilton. "Art: A Return to Modernism," *The Soviet Union: The Fifty Years.* Ed. Harrison Salisbury. New York: New American Library, 1967.

MacLeod, Joseph. *Actors Across the Volga.* London: Allen and Unwin, 1946.

MacLeod, Joseph. *The New Soviet Theatre.* London: Allen and Unwin, 1943.

Markov, Pavel. *The Soviet Theatre.* London: V. Gollancz, 1934.

Mayakovsky, Vladimir. *The Complete Plays of Mayakovsky.* Trans. Guy Daniels. New York: Washington Square Press, 1968.

Meyerhold, V. E. *Meyerhold on Theatre.* Trans. Edward Braun. New York: Hill and Wang, 1969.

Meyerhold, V. E. *O Teatr.* St. Petersburg: n.p., 1913.

Meyerhold, V. E. *Le théâtre théâtral.* French trans. Nina Gourfinkle. Paris: Gallimard, 1963.

Meyerhold, V. E. *V. E. Meyerhold: statyi, pisma, rechi, besedy.* Ed. A. V. Fevralsky, B. I. Rostotsky, et al. 2 vols. Moscow: Iskusstvo, 1968.

Miller, Anna Irene. *The Independent Theatre in Europe.* New York: Benjamin Blom, 1931.

Miller, Arthur. "In Russia." *Harper's Magazine,* 239 (September 1969), 37-78.

Mirsky, D. S. *A History of Russian Literature from Its Beginnings to 1900.* Ed. Francis J. Whitfield. New York: Vintage, 1958.

Nemirovich-Danchenko, Vladimir. *My Life in the Russian Theatre.* Trans. John Cournos. Boston: Theatre Arts, 1936.

Nikitina, Yelena (ed.). *Gogol i Meyerhold.* Moscow: n. p., 1927.

Olesha, Yur. *Envy and Other Works.* Trans. Andrew R. MacAndrew. Garden City: Doubleday, 1967.

Ostrovsky, Alexander. *Five Plays of Alexander Ostrovsky.* Trans. Eugene K. Bristow. New York: Pegasus, 1969.

Reeve, F. D. (ed.). *An Anthology of Russian Plays.* Trans. F. D. Reeve. 2 vols. New York: Random House, 1963.

Rostotsky, Vasily. *O rezhissorskom tvorchestve V. E. Meyerholda.* Moscow: Iskusstvo, 1960.

Rudnitsky, Konstantine. *Rezhissor Meyerhold.* Moscow: Nauka, 1969.

Salisbury, Harrison. "Theatre: The Naked Truth," *The Soviet Union: The Fifty Years.* Ed. Harrison Salisbury. New York: New American Library, 1967.

Sayler, Oliver. *The Russian Theatre.* New York: Brentano's, 1922.

Simonov, Ruben, *Stanislavsky's Protege: Eugene Vakhtangov.* Trans. Miriam Goldina. New York: DBS Publications, 1969.

Slonim, Marc. *Russian Theatre From the Empire to the Soviets.* New York: Crowell-Collier, 1962.

Smith, Winifred. *The Commedia dell'Arte.* New York: Columbia Univ. Press, 1912.

Sovietsky Teatr–Dokumenty i Materialy, 1917-1967. Ed. A. E. Yufit et al. Leningrad: Iskusstvo, 1968.

Stansilavsky, Constantin. *My Life In Art.* Trans. J. J. Robbins. New York: Meridian, 1956.

Sukhovo-Kobylin, Alexander. *The Trilogy of Alexander Sukhovo-Kobylin.* Trans. Harold B. Segel. New York: Dutton, 1969.

Tairov, Alexander. *Notes of a Director.* Trans. William Kuhlke. Coral Gables: Univ. of Miami Press, 1969.

Teatralnaya Entsiklopediya. Ed. S. S. Mokulsky. 5 vols. Moscow: Sovietskaya Entsiklopediya, 1961.

Two Great Belgian Plays, about Love. Trans. Marnix Gijsen. New York: J. H. Heineman, 1966.

Varneke, B. V. *History of the Russian Theatre.* New York: Macmillan, 1951.

Volkov, Nikolai. *Meyerhold.* 2 vols. Moscow: Akademiya, 1929.

Volkov, Nikolai. *Meyerhold.* Moscow: Akademiya, 1923. A small pamphlet commemorating Meyerhold's twenty-fifty anniversary in the Russian theatre.

Vstrechi s Meyerholdom: sbornik vespominany. Ed. M. A. Valentey, et al. Moscow: Vserossiyskoye Tentralnoze Obchestro, 1967.

Zakhava, Boris. *Sovremniki.* Moscow: Iskusstvo, 1969.

Index